THE EVERYTHING. Low-Fat, High-Flavor Cookbook

Dear Reader,

Americans are getting fatter. This is an indisputable fact, and it's happening despite lots of focus on no fat, high-protein, low-carb, and low-fat diets. What is going on? Read on and you'll find some possible answers and solutions in this book.

As processed food production soared in the last century, heart disease rates started going up along with obesity. I remember when visiting a fast-food outlet for dinner was an occasional (and I do mean occasional!) treat. Now many Americans eat that way every day for at least one meal a day.

My mother started cooking healthy foods—not necessarily low-fat foods—in the 1960s. She added lots of vegetables, fruits, whole grains, and healthy meats to our diet and eliminated, as much as possible, sweets, processed foods, soft drinks, and salty snacks. I don't remember drinking very much soda, and potato chips were served only during summer cookouts and Christmas Eve dinner (but that's another story!).

Researchers are discovering that it's not so much the amount of fat as the kind of fats we eat. The healthiest diet in the world is the Mediterranean diet. This diet isn't low in fat, but it's high in "good" fats like olive oil and nut oils, as well as fresh fruits and vegetables. That's the framework we should base our diets upon. The foods in this book follow that pattern.

Whole foods, cooked simply with lots of flavor from herbs, spices, condiments, and just plain high-quality produce, seems to be key to feeling and looking good. You'll find that as you reduce the fat and sodium in your meals, you'll start to taste the wonderful flavors fresh food offers. It's a win-win situation. Let's get started!

Linda Larsen

Welcome to the EVERYTHING Series!

These handy, accessible books give you all you need to tackle a difficult project, gain a new hobby, comprehend a fascinating topic, prepare for an exam, or even brush up on something you learned back in school but have since forgotten.

You can read an *Everything*® book from cover to cover or just pick out the information you want from our four useful boxes: e-questions, e-facts, e-alerts, e-ssentials. We give you everything you need to know on the subject, but throw in a lot of fun stuff along the way, too.

We now have more than 400 *Everything*® books in print, spanning such wideranging categories as weddings, pregnancy, cooking, music instruction, foreign language, crafts, pets, New Age, and so much more. When you're done reading them all, you can finally say you know *Everything*®!

QUESTION?

Answers to
common questions

FACT

Important snippets
of information

ALERT!

Urgent
warning

Quick
handy tips

PUBLISHER Karen Cooper

DIRECTOR OF ACQUISITIONS AND INNOVATION Paula Munier

MANAGING EDITOR, EVERYTHING SERIES Lisa Laing

COPY CHIEF Casey Ebert

ACQUISITIONS EDITOR Brielle K. Matson

DEVELOPMENT EDITOR Elizabeth Kassab

EDITORIAL ASSISTANT Hillary Thompson

Visit the entire *Everything*® series at *www.everything.com*

THE
EVERYTHING®
LOW-FAT, HIGH-FLAVOR COOKBOOK

2nd Edition

Simple and satisfying meals you won't
believe are good for you!

Linda Larsen
B.S. in Food Science and Nutrition

Aadamsmedia
Avon, Massachusetts

Dedication

To my sweet husband
Doug, who is my strength
and happiness.

An Everything® Series Book.
Everything® and everything.com® are registered trademarks of F+W Publications, Inc.

Published by Adams Media, an F+W Publications Company
57 Littlefield Street, Avon, MA 02322. U.S.A.
www.adamsmedia.com

ISBN 10: 1-59869-604-1
ISBN 13: 978-1-59869-604-2
Printed in the United States of America.

J I H G F E D C B A

Library of Congress Cataloging-in-Publication Data
available from the publisher.

This publication is designed to provide accurate and authoritative information with regard to the subject matter covered. It is sold with the understanding that the publisher is not engaged in rendering legal, accounting, or other professional advice. If legal advice or other expert assistance is required, the services of a competent professional person should be sought.

—From a *Declaration of Principles* jointly adopted by a Committee of the American Bar Association and a Committee of Publishers and Associations

Many of the designations used by manufacturers and sellers to distinguish their products are claimed as trademarks. Where those designations appear in this book and Adams Media was aware of a trademark claim, the designations have been printed with initial capital letters.

This book is available at quantity discounts for bulk purchases.
For information, please call 1-800-289-0963.

Contents

Introduction • vii

1 Low-Fat Cooking • 1

2 Appetizers • 19

3 Breads • 31

4 Beef • 45

5 Pork • 65

6 Chicken • 77

7 Turkey • 93

8 Seafood • 105

9 Vegetarian Entrees • 123

10 Sandwiches and Pizza • 139

11 Rice • 153

12 Pasta • 169

13 Pasta and Bean Salads • 183

14 Side Salads • 195

15 Soups • 209

16 Side Dishes • 225

17 Chilled Desserts, Puddings, and Sorbets • 237

18 Baked Desserts • 253

19 Sauces and Dressings • 269

20 Condiments and Extras • 283

Appendix A: Glossary • 295

Appendix B: Menus • 302

Appendix C: Resources • 303

Index • 305

Introduction

Low fat, no fat, high fat, fake fat: it seems that dietary recommendations over the last twenty years have changed with the wind. What are we supposed to eat? Are fats bad for us, and how much is too much? These are all fair questions, and researchers are trying to answer them.

Decades ago, everyone ate butter, eggs, and meat, yet obesity rates were much lower than they are now. Fad diets have come and gone, and Americans are still getting fatter. It seems that scientists can agree on a few facts. One is that fat, gram for gram, provides more than twice the calories as carbohydrates and protein, the other main molecules in food. And another is that we need fat in our diets.

In the middle of the last century, people ate mostly whole foods, that is, foods that are not processed or that have artificial ingredients and added chemicals. Snack foods, fast food, and junk food were not readily available. Many of us, in fact, had fast-food meals just as a treat, about once a month or so! And we were much more active than we are today.

Today the emphasis is more on good fat than super-low or no fat. We have to eat fat in order to absorb vitamins and obtain the essential fatty acids that are necessary for cell growth and production. The trick is to eat fats that are healthy. Monounsaturated fats, found in olive oil, nuts, and avocados, among other foods, may actually help reduce the risk of heart disease—and they're delicious! It's easy to transform recipes to use these healthy fats, and you'll love how your food tastes.

Low fat is defined as 30 percent of calories from fat. Most Americans currently get 35 to 40 percent of their daily calories from fat, so while transforming your diet to a low-fat diet is a change, it's not that drastic. Simple changes in the way you cook, cutting down on fat in recipes, and adding flavor with healthy, delicious ingredients will soon become second nature.

The only truly bad fat is hydrogenated fat, also known as trans fat. These artificial fats should be avoided as much as possible. Other fats, including saturated and polyunsaturated fats, can be eaten in moderation. In fact, moderation is the key to eating well.

Building a colorful plate, eating whole foods, consuming good fats, and getting moderate, regular exercise are the keys to living a good life. The key is to start small. Make small changes; as you incorporate these into your life, gradually add more. Soon you'll be fit, trim, healthy, and happier!

Chapter 1
Low-Fat Cooking

For many people, the very term "low-fat" means boring, flavorless food that is good for you, but that nobody wants to eat. That doesn't have to be the truth. Low-fat foods, made using good, healthy fats, can be delicious. You can use them to form the basis for a healthy diet. By now, everyone with a television or Internet connection knows that we are supposed to eat a diet that is low in fat. But what does that mean? What is low-fat? How much fat should we eat for the best health? Are there differences in the health effects of different fats? And how can we make a low-fat diet appetizing and delicious so we can live with it for life?

What Is Fat?

Fat is an essential component of a healthy diet. Our brains are made up of 70 percent fat, and a layer of fat surrounds the heart and acts as an emergency source of energy. Fat is a component of all of our cells. We need it to absorb fat-soluble nutrients. It helps regulate our body temperature. Fat is used in cell growth and in the maintenance of our nervous system. And essential fatty acids (EFAs) are found only in some foods; these compounds are used to regulate metabolism and our immune systems. We need fat to live.

ALERT!

Do not feed children under the age of two a low-fat diet! They need to consume a good amount of fat to help their brains develop and to help sustain their bodies' growth rate. The American Academy of Pediatrics states that fat intake should not be limited until a child is at least two years old.

There are three main types of molecules in food: carbohydrates, protein, and fat (alcohol is another, but it doesn't factor into this discussion). Carbohydrates provide 4 calories per gram, protein also provides 4 calories per gram, and fat provides 9 calories per gram of food. That difference alone is what makes restricting fat in our diets important.

Good Fat, Bad Fat

There is only one true bad fat: trans fat. This artificial substance is created by pumping hydrogen gas through oil, resulting in a tasteless, extremely stable fat that is very valuable to the food processing industry—and very bad for your body. Hydrogenated fats are the only fat you really have to avoid, no matter what.

ESSENTIAL

Even *Cooking Light*, one of the oldest low-fat recipe magazines, is including butter and olive oil in many of its recipes. This reflects the newer research and opinions that these natural fats are not bad for you as long as they are eaten in moderation. In fact, some of their recipes have 39 percent or more calories from fat!

Don't look at fat as the enemy. Rather, think of fat as a necessary substance you have to consume, and include fats that are actually good for you in your diet. Naturally occurring fats, including vegetable oils, monounsaturated oils, and oils found in nuts, fish, and avocados, are delicious and healthy. One of the healthiest diets on earth, the Mediterranean diet, is fairly heavy in monounsaturated fats like olive oil.

Saturation

There are two basic types of fat: saturated and unsaturated. There is a controversy in the medical and scientific communities about whether saturated fats are bad for your health.

The term *saturated* refers to the presence or absence of double bonds between carbon molecules in a fat. Saturated fat is simply a chain of triglycerides, or fat molecules, which has all of its carbon molecules bound to hydrogen molecules, with no double bonds between the carbon molecules. Saturated fats are usually solid at room temperature.

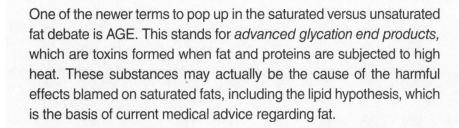

One of the newer terms to pop up in the saturated versus unsaturated fat debate is AGE. This stands for *advanced glycation end products,* which are toxins formed when fat and proteins are subjected to high heat. These substances may actually be the cause of the harmful effects blamed on saturated fats, including the lipid hypothesis, which is the basis of current medical advice regarding fat.

Unsaturated fats are divided into two groups: monounsaturated and polyunsaturated. These molecules have one (monounsaturated) or more (polyunsaturated) double bonds between the carbon molecules because they are missing two or more hydrogen molecules. These fats are usually liquid at room temperature.

Some studies have shown that a diet containing moderate amounts of saturated fat can help protect your health. Butter contains vitamins and minerals, and some of the medium-chain saturated fats like coconut and palm oil have antimicrobial and antiviral properties and can help prevent oxidation of cholesterol.

Moderation Is Key

If you consume too much of any one food or ingredient, you can get sick. Even drinking too much water, one of the most innocuous substances on earth, can be bad for you. It's also possible to not consume enough of any one substance, which leads to nutritional deficiencies and health problems. Moderation is key.

Most experts think that a diet that contains 25 to 35 percent of your calories from fat is the healthiest. For our purposes, the limit will be 30 percent calories from fat. Saturated fat has its own limit; most experts think that less than 10 percent of your total daily calories should come from saturated fat.

Table 1-1 Fat Grams per Calorie Intake			
Calories per Day	Calories from Fat	Fat Grams	Saturated Fat Grams
2,600	780	86.7	28.89
2,400	720	80.0	26.67
2,200	660	73.3	24.44
2,000	600	66.7	22.22
1,800	540	60.0	20.00
1,500	450	50.0	16.67

Recent Studies

Some high-profile large scientific studies have showed no difference in the risks associated with cancer, heart attack, and stroke between a group of women who ate low-fat diets and those who ate whatever they wanted. This study, like many others, just proves that a diet rich in variety and whole foods is probably the best for you throughout your life.

It seems that almost every day the media report on a new scientific study that directly contradicts established wisdom. What are you supposed to do? Science doesn't progress in an orderly fashion. Theories change as new studies prove different conclusions. All you can do is keep eating whole foods, a balanced diet, and fresh foods. If you eat a colorful plate and vary your diet, you'll automatically eat about 30 percent calories from fat. You'll also feel satisfied, have more energy, and be able to maintain a healthy weight.

Think of food as a balloon. Food is made up of fat, proteins, and carbohydrates. If you cut down on one, the others automatically must increase. If fat in a food is reduced, it has to be replaced with something. Just make sure the fat replacements you eat are natural and healthy.

How Low Is Too Low?

It's possible to eat a diet that is too low in fat. Since fats carry important nutrients and your body needs fat to function and maintain optimal health, a diet too low in fat can make you malnourished. A diet too low in fat will cause:

- Dry hair
- Dry skin
- Tiredness
- Eye problems
- Hair loss
- Pour wound healing
- Susceptibility to infection
- Signs of malnutrition

If your diet is too low in fat, you run the risk of becoming deficient in several critical vitamins. Vitamins A, D, K, and E are fat-soluble. That means they are carried by fat in food and stored in the fatty tissue in your body. Other nutrients, including vitamin C, are absorbed better by your body if they are accompanied by a small amount of fat. And then there are essential fatty acids. These compounds, which your body cannot make, must come from food. Essential fatty acids are used in tissue repair and cell function.

Some researchers think that no more than 10 percent of calories should come from fat. A diet that low in fat will cause weight loss, although the general effects are disputed. It is very difficult to maintain a diet that low in fat, because it's hard to make your body feel full.

How High Is Too High?

Eating a diet too high in fat—one in which you get more than the recommended 20 to 35 percent of your calories from fat—can lead to problems like weight gain. In its extreme, obesity, weight gain increases your risk for a multitude of health problems. Put simply, eating too much fat makes it too easy to go over the amount of calories your body needs in a day. Those excess calories, whether from sugar, fat, or protein, will be stored in your cells as fat. And once there, it's difficult to get rid of fat and shrink those cells.

Diets very low in carbohydrates have been popular in recent years. Since these diets cut carbs from the diet, fat intake had to increase. The American Heart Association has stated that long term adherence to a low-carb, high-fat diet can increase the risk of heart disease. The risks of bone, liver, and kidney disease can also increase the longer this diet is followed.

A recent study at the University of Minnesota shows that eating too much fat can damage your liver. Excess fat is stored in the liver; this can lead to metabolic syndrome, which causes insulin resistance and other health problems.

What Is Flavor?

We sense flavor foods in several different ways. Unfortunately, in many foods like chicken, beef, and baked goods, fats provide much of the flavor. Fats are a good flavor carrier. Many organic molecules that provide flavor do not dissolve in water but do dissolve in fat. When the molecules are carried in fat, the flavor can be spread easily throughout the food.

It's better to have a small amount of real fat in your food, rather than relying on artificial substitutes. Scientists may find problems with these substitutes in the future; these products use lots of artificial and manufactured ingredients, and they just don't taste the same.

Smell

Much of the flavor in foods is actually produced by the aroma, not your taste buds. That's why foods don't taste as flavorful when you are suffering from a cold or allergies. Receptors in your nose react with aromatic compounds given off by food. These receptors send signals to your brain that are registered as smell.

FACT

Artificial flavors actually get their start in the real thing. The smell flavorants, or chemicals which create the aroma, are extracted from the natural source. Scientists then purify and analyze them. Different combinations of thousands of chemicals are tried and tested to see if they resemble the original odor.

Nerve endings in the eyes and in the mucous membranes of the nose, mouth, and throat identify aromatic compounds like mint, spicy foods, and ammonia. The sense of smell can be affected by illness, injury, or disease. This sense also lessens as we age. This can be a problem when counseling older people about healthy eating habits. Food just doesn't taste as good as it used to because their sense of smell has diminished.

Color

Believe it or not, color is a flavor cue. Scientific tests have determined that if people cannot see the color of a food or drink when they eat it, they make mistakes about the flavor. Scientists have found that the color green increased sweet taste sensitivity, while red decreased bitter taste sensitivity. One study discovered that subjects were more attuned to the color of orange juice when sensing sweetness than they were to the actual sugar level.

Temperature

When foods are cold, their spice and flavor level diminishes. So when you're making low-fat salad dressings, make them spicier than you would ordinarily. As with texture, we have expectations of the temperature of many foods. Eating a cold hamburger just doesn't taste as good as eating one that is hot and juicy.

Is low fat the same as low calorie?
Low fat doesn't mean low calorie. It's perfectly possible to eat a diet very high in calories while eating a low-fat diet. The total number of calories consumed during the day is the final determinant as to whether you gain or lose weight. Eating a ton of low-fat food is just as bad as eating more moderate amounts of high-fat food.

Temperature also helps determine texture of foods. If you use a small amount of butter to brush on the top of a loaf of bread, for instance, it will taste different when it's hot compared to when the loaf has cooled.

The temperature a food is cooked to also affects its flavor. In many foods, compounds need to reach a certain temperature in order to combine or break down to form flavor compounds. Think of eating a French fry that is barely cooked and not browned, compared to one that is well browned. Or take a bite of a raw onion compared to one that is cooked. The difference is in the temperature.

Taste

There are several different types of taste buds in your mouth. Basically, flavor is divided into five major categories: salty, sweet, sour, bitter, and umami. All of these taste buds are scattered throughout and underneath the surface of your tongue.

FACT

Taste buds have a life span of about ten days. They regenerate quickly because they played an important part in our evolutionary survival. Many poisonous plants have a bitter taste, so it used to be important that we be able to sense bitterness to avoid those plants. That's also why, when you burn your tongue on something hot, you get the taste sensation back quickly.

You also have other nerve endings, called the trigeminal sense, to detect spiciness or heat. Those nerves are slightly recessed in your tongue, which is why it can take a few seconds for your brain to register when a food is very spicy hot. Umami, which registers as a meaty taste, is also accessed only through taste buds. Compounds that react with umami taste buds include glutamates and glycine salts found in soy sauce and monosodium glutamate (MSG).

We're born with the taste buds we'll have all throughout life. The number of these taste buds is genetically determined. Taste buds are measured per square centimeter of tongue. Some people have thousands of taste buds per centimeter, while others have only hundreds. That is why it is so difficult to accurately describe taste, and it's also why so many recipes end with the instruction "season to taste."

Don't make the mistake of oversalting your food when you cook low fat. Too much salt can mute and overwhelm the other flavors in food, and too much sodium in your diet can increase the risk of heart disease. Most of the sodium in our diets comes from processed foods and hidden sources, so adding a lot more in cooking throws off the balance between sodium and other minerals.

Texture

Texture is a component of flavor mainly because of our expectations and learned responses. For instance, when you bite into a potato chip, it should be crisp and break apart easily. A soggy potato chip doesn't taste the same as a crisp one. Your jaw and teeth are very sensitive to thickness, texture, and pressure. Crispness is perceived by the amount of vibration a food emits when you bite into it.

The most common texture descriptors include *chewy*, *viscous*, *crunchy*, *crisp*, *smooth*, *tender*, *creamy*, *slippery*, and *tough*. Different foods should possess the appropriate textures for the best taste.

High-Flavor Substitutions for Fat

There are many ingredients you can use in your cooking that add flavor but not fat. Remember, fat is a flavor carrier and enhancer, so when you reduce it in a recipe or formula you must compensate by adding high-flavor foods. Luckily, there are many of these foods that not only add flavor, but also add vitamins, fiber, and other nutrients to your diet.

Herbs

Herbs are some of the best ways to punch up flavor in low-fat recipes. There is a huge selection to choose from, both fresh and dried. Many are easy to grow, on the windowsill or in your backyard. Some of the newer culinary trends call for using herbs in sweet baked goods and sweet spices in main dishes.

Table 1-2 Herbs and Food		
Herb	Flavor	Complements These Foods
Basil	Lemony, peppery	Tomatoes, chicken, greens
Oregano	Assertive, peppery	Tomatoes, vegetables, lamb
Thyme	Lemony, minty	Fish, chicken, fruit desserts
Marjoram	Woodsy, earthy	Beef, vegetables, pasta, pork
Rosemary	Lemony, warm	Chicken, nuts, pork, lamb
Dill Weed	Earthy, fresh	Vegetables, salmon, carrots
Sage	Warm, earthy	Chicken, turkey, potatoes, soup
Mint	Fresh, clean	Fruit, chocolate, tomatoes
Bay	Woodsy, spicy	Beans, soup, tomatoes, fish
Tarragon	Licorice, earthy	Fish, stews, chicken, vegetables

When using dried herbs, crumble the leaves between your fingers to help release the aromatic oils. This pressure and the heat from your fingers will make the herbs taste more intense. Dried herbs are three times more concentrated than fresh, so adjust recipes accordingly. If a recipe calls for 1 teaspoon of dried herbs, 1 tablespoon of fresh is the appropriate equivalent.

Condiments

Condiments are mixtures of ingredients that developed in various cultures. These can be added to many foods, including baked goods, meat dishes, pasta, and sandwiches, to add lots of great flavor. Some low-fat and fat-free condiments include:

- Mustard
- Asian sauces
- Salsa
- Ketchup
- Jams and jellies
- Chutney
- Pickles
- Mole sauce
- Flavored vinegars
- Barbecue sauce

Read the labels of these products and choose those which are lower in fat and especially sodium. Many condiments can be quite high in sodium, but you can find lower-salt varieties in health food stores and co-ops.

Heat

Adding peppers, hot sauce, cayenne, white pepper, and other spices to your food will let you reduce fat. These ingredients may also be good for you; studies have shown that eating spicy-hot foods can help lower blood pressure. Remember, the smaller the pepper, the hotter it will be. There's a slight delay between the time you put the food on your tongue and the time you taste the heat because the receptors for heat are located slightly under your tongue's surface. For less heat, remove the seeds and membranes from peppers before you chop or mince them.

Vinegar

Vinegar adds a tart and bitter flavor to food along with some sweetness. You can choose from a wide variety of flavored vinegars that add flavor to foods. Some aromatic compounds that won't dissolve in water will dissolve in vinegar because of vinegar's acid content. Tarragon vinegar, garlic vinegar, herbed vinegar, and fruit vinegars are all easy to make at home. Just place the well-washed flavoring ingredients in a clean bottle and add distilled vinegar. Cover and let stand for 1 to 2 weeks to develop flavors before you use them in salad dressings and sandwich fillings.

Spices

In addition to single spices, a number of spice blends make seasoning your food very easy. They range from super spicy Cajun blends to milder grill seasoning blends.

Some spices have a nutritional component. For instance, curcumin, found in turmeric and curry powder blends, may help prevent the onset of Alzheimer's disease. Cinnamon can lower blood pressure and help reduce cholesterol levels.

Table 1-3 Spices		
Spices	**Flavor**	**Complements These Foods**
Cinnamon	Warm, nutty	Baked goods, poultry, curries
Nutmeg	Lemony, warm	Baked goods, greens, potatoes, beef
Cardamom	Aromatic, pungent	Desserts, bread, fish, fruit
Ginger	Warm, spicy	Ham, curries, fish, fruit, cakes
Allspice	Earthy, citrus	Baked goods, eggs, fish
Anise	Licorice	Stone fruits, eggs, chicken, tomatoes
Saffron	Warm, nutty	Fish, rice, chicken, seafood
Cloves	Spicy, orange	Chicken, fruit, breads, pork
Cumin	Smoky, earthy	Beef, soup, chicken, rice, vegetables
Coriander	Lemony, woodsy	Pork, curry, chutney, lentils

Citrus

Lemon juice, oranges, and grapefruits all are wonderful flavor enhancers that brighten foods and add vitamin C as well as fiber to your diet. Lemon pairs beautifully with fish and chicken and enhances many baked goods. Lemon juice as a glaze, combined with sugar and other ingredients, adds another layer of flavor to baked goods. In fact, lemon can even make foods taste salty, letting you reduce sodium as well as fat.

Alcohol

Alcohol, like fat, is a flavor carrier. Most of the extracts and flavorings we use are made by using alcohol to extract non-water-soluble aromatic compounds and flavors from spices and herbs. If you soak mint in alcohol and compare it to mint soaked in water, you'll see that the alcohol has picked up the mint flavor, while the water has not. Adding alcohol-based extracts like vanilla will brighten food as well and add flavor without adding fat.

You can use alcohol to sauté foods instead of fats and oils. Alcohol can also carry flavor molecules, so some low-fat recipes use alcohol as a flavor carrier. Remember, not all of the alcohol will burn off during the cooking process.

Caramelization

When sugars and proteins are subjected to high heat, the compounds in them break down and reassemble to form hundreds of different molecules that add flavor and aroma to foods. To add a caramel flavor to food, you can add caramel flavoring, but it's also attained by thoroughly browning meats, which caramelizes the sugars and proteins on the meat surface, and by caramelizing sugar, which occurs during baking, grilling, and broiling.

Smokiness

A smoky flavor is a complex flavor involving your taste buds and your nose. It tastes rich, brown, and nutty, with a slightly burned flavor. You can add smokiness to foods by grilling, and by adding certain ingredients. Chipotle peppers, cumin, chili powder, and liquid smoke add a smoky flavor to foods.

Foods High in Fat and Low in Fat

The kind of fat in these foods is just as important as the amounts. For instance, avocados are a fruit, but they are high in fat. That fat, however, is monounsaturated and very good for you. There's a similar issue with fish. Fatty fish, like salmon, mackerel, and tuna, is high in fat: good fat.

You can also choose different foods within the groups. Chicken sausage is going to have more fat than chicken breasts. And whole grain breads are better for you than white bread or croissants.

Low-Fat Foods

Many foods are naturally low in fat or have no fat at all. By including more of these foods in your diet, you will automatically eat less fat without having to turn to fat alternatives or drastically reworking your diet. Naturally low-fat foods include

- Fruits
- Vegetables
- Rice
- Legumes
- Fish
- Chicken
- Cereals
- Breads
- Whole grains
- Spices and herbs

When you look at that list, you probably see many colors in your mind. That's another trick; assemble colorful recipes and a colorful plate to eat the most balanced diet and to naturally reduce fat intake. In fact, eating a varied diet is one of the best ways to automatically eat a lower-fat, healthier-fat diet.

High-Fat Foods

Some foods are naturally high in fat. You can still eat these foods, but do so in moderation. Even if a food is high in fat, if it's a fat that is good for you like the monounsaturated fat in avocados and nuts, you can enjoy it in your regular diet. High-fat foods include:

- Red meat
- Butter
- Egg yolks
- Cheese
- Oils
- Dairy foods
- Nuts
- Cookies, cakes, and pies
- Ice cream

When you choose to eat high-fat foods, remember portion sizes. Most Americans don't understand what a portion is, and they usually eat two to three portions in one sitting. A portion of red meat is 3 ounces. A serving of ice cream is ½ cup. One serving of cheese is 1 ounce, about the size of a pair of dice. Learn these sizes and you'll automatically eat less fat.

Cooking Tricks and Tips

You'll find that most cooking and baking recipes are easily adapted to a lower-fat lifestyle. Look for recipes that use leaner meats, and reduce the amount of oil or butter used in sautéing foods. Most baked goods can be altered slightly to reduce the fat, and it's easy to add flavor with condiments, herbs, and spices.

Substitute Fruit Purées

Fruit purées, including applesauce, puréed pears, raisins, and prunes, are a good substitute for fat in baking. Reduce the fat by one-third to one-half and add an equal amount of the purée. Lighter purées like applesauce work well in light goods like sugar cookies and vanilla cakes, while prune purées add flavor and moisture to chocolate recipes.

Reduce Fat in Baked Goods

Many baked goods, especially breads, can be made with less fat without changing anything else in the recipe. Start by reducing the fat, whether it's butter, margarine, or oil, by 25 percent. If the finished product is acceptable, reduce it by 10 percent more. There is a limit to the amount you can omit, however, since fat plays an important part in the structure of baked goods.

Meat as Flavor

Meats, especially red meat and pork, are quite high in fat no matter how you trim them. The best solution is to reduce their presence in the recipes you make. Use meat as a flavoring instead of as the main ingredients in casseroles and soups. If a recipe calls for whole pork chops to be baked on scalloped potatoes, for instance, think about cubing half the number of chops and stirring them into the potatoes.

FACT

There are two kinds of fat in meat: intra-muscular and extra-muscular. Intra-muscular fat is the white streaks and spots that appear within the cut. Extra-muscular is the meat on the outside of the cut that can be trimmed away. Meats with more intramuscular fat are more tender and juicy, but those cuts with less fat can be delicious when cooked properly.

Trim visible fat from meats, and be sure to drain saucepans after browning meats. By doing this you can cut as much as 10 percent of the fat from a recipe without having to change anything else. Also choose cuts of meat that are naturally lower in fat. The cheaper cuts of beef, including top and bottom round as well as flank steak, are less expensive than filet mignon because they have less internal marbling. Cooked properly, they are just as delicious.

Drink Lower-Fat Milk

Lowering the amount of fat in your milk can be accomplished gradually, so your family won't even know. If you currently drink whole milk, switch to a combination of whole and 2% milk. Then gradually increase the 2% and reduce the whole. Once that transition is completed, continue the process with 1% milk. Eventually, you may be able to get your family to drink skim milk. By switching from whole to skim milk, you'll save almost 7 grams of fat per cup.

Even if your family doesn't want to switch, use lower-fat dairy products in baking and cooking. It's hard to tell the difference between full-fat and low-fat sour cream in a potato salad.

Cook in Alcohol and Stocks

Since alcohol transmits volatile flavors just as well as fat does, sautéing onions and other vegetables in a bit of alcohol adds no fat and does add flavor to a recipe. You can also sauté in chicken, beef, and vegetable stocks instead of butter, margarine, or oils. However, note that the alcohol content will not completely cook out, even if it evaporates.

Marinades and Brining

Marinades and rubs will help add flavor and tenderize meats that have a lower-fat content. With less fat in meat, acidic ingredients like lemon juice, wine, and vinegar are used to help break down some of the fibers before cooking, resulting in a more tender finish. Marinades also add flavor to meats.

Matching a Marinade to Food
Refer to the charts of herbs and spices to choose the ones to use with the meat you are marinating. Robust herbs like oregano and rosemary are better with strongly flavored meats like beef and lamb, while delicate herbs like basil and dill work best with chicken and fish. Use lighter vinegars and alcohols for fish and chicken. And don't marinate too long, or the meat can become mushy.

Brining is another way to add flavor and moisture to meat. When you make a brine, you usually add tablespoons or cups of salt and sugar, but most isn't absorbed into the meat and so the method does not add much sodium or calories.

Slow Cooker

When you use a slow cooker, not only will your food have few AGEs, but you will need less fat. Slow cooking is an excellent choice for leaner, cheaper cuts of meat that naturally have less fat. It also helps capture all of the flavor, including volatile compounds.

About the Recipes

These recipes are quite tolerant and variable. You can substitute other vegetables and fruits for those called for, try a marinade for beef with chicken or pork, and use different cheeses and seasonings.

One caveat: if a food has very few calories, the fat content may be over 30 percent. In salad dressings and some flavorings and condiments, there's no way to reduce the fat enough if a serving has 30 to 40 calories or fewer. Don't be afraid of using these recipes, especially if the fat used is a good fat like olive oil or nut oils.

The nutrition information for the recipes in this book has been calculated by NutriBase Clinical version 7.0 (*www.dietsoftware.com*). Total calories, fat, saturated fat, cholesterol, and sodium amounts are included for each recipe.

Now let's get started on changing your diet to include healthy whole foods, the best amount of healthy fats, and more taste and flavor than you dreamed possible!

Chapter 2
Appetizers

Tortilla Chips 20

Black Bean Dip 20

Black Bean Veggie Dip 21

Creamy Mustard Dip 21

Yogurt Cheese 22

Chili Bean Dip 22

Herbed Clam Dip 23

Roasted Garlic 23

Baked Mushroom Dip with Spinach 24

Garlic Red Pepper Dip 24

Tropical Salsa Bruschetta 25

Oven-Baked Fries 25

Mozzarella Basil Crostini 26

Quick Crab Cakes 26

Stuffed Celery 27

Bean and Corn Tartlets 27

Stuffed Triangles 28

Lemon Sesame Tuna 28

Sweet Potato Sticks with Lime 29

Stuffed Parmesan Mushrooms 30

Tortilla Chips

Serve these chips with a Mexican dinner along with a selection of salsas from the Sauces and Dressings chapter (page 269).

Yields 4 cups of chips; 8 servings

Calories: 71.26
Fat: 3.02 grams
Saturated Fat: 0.55 grams
Cholesterol: 0.0 mg
Sodium: 153.96 mg

8 (6-inch) corn tortillas
2 tablespoons olive oil
1 tablespoon chili powder
1 teaspoon garlic powder
1 teaspoon ground cumin
½ teaspoon fine salt
¼ teaspoon cayenne pepper

1. Preheat oven to 350°F. Place tortillas on work surface and brush all sides very lightly with the olive oil. Cut tortillas into 8 wedges each.

2. Arrange tortillas in a single layer on a cookie sheet. Sprinkle with chili powder, garlic powder, cumin, salt, and cayenne pepper and toss to coat. Bake for 4 minutes, then turn and toss the chips and return to oven. Bake for 2 to 4 minutes longer until tortillas are crisp and light golden brown. Remove to wire rack to cool.

Make It Your Own

You can flavor these quick and easy chips with anything you'd like. Some finely grated Romano cheese sprinkled on the chips while they're hot adds great flavor. And think about using different flavors and types of tortillas. This recipe can be used with everything from flour tortillas to blue corn tortillas.

Black Bean Dip

This hearty dip can be served on its own or used as the basis for layered dips. Use bell pepper strips and crackers for dippers.

Yields 2 cups; serving size ¼ cup

Calories: 108.34
Fat: 0.44 grams
Saturated Fat: 0.11 grams
Cholesterol: 0.0 mg
Sodium: 309.94 mg

2 (15-ounce) cans black beans, rinsed and drained
2 jalapeño peppers, minced
2 cloves garlic, minced
1 large tomato, chopped
1 red bell pepper, chopped
2 tablespoons minced cilantro
¼ teaspoon pepper

1. In a food processor, combine beans, jalapeños, and garlic; process until smooth.

2. Transfer to a medium bowl and stir in remaining ingredients. Cover and chill for 2 to 3 hours before serving.

Black Bean Veggie Dip

This colorful dip can be served with Tortilla Chips (page 20) or fresh vegetables cut into strips.

1. Place rinsed and drained black beans in a medium bowl; add chili powder, cumin, and pepper and mash until smooth. Spread on a serving plate.

2. In a small bowl, combine yogurt and basil leaves. Spread over the beans. Top with the vegetables and cheese. Serve immediately.

Cotija Cheese

Cotija cheese is a hard grating cheese similar to Parmesan or Romano, but less expensive and with more flavor. You can find it in ethnic grocery stores, especially Mexican and Latino markets, and sometimes in the regular grocery store in the dairy aisle. It's a good substitute for other hard grating cheeses because you can use less.

Creamy Mustard Dip

This dip is excellent with fresh crisp vegetables like baby carrots, celery sticks, and bell pepper strips. You can also serve it as a topping for grilled fish.

Combine all ingredients in a blender or food processor; blend or process until smooth. Cover and refrigerate for 2 to 3 hours to blend flavors before serving.

Serves 6

Calories: 160.84
Fat: 6.09 grams
Saturated Fat: 1.45 grams
Cholesterol: 4.57 mg
Sodium: 365.57 mg

1 (15-ounce) can black beans, rinsed and drained
1 tablespoon chili powder
1 teaspoon cumin
¼ teaspoon cayenne pepper
½ cup Yogurt Cheese (page 22)
½ cup chopped fresh basil leaves
1 red bell pepper, diced
1 green bell pepper, diced
1 tomato, diced
1 avocado, diced
2 tablespoons grated Cotija cheese

Yields 1½ cups; serves 12

Calories: 42.61
Fat: 2.50 grams
Saturated Fat: 0.41 grams
Cholesterol: 0.51 mg
Sodium: 147.91 mg

⅓ cup plain nonfat yogurt
½ cup 1% cottage cheese
⅓ cup low-fat mayonnaise
3 tablespoons Dijon mustard
1 tablespoon yellow mustard
⅛ teaspoon white pepper

Yogurt Cheese

Yogurt cheese is a great substitute for cream cheese or other soft cheeses in any recipe—and it's easy to make.

Yields 1½ cups; serving size 2 tablespoons

Calories: 87.66
Fat: 4.02 grams
Saturated Fat: 0.91 grams
Cholesterol: 4.49 mg
Sodium: 126.33 mg

4 cups natural yogurt

1. Place the yogurt in a strainer or a colander lined with a couple of coffee filters or some dampened cheesecloth. Place the strainer in a large bowl, cover tightly with foil, and refrigerate for 24 hours until the mixture thickens.

2. The yogurt cheese will keep, tightly covered, in the refrigerator for 3 to 4 days. The whey can be reserved and frozen; use it in soups and marinades.

Chili Bean Dip

Kidney beans are a healthy choice for an appetizer dip; they're full of fiber and protein. Serve this dip with Tortilla Chips (page 20).

Yields 1½ cups; serving size ¼ cup

Calories: 67.17
Fat: 0.51 grams
Saturated Fat: 0.07 grams
Cholesterol: 0.0 mg
Sodium: 308.52 mg

1 (15-ounce) can kidney beans, rinsed and drained
2 chipotle peppers in adobo sauce, minced
2 tablespoons adobo sauce
1 tablespoon red wine vinegar
2 teaspoons chili powder
¼ teaspoon cumin
1 tablespoon minced onion
2 tablespoons minced flat-leaf parsley

1. Using a potato masher, mash the beans until smooth but some texture remains. Stir in remaining ingredients except parsley.

2. Transfer mixture to serving bowl and sprinkle with parsley. Cover and chill for 3 to 4 hours before serving.

Herbed Clam Dip

This fresh-tasting dip is excellent served with breadsticks, Tortilla Chips (page 20), or red and green bell pepper strips.

1. In a food processor or blender, process cottage cheese until smooth, then transfer to small bowl.

2. Drain clams, reserving 1 tablespoon of the juice. Add clams and reserved juice to cottage cheese mixture along with parsley, yogurt cheese, and basil; mix well. Stir in remaining ingredients and stir.

3. Cover tightly and refrigerate for 2 to 3 hours before serving.

Yields 1½ cups; serving size ¼ cup

Calories: 120.24
Fat: 2.33 grams
Saturated Fat: 0.67 grams
Cholesterol: 43.15 mg
Sodium: 237.18 mg

1 cup low-fat cottage cheese
1 (10-ounce) can minced clams
⅓ cup chopped flat-leaf parsley
3 tablespoons Yogurt Cheese (page 22)
2 teaspoons dried basil leaves
2 tablespoons minced onion
1 tablespoon lemon juice
Dash Tabasco sauce
⅛ teaspoon white pepper

Roasted Garlic

Spread this fragrant soft garlic on bread, combine it with nonfat sour cream for an appetizer dip, or add it to Portobello Sandwiches (page 134)

1. Preheat oven to 375°F. Cut the garlic heads in half, parallel to the root end. Place, cut-side up, on a cookie sheet. Drizzle with olive oil and sprinkle with salt and pepper.

2. Bake for 55 to 65 minutes until garlic is light golden brown and soft. Cool for 10 minutes, then squeeze cloves out of the papery skins; spread on bread or crackers. Cover and store in refrigerator for 3 days, or freeze for up to 3 months.

Serves 8

Calories: 36.08
Fat: 0.44 grams
Saturated Fat: 0.11 grams
Cholesterol: 0
Sodium: 309.94 mg

2 full heads garlic
2 teaspoons olive oil
¼ teaspoon salt
⅛ teaspoon pepper

Baked Mushroom Dip with Spinach

You can use different types of mushrooms in this easy, creamy dip. Cremini, or brown mushrooms, are baby portobellos, and are very flavorful.

Serves 6

Calories: 83.32
Fat: 3.94 grams
Saturated Fat: 2.29 grams
Cholesterol: 9.44 mg
Sodium: 134.69 mg

1 tablespoon olive oil
24 medium button
    mushrooms, quartered
1½ cups frozen spinach,
    thawed and drained
½ cup Basic Low-Fat White
    Sauce (page 278)
¼ cup shredded sharp
    Cheddar cheese
¼ cup shredded part-skim
    mozzarella cheese
⅛ teaspoon white pepper

1. Preheat oven to 350°F. In a large skillet over medium heat, combine olive oil and mushrooms. Cook and stir until mushrooms are tender and lightly browned, about 5 to 6 minutes. Set aside.

2. Drain spinach very well by pressing between paper towels. Line bottom of a 1-quart baking dish with the spinach. Arrange mushrooms on top. Pour white sauce over mushrooms, then sprinkle with cheeses and pepper.

3. Bake until dip is hot and bubbly and cheeses melt and begin to brown, about 20 to 25 minutes. Serve immediately.

Garlic Red Pepper Dip

If you love garlic, add more! This beautifully colored dip is sweet and tangy at the same time.

Yields 1 cup; serving
size 2 tablespoons

Calories: 38.42
Fat: 1.93 grams
Saturated Fat: 0.34
grams
Cholesterol: 0.56 mg
Sodium: 397.72 mg

1 tablespoon olive oil
4 cloves garlic, minced
1 onion, chopped
1 (7-ounce) jar roasted
    red peppers, drained
1 tablespoon balsamic
    vinegar
½ cup low-fat cottage
    cheese
⅛ teaspoon pepper

1. In a small microwave-safe bowl, combine olive oil, garlic, and onion. Microwave on high for 2 to 3 minutes, stirring once during cooking time, until garlic and onions are tender; set aside.

2. In a food processor, combine peppers, vinegar, cottage cheese, and pepper and blend until smooth. In a small bowl, combine pepper mixture with onion mixture and stir well. Cover and chill for 2 to 3 hours before serving.

Tropical Salsa Bruschetta

This sweet and spicy salsa is fresh and invigorating. Serve it with apple and pear slices, pineapple slices, and sweet crackers.

1. For salsa, combine cantaloupe, melon, green chilies, green onion, lime juice, cayenne pepper, cilantro, and salt in medium bowl. Using a potato masher, mash about one-third of the fruits into a sauce. Stir well, cover, and chill for at least 1 hour before serving.

2. Toast the bread until golden brown, under the broiler or in a toaster oven. While still warm, spread with the cream cheese and top each with a large spoonful of the salsa. Serve immediately.

Ripening Melons

A ripe melon smells sweet and the blossom end will give slightly when pressed. To ripen, let the melon stand at room temperature for 1 to 2 days, turning occasionally. Once ripe, refrigerate it to slow the process.

Oven-Baked Fries

Even with oil, butter, and cheese, these crisp little fries have less than 30 percent calories of fat per serving.

1. Preheat oven to 475°F. Scrub potatoes and cut into strips ¼ inch by ¼ inch by 4 inches long. In a medium bowl, toss together the potatoes, oil, paprika, chili powder, salt, pepper, butter, and cheese and mix Add potatoes and toss well.

2. Spread out on a baking sheet in a single layer. Bake, turning occasionally with a spatula, until golden brown, about 25 to 30 minutes. Serve hot.

Serves 12

Calories: 150.45
Fat: 4.38 grams
Saturated Fat: 2.32 grams
Cholesterol: 10.58 mg
Sodium: 466.60 mg

1 cup diced cantaloupe
1 cup diced honeydew melon
1 (4-ounce) can chopped green chilies
⅓ cup chopped green onion
2 tablespoons lime juice
¼ teaspoon cayenne pepper
¼ cup chopped fresh cilantro
½ teaspoon salt
1 (8-ounce) package low-fat cream cheese
12 thin slices Oat Bran French Bread (page 37)

Serves 8

Calories: 184.79
Fat: 5.12 grams
Saturated Fat: 2.33 grams
Cholesterol: 8.73 mg
Sodium: 199.89 mg

4 large potatoes
1 tablespoon olive oil
1 teaspoon paprika
1 tablespoon chili powder
½ teaspoon salt
¼ teaspoon cayenne pepper
2 tablespoons melted butter
2 tablespoons grated Parmesan cheese

Mozzarella Basil Crostini

This excellent tomato spread can be used as an appetizer all on its own. Stir in some nonfat sour cream for a delicious dip.

Serves 8

Calories: 249.85
Fat: 6.64 grams
Saturated Fat: 2.46 grams
Cholesterol: 7.63 mg
Sodium: 536.72 mg

½ cup chopped dry-packed sun-dried tomatoes
3 cloves garlic, minced
1 tablespoon olive oil
2 tablespoons lemon juice
1/8 teaspoon crushed red pepper flakes
8 slices Oat Bran French Bread (page 37)
1 cup shredded part-skim mozzarella cheese
1 cup grape tomatoes, chopped
1 tablespoon balsamic vinegar
1 cup fresh basil leaves, torn

1. Place sun-dried tomatoes in a bowl and cover with boiling water. Let stand for 10 minutes, then drain well.

2. In a food processor, combine drained rehydrated tomatoes, garlic, olive oil, lemon juice, and red pepper flakes and process until smooth.

3. Preheat broiler. Toast the French bread on both sides. Spread side with the tomato mixture and the cheese. Place on broiling pan; broil 6 inches from heat for 4 to 6 minutes until cheese melts and bubbles.

4. While bruschetta is toasting, combine tomatoes, vinegar, and basil in small bowl. Remove bruschetta from broiler, top with basil mixture, and serve immediately.

Quick Crab Cakes

Crab is such a luxurious meat; it's a good choice for an appetizer because you use less of it. Serve these little cakes with cocktail sauce and lemon wedges.

Serves 6

Calories: 127.42
Fat: 4.33 grams
Saturated Fat: 0.81 grams
Cholesterol: 67.46 mg
Sodium: 772.69 mg

12 soda crackers, crushed
1 egg, lightly beaten
3 tablespoons plain yogurt
1 teaspoon Worcestershire sauce
1 tablespoon lemon juice
1½ teaspoons Old Bay Seasoning
¼ teaspoon crushed red pepper flakes
1 pound lump crabmeat
1 tablespoon olive oil

1. In a large bowl, combine cracker crumbs, egg, yogurt, Worcestershire sauce, lemon juice, seasoning, and red pepper flakes and mix well.

2. Add the crabmeat and gently fold mixture together. Form into six patties.

3. Heat olive oil in large nonstick skillet over medium heat. Add the patties and cook, turning once, until patties are brown and crisp and hot, about 10 to 15 minutes. Serve immediately.

Stuffed Celery

Celery is full of fiber and has no fat and hardly any calories. Its fresh crunchy texture is very satisfying.

1. Cut the celery stalks in half to make 24 pieces. Rinse and dry, then arrange on serving platter, hollow-side up.

2. In a food processor, combine cream cheese, cottage cheese, and onion; process until smooth. Add paprika and pepper; process briefly to combine.

3. Fill celery with the cheese mixture, and top with olives. Cover and chill for 2 to 3 hours before serving.

Serves 6

Calories: 83.82
Fat: 2.12 grams
Saturated Fat: 0.68 grams
Cholesterol: 3.78 mg
Sodium: 479.60 mg

12 long celery stalks with leaves
1 (8-ounce) package nonfat cream cheese, softened
½ cup low-fat cottage cheese
¼ cup minced onion
⅛ teaspoon paprika
Dash white pepper
½ cup pimiento-stuffed olive slices

Bean and Corn Tartlets

These little tartlets are cute and bite-sized. Place them on a serving tray and garnish with chopped chives or cilantro.

1. Drain the corn and black beans very well. Combine with tomato, lemon juice, and pepper in small bowl, then stir in sour cream. Cover and chill until serving time.

2. To serve, spoon a tablespoon of the corn mixture into each tartlet shell. Serve immediately.

Yields 32 tartlets

Calories: 23.69
Fat: 0.66 grams
Saturated Fat: 0.24 grams
Cholesterol: 2.98 mg
Sodium: 38.70 mg

¾ cup frozen corn, thawed
1 cup canned black beans, rinsed
¼ cup chopped tomato
1 tablespoon lemon juice
⅛ teaspoon pepper
⅓ cup low-fat sour cream
32 mini frozen phyllo tartlet shells, thawed

Mini Phyllo Shells

You can find mini phyllo tartlet shells in the freezer section of supermarkets. They are made from phyllo (or filo or fillo) dough and are very crisp. They're already prepared, so all you have to do is let them thaw. They can be filled with just about anything and served as appetizers or dessert.

Stuffed Triangles

You can make the wontons ahead of time; cover with a damp towel and refrigerate until it's time to bake them.

Serves 12

Calories: 142.86
Fat: 5.78 grams
Saturated Fat: 1.97 grams
Cholesterol: 27.61 mg
Sodium: 292.23 mg

*1 cup part-skim ricotta
    cheese
1 cup frozen chopped
    spinach, drained
¼ cup chopped green
    onions
½ teaspoon nutmeg
1 egg
1 egg white
¼ cup grated Parmesan
    cheese
30 wonton wrappers
2 tablespoons olive oil
1 cup chunky pasta sauce*

1. In a small bowl, combine ricotta with spinach, green onions, nutmeg, egg, egg white, and Parmesan cheese and beat well.

2. Arrange a few wonton wrappers on work surface. Brush edges with a bit of water to moisten, then place a tablespoon of the cheese mixture in the center. Fold wrappers in half and press edges to seal.

3. Brush wontons lightly with oil and place on parchment paper-lined cookie sheet. Bake for 5 minutes, then carefully turn and bake for 6 to 8 minutes longer until wontons are lightly browned.

4. While wontons are baking, heat pasta sauce in small saucepan over medium heat. Serve the wontons with warm pasta sauce for dipping.

Lemon Sesame Tuna

Tuna is delicious as an appetizer when it's cut into cubes and marinated in a lemon mixture.

Serves 8

Calories: 99.51
Fat: 6.07 grams
Saturated Fat: 1.09 grams
Cholesterol: 14.80 mg
Sodium: 92.60 mg

*2 tablespoons lemon juice
1 tablespoon low-sodium
    soy sauce
1 tablespoon sesame oil
2 green onions, minced
2 (⅓-pound) tuna fillets
¼ cup sesame seeds,
    toasted*

1. In shallow bowl, combine lemon juice, soy sauce, sesame oil, and green onions and mix well. Cut the tuna into 1-inch cubes and add to the marinade; toss to coat and let stand for 15 minutes.

2. Preheat oven to 400°F. Arrange the fish in a single layer on a baking sheet. Bake until fish is just opaque, about 5 to 7 minutes. Sprinkle with sesame seeds and serve immediately with toothpicks.

Sweet Potato Sticks with Lime

These crisp and tender sticks of potato pack a nutritional punch. Each serving gives you 200 percent of the recommended daily value of vitamin A required in one day.

Serves 8

Calories: 76.63
Fat: 1.79 grams
Saturated Fat: 0.27 grams
Cholesterol: 0.0 mg
Sodium: 169.75 mg

3 sweet potatoes, peeled
2 tablespoons lime juice
1 tablespoon olive oil
½ teaspoon salt
⅛ teaspoon cayenne pepper
2 limes, each cut into quarters

1. Preheat oven to 400°F. Line a cookie sheet with a Silpat liner and set aside.

2. Cut sweet potatoes into ½-inch sticks, each about 3 inches long. In a small bowl, combine lime juice, olive oil, salt, and pepper and mix well until salt dissolves. Sprinkle this mixture over the sweet potatoes and toss to coat.

3. Arrange sweet potatoes on the prepared cookie sheet. Bake for 20 to 30 minutes, turning twice with a spatula during baking time, until potatoes are crisp and tender on the inside. Serve immediately with lime wedges.

Sweet Potatoes or Yams?

Sweet potatoes and yams are two different root vegetables. What we in the United States call yams are actually sweet potatoes. Yams are members of the lily family, native to Africa and Asia. They are not as sweet as sweet potatoes. Sweet potatoes are members of the morning glory family. The soft varieties are most commonly sold in the United States.

Stuffed Parmesan Mushrooms

Serves 6

Calories: 84.22
Fat: 3.81 grams
Saturated Fat: 0.86 grams
Cholesterol: 1.47 mg
Sodium: 76.82 mg

12 large mushrooms
1 tablespoon olive oil
1 onion, minced
½ cup minced green bell pepper
2 cloves garlic, minced
½ cup crushed saltine crackers
2 tablespoons grated Parmesan cheese
1 tablespoon minced flat-leaf parsley
½ teaspoon dried oregano leaves
⅛ teaspoon pepper
⅓ cup fat-free chicken broth

Stuffed mushrooms are a classic appetizer. This version is full of flavor and color; it looks beautiful on an appetizer tray.

1. Preheat oven to 350°F. Wipe mushrooms with damp paper towels and remove stems. Mince stems and combine in small saucepan with olive oil, onion, green bell pepper, and garlic. Cook and stir until tender, about 5 to 6 minutes.

2. Remove pan from heat and add cracker crumbs, cheese, parsley, oregano, and pepper.

3. Spoon mixture into mushroom caps, rounding the tops. Place in large baking dish and pour chicken broth around mushrooms.

4. Bake, uncovered, until mushrooms are tender and filling is hot, about 18 to 22 minutes. Serve immediately.

Chapter 3
Breads

Apple Date Bread 32

Pear Tea Bread 33

Whole Grain Bread 34

Herbed Buttermilk Quick Bread 35

Pumpkin Nut Bread 36

Oat Bran French Bread 37

Cheese Coins 38

Spicy Corn Bread 38

Rosie's Pizza Dough. 39

Chewy Pizza Crust 40

Baked Apple Pancake. 41

Apple Bread Pudding 42

Rhubarb Muffins 43

Blueberry Muffins. 44

Apple Date Bread

This hearty bread is so satisfying, one slice spread with some jam or whipped honey will keep you going until lunch.

Calories: 362.33
Fat: 7.86 grams
Saturated Fat: 1.94 grams
Cholesterol: 24.35 mg
Sodium: 148.92 mg

¾ cup brown sugar
¾ cup chopped walnuts
2 tablespoons butter,
  softened
¼ cup flour
½ teaspoon cinnamon
1½ cups flour
1¼ cups whole wheat
  flour
½ cup sugar
½ cup brown sugar
2 teaspoons baking
  powder
1 teaspoon baking soda
½ teaspoon salt
1 egg
1 egg white
1 cup buttermilk
¼ cup orange juice
1 cup chopped dates
1 cup finely chopped,
  peeled apples

1. Preheat oven to 350°F. Spray a 9" × 5" loaf pan with nonstick baking spray containing flour and set aside. In a small bowl, combine ¾ cup brown sugar, walnuts, 2 tablespoons butter, ¼ cup flour, and cinnamon and mix until crumbly; set aside.

2. In a large bowl, combine 1½ cups flour, whole wheat flour, sugar, ½ cup brown sugar, baking powder, baking soda, and salt and mix well.

3. In a small bowl, combine egg, egg white, butter, milk, and orange juice and beat until combined. Stir into flour mixture until combined, then add dates and apples.

4. Turn into prepared loaf pan and sprinkle with the walnut mixture. Bake until loaf is golden brown and firm, about 60 to 70 minutes. Cool on wire rack.

Pear Tea Bread

This delicious bread has a wonderful pear and lemon aroma and flavor. Serve it for a quick breakfast or part of a holiday breakfast buffet.

Yields 1 Loaf; serves 12

Calories: 257.68
Fat: 6.68 grams
Saturated Fat: 1.19 grams
Cholesterol: 17.63 mg
Sodium: 106.98 mg

1 (16-ounce) can pear halves
2½ cups flour
½ cup sugar
¼ cup brown sugar
2 teaspoons baking powder
1 teaspoon baking soda
½ teaspoon salt
⅛ teaspoon cardamom
⅓ cup vegetable oil
1 egg
1 teaspoon grated lemon zest
2 tablespoons lemon juice
½ cup powdered sugar

1. Preheat oven to 350°F. Spray a 9" × 5" loaf pan with nonstick baking spray containing flour and set aside.

2. Drain pears, discarding liquid. In blender or food processor, blend or process pears until smooth. Measure out 1 cup of puree. Reserve remaining puree for another use.

3. In a large bowl, combine flour, sugar, brown sugar, baking powder, baking soda, salt, and cardamom. In a small bowl, combine puréed pear mixture, oil, egg, and lemon zest.

4. Combine the two mixtures, stirring until just mixed. Pour into prepared loaf pan. Bake for 50 to 60 minutes or until loaf is golden brown and firm.

5. While the bread is baking, combine lemon juice and powdered sugar in small bowl and spoon over hot bread. Remove bread from pan and cool completely on wire rack.

Fat Substitutes

Puréed fruit has long been used as a fat substitute. Puréed pears or applesauce are used in light breads and baked goods, while puréed prunes or raisins are a good choice in chocolate products. They add moisture and bolster the structure of the product, as well as preventing drying of the finished baked good.

Whole Grain Bread

Homemade bread is one of the great joys of life—and this one is low-fat too! The aroma that fills your house while the bread is baking will make your swoon, and the bread makes great toast the next day.

**Yields 2 loaves;
20 servings**

Calories: 101.71
Fat: 3.39 grams
Saturated Fat: 1.39 grams
Cholesterol: 15.64 mg
Sodium: 81.40 mg

1 (0.25-ounce) package
    dry yeast
¼ cup warm water
1¼ cups whole wheat
    flour
1 cup bread flour
¼ cup flaxseed
½ cup quick cooking
    oatmeal
½ teaspoon salt
3 tablespoons brown
    sugar
½ cup buttermilk
½ cup warm water
¼ cup orange juice
3 tablespoons butter
1 egg
1 to 2 cups all-purpose
    flour

1. Grease two 8" × 4" loaf pans with solid shortening; set aside. In a small bowl, combine yeast and ¼ cup warm water; mix and let stand for 10 minutes.

2. In a large bowl, combine whole wheat flour, bread flour, flaxseed, oatmeal, salt, and brown sugar and mix well.

3. In a small saucepan, combine buttermilk, ½ cup water, orange juice, and butter; heat over low heat until butter melts. Add to flour mixture along with egg; beat for 1 minute. Then stir in yeast mixture.

4. Gradually add enough all-purpose flour to make a firm dough. Knead on floured surface for 6 to 7 minutes until smooth. Place in greased bowl, turning to grease top. Cover and let rise for 1 hour.

5. Punch down dough and divide in half. Roll out to 7" by 5" rectangles. Roll up, starting with short side; pinch edges to seal. Place in prepared pans. Cover and let rise until doubled, about 45 to 50 minutes. Preheat oven to 350°F.

6. Bake bread for 30 to 40 minutes, or until tops are deep golden brown. Remove from pans and brush with melted butter. Cool completely on wire rack.

Herbed Buttermilk Quick Bread

Choose this recipe for a quick and easy bread recipe to serve with dinner. Serve it warm from the oven with olive oil for dipping.

Yields 1 loaf; Serves 12

Calories: 121.34
Fat: 3.04 grams
Saturated Fat: 0.61 grams
Cholesterol: 1.63 mg
Sodium: 88.27 mg

*1¼ cups whole wheat
   flour
¾ cup flour
½ teaspoon baking
   powder
½ teaspoon baking soda
¼ teaspoon salt
½ teaspoon dried thyme
   leaves
½ teaspoon dried dill
   weed
2 tablespoons corn oil
1 cup buttermilk*

1. Preheat oven to 425°F. Spray a nonstick baking sheet with nonstick baking spray containing flour and set aside.

2. In a medium bowl, combine whole wheat flour, flour, baking powder, baking soda, salt, thyme, and dill and mix well. Add corn oil and buttermilk and mix just until a dough forms.

3. Turn dough out onto floured work surface and knead ten times. Shape into a flat, round loaf on prepared baking sheet. Bake for 40 to 45 minutes or until bread is deep golden brown. Cool on wire rack for 15 minutes before serving.

Buttermilk in Baking

Buttermilk adds tang and rich flavor to baked goods. But you don't have to keep it on hand; you can make your own. Just put 1 to 2 tablespoons vinegar or lemon juice in a measuring cup and add enough regular milk to make 1 cup. Stir and let stand for 10 minutes, then use as directed in recipes.

Pumpkin Nut Bread

Yields 1 loaf; serves 10

Calories: 287.87
Fat: 7.85 grams
Saturated Fat: 3.28 grams
Cholesterol: 33.35 mg
Sodium: 119.28 mg

1 cup canned solid-packed pumpkin
¼ cup butter, softened
¼ cup applesauce
1 cup brown sugar
½ cup sugar
½ teaspoon grated orange zest
1 egg
2 egg whites
2 cups flour
1 teaspoon baking soda
¼ teaspoon salt
1 teaspoon pumpkin pie spice
¼ teaspoon cinnamon
⅓ cup chopped toasted walnuts

This gorgeous bread is so moist and tender. For only 5.40 grams of fat per slice, you can omit the nuts or try dried cherries instead.

1. Preheat oven to 325°F. Spray one 9" × 5" loaf pan with nonstick cooking spray containing flour and set aside.

2. In a large bowl, combine pumpkin purée, butter, and applesauce and beat well. Add brown sugar, sugar, and orange zest; mix until combined. Then add egg and egg whites; beat until smooth.

3. In a sifter, combine flour, baking soda, salt, pumpkin pie spice, and cinnamon. Sift over the pumpkin mixture and stir just until combined. Fold in walnuts. Spread in prepared pan.

4. Bake for 60 to 70 minutes, or until bread is golden brown and firm, and a toothpick inserted in center comes out clean. Cool in pan for 5 minutes, then remove to wire rack to cool completely.

How to Chop Nuts

There are several ways to chop nuts. You can use a food processor, adding a bit of flour so the nuts don't stick. A chef's knife does a good job; place the nuts on the work surface and run the knife over them until they reach the desired consistency. And then there are nut choppers, which you can find at grocery stores.

Oat Bran French Bread

Toast slices of this bread and serve with extra-virgin olive oil sprinkled with pepper for a great appetizer or meal starter.

**Yields 2 loaves;
24 servings**

Calories: 106.37
Fat: 0.91 grams
Saturated Fat: 0.24 grams
Cholesterol: 9.43 mg
Sodium: 119.29 mg

3 to 4 cups bread flour
1 cup whole wheat flour
¼ cup oat bran
1 tablespoon brown sugar
1 teaspoon salt
*2 (0.25-ounce) packages
    dry yeast*
1 cup warm water
¾ cup buttermilk
1 egg
*2 tablespoons orange
    juice*
2 tablespoons cornmeal

1. In a large mixing bowl, combine 1 cup bread flour, the whole wheat flour, oat bran, brown sugar, and salt and mix well. In a small bowl, combine yeast and warm water; stir and let stand for 5 minutes until bubbly.

2. Add yeast to dry ingredients along with buttermilk, egg, and orange juice; beat for 2 minutes. Then gradually add enough remaining bread flour to form soft dough.

3. Turn onto floured surface and knead until smooth and elastic, about 8 to 10 minutes. Place in greased bowl, turning to grease top. Cover and let rise until doubled, about 30 to 40 minutes.

4. Punch down dough and turn onto floured surface; let rest for 10 minutes. Then divide dough in half. Roll out each half to a 12" × 7" rectangle, then roll up, starting with long side. Grease two 12" × 3" shapes on a cookie sheet with solid shortening and sprinkle with cornmeal. Place loaves on the cornmeal.

5. Cover and let rise in warm place until doubled, about 20 to 25 minutes. Preheat oven to 375°F. Cut slashes in the top of the loaf using a sharp knife. Bake bread for 30 to 40 minutes or until deep golden brown. Cool completely on wire rack.

French Bread Tins

You can buy French bread tins in baking supply stores and kitchenware stores. These are curved pieces of nonstick material, which helps form French bread into perfect round shapes. They are often perforated so the hot oven air can circulate all around the dough as it cooks, producing a nice crisp crust.

Calories: 63.47
Fat: 2.50 grams
Saturated Fat: 0.69 grams
Cholesterol: 2.05 mg
Sodium: 98.27 mg

¼ cup reduced-fat
   margarine
1½ cups shredded low-fat
   sharp Cheddar cheese
⅔ cup shredded nonfat
   mozzarella cheese
1 tablespoon mustard
2 tablespoons 1% milk
½ teaspoon seasoned salt
1 jalapeño pepper,
   minced
1½ cups flour

Serves 9

Calories: 263.90
Fat: 8.09 grams
Saturated Fat: 1.57 grams
Cholesterol: 25.68 mg
Sodium: 504.62 mg

1¼ cups flour
1¼ cups cornmeal
⅓ cup sugar
2 teaspoons baking
   powder
1 teaspoon baking soda
½ teaspoon salt
1 tablespoon chili powder
⅛ teaspoon Tabasco
   sauce
1 jalapeño pepper,
   minced
¼ cup vegetable oil
1 egg
2 egg whites
1 cup buttermilk, divided
½ cup frozen corn, thawed

Cheese Coins

These little crackers are excellent served warm with soup.
They can be reheated in a toaster oven until they sizzle.

1. In a large bowl, combine margarine with cheeses, mustard, milk, salt, and jalapeño pepper; beat until combined. Add flour and mix just until a dough forms.

2. Preheat oven to 350°F. Shape dough into ½-inch balls and place on ungreased baking sheets. Press each ball with the bottom of a drinking glass to flatten to a ⅛-inch thickness. Prick with the tines of a fork.

3. Bake crackers until light golden brown around edges, about 12 to 16 minutes. Remove from cookie sheet and let cool completely on wire rack. Store in airtight container at room temperature for up to 1 week.

Spicy Corn Bread

Corn bread is the perfect accompaniment to chili or any hot soup
or stew. Serve this one with salsa.

1. Preheat oven to 400°F. Spray a 9" square pan with nonstick baking spray containing flour and set aside.

2. In a large bowl, combine flour, cornmeal, sugar, baking powder, baking soda, salt, and chili powder. In a small bowl, combine Tabasco, jalapeño pepper, oil, egg, egg whites, and ¾ cup buttermilk and mix well.

3. In a food processor or blender, place corn and ¾ cup buttermilk. Process or blend until smooth; add to oil mixture.

4. Pour oil mixture into dry ingredients and mix until a batter forms. Spoon and spread into prepared pan. Bake for 20 to 25 minutes or until deep golden brown. Let cool for 10 minutes, then cut into squares to serve.

Rosie's Pizza Dough

You can top this dough with anything you'd like. Go gourmet and use nonfat cream cheese with roasted asparagus, or make a typical pepperoni pizza.

1. In a medium bowl, combine water and honey and stir to combine. Add yeast and stir again; let stand until bubbly, about 5 to 10 minutes.

2. In a large bowl, combine ½ cup bread flour, semolina flour, salt, and ½ cup cornmeal. Add yeast mixture and olive oil; beat well. Gradually add enough remaining bread flour to form a firm dough.

3. Knead on floured surface for 6 to 7 minutes until smooth. Place in greased bowl, turning to grease top. Cover and let rise for 1 hour.

4. Punch down dough and divide in half. Divide each half into eighths if making small crusts. Coat work surface with remaining cornmeal. Roll out dough in the cornmeal to a ¼-inch thickness.

5. Place on ungreased cookie sheets. Cover and let rise for 20 minutes. Preheat oven to 400°F. Bake small crusts for 5 to 8 minutes, large crusts for 10 to 12 minutes, until set but not brown. Cool on wire racks and use as directed in recipes.

Make it Ahead

You can make a bunch of these crusts and keep them in your freezer for your own pizza shop. Just prebake the rounds, then cool completely, place in large freezer bags, label, and freeze until you're ready to eat. Then just top and bake at 400°F for 10 to 15 minutes (small crusts) or 20 to 30 minutes (large crusts).

16 Individual Crusts or 2 Large Crusts; serves 16

Calories: 154.18
Fat: 3.23 grams
Saturated Fat: 0.45 grams
Cholesterol: 0.0 mg
Sodium: 241.48 mg

1½ cups warm water
1 tablespoon honey
4 teaspoons active dry yeast
2 cups bread flour, divided
1 cup semolina flour
1 teaspoon salt
1 cup cornmeal, divided
3 tablespoons olive oil

Chewy Pizza Crust

Serves 8

Calories: 164.19
Fat: 3.98 grams
Saturated Fat: 0.55 grams
Cholesterol: 0.0 mg
Sodium: 291.88 mg

1 (0.25-ounce) envelope active dry yeast
1 cup lukewarm water
2 cups bread flour
4 teaspoons sugar
1 teaspoon salt
2 tablespoons olive oil

Because it rises slowly overnight in the refrigerator, this crust develops a fabulous wheaty taste and texture.

1. In a small bowl, sprinkle the yeast over the water, stir, and set aside. Combine flour, sugar, and salt in a large bowl. Make a well in the center and add the yeast mixture and olive oil. Gradually combine the wet and dry ingredients.

2. When dough has formed, lightly oil your hands and knead the dough for 5 minutes. It should be slightly tacky. Place dough in a greased bowl, turning to grease top. Cover the bowl and set aside at room temperature until doubled in size, about 2 hours. Then punch it down and return it to the same bowl. Cover again airtight with plastic wrap, and place in the refrigerator overnight.

3. About 2 hours before you are ready to eat, remove the dough from the refrigerator and divide it into two equal portions. Roll each portion into a round ball. Let rise at room temperature until they start to puff a bit, about 40 minutes.

4. Place a pizza stone in an oven and preheat to 500°F. On floured work surface, place one ball of dough. Using your hands or a rolling pin, press down on dough, gently stretching it, until you have formed a 12-inch round.

5. Using a pizza peel, transfer to the hot pizza stone in the oven. Bake until set, about 2 to 3 minutes. Remove from oven and let cool. Repeat with second ball of dough. To use, top as directed in individual recipes, then bake at 400°F until cheese is bubbly and toppings are hot, about 8 to 10 minutes.

Baked Apple Pancake

This pancake is a great choice for a holiday breakfast because you don't have to stand at the stovetop making pancakes!

1. Preheat oven to 425°F. In a large ovenproof skillet, melt butter over medium heat. Add apples to the pan and sprinkle with brown sugar. Cook, stirring frequently, until apples are soft, about 12 to 15 minutes. Sprinkle apples with cinnamon and remove from heat.

2. Meanwhile, in medium bowl combine flour and sugar. Add milk, egg whites, eggs, and vanilla and beat just until smooth. Pour over apples in skillet.

3. Place pan in oven and bake for 20 minutes. Reduce heat to 350°F and bake for 12 to 18 minutes longer or until pancake is golden brown. Sprinkle with powdered sugar and serve immediately.

Serves 4

Calories: 380.41
Fat: 6.53 grams
Saturated Fat: 3.07 grams
Cholesterol: 116.43 mg
Sodium: 115.76 mg

1 tablespoon butter
4 medium tart apples, peeled and sliced
3 tablespoons brown sugar
½ teaspoon cinnamon
1 cup flour
3 tablespoons sugar
1 cup 1% milk
2 egg whites
2 eggs
2 teaspoons vanilla
3 tablespoons powdered sugar

Apple Bread Pudding

Serves 8

Calories: 215.45
Fat: 4.38 grams
Saturated Fat: 1.77 grams
Cholesterol: 90.95 mg
Sodium: 105.53 mg

4 cups crumbled Whole
    Grain Bread (page 34)
2 apples, peeled and
    grated
½ cup raisins
½ cup chopped pecans
1½ cups 1% milk
3 eggs
2 teaspoons vanilla
¾ cup brown sugar
3 tablespoons honey
1 teaspoon cinnamon
½ teaspoon nutmeg
2 tablespoons lemon juice

Bread pudding is such a comforting dessert. Serve it on a cold winter day when the kids come home from school.

1. The bread should be at least 1 day old so it's fairly firm. Preheat oven to 350°F. Spray a 9" square baking pan with nonstick baking spray containing flour.

2. Combine bread crumbs, apples, raisins, and pecans in the prepared pan and spread in even layer. Combine remaining ingredients in a medium bowl and mix until well blended. Be sure the bread is saturated; push it down into the liquid mixture if necessary. Let stand for 10 minutes.

3. Bake the pudding until top is golden brown, about 35 to 45 minutes. Serve warm with warmed honey or maple syrup.

Bread Pudding Toppings

Bread pudding can be topped with everything from nonfat whipped topping to a fruit sauce or Hard Sauce. To make Hard Sauce, combine 2 tablespoons butter with ½ cup powdered sugar, ½ teaspoon vanilla, and about 2 to 3 tablespoons skim milk, enough to make a stiff sauce. The sauce melts over the hot dessert. Yum!

Rhubarb Muffins

Rhubarb is one of the first fruits or vegetables to appear in the spring. It is a great source of vitamin C and dietary fiber, and a great addition to a low-fat diet.

Yields 12 muffins

Calories: 208.39
Fat: 4.26 grams
Saturated Fat: 2.27 grams
Cholesterol: 43.69 mg
Sodium: 141.09 mg

2 cups finely chopped rhubarb
¾ cup sugar, divided
1 teaspoon grated orange zest
¼ cup brown sugar
2 cups all purpose flour
½ cup whole wheat flour
1 teaspoon baking soda
½ teaspoon baking powder
½ teaspoon salt
2 eggs, beaten
½ cup low-fat buttermilk
¼ cup orange juice
1 teaspoon vanilla
3 tablespoons butter, melted
½ teaspoon cinnamon

1. Preheat oven to 375°F. Spray a 12-cup muffin tin with nonstick baking spray containing flour and set aside. In a small bowl, combine rhubarb, ¼ cup sugar, and orange zest; let stand for 5 minutes.

2. In a large bowl, combine 6 tablespoons sugar, brown sugar, and all purpose flour, whole wheat flour, baking soda, baking powder, and salt and mix well. Make a well in the center of the dry ingredients and add rhubarb mixture, eggs, buttermilk, orange juice, vanilla, and melted butter. Mix just until combined.

3. Spoon batter into prepared muffin tin, filling each cup two-thirds full. In a small bowl combine remaining 2 tablespoons sugar and ½ teaspoon cinnamon; sprinkle over each muffin. Bake for 20 to 25 minutes or until muffins are golden brown and firm. Remove from muffin tin and cool on wire rack for 15 minutes before serving.

Muffins

All muffin batter should be mixed just until the dry ingredients are moistened, but you have to be even more careful with low-fat muffins. There will be some lumps in the batter; that's okay. They will disappear during baking time. Be sure to remove muffins from the tins as soon as they are baked or they will steam and become sticky.

Blueberry Muffins

Calories: 186.55
Fat: 4.36 grams
Saturated Fat: 0.56 grams
Cholesterol: 1.23 mg
Sodium: 73.65 mg

1½ cups flour
½ cup whole wheat pastry flour
¼ cup brown sugar
⅓ cup plus 2 tablespoons sugar
½ cup oat bran
1 teaspoon baking powder
1 teaspoon baking soda
¼ teaspoon salt
⅓ cup applesauce
¾ cup buttermilk
2 tablespoons orange juice
2 egg whites
3 tablespoons canola oil
½ teaspoon grated orange zest
¾ cup fresh or frozen blueberries
½ cup dried blueberries
2 teaspoons vanilla
½ teaspoon cinnamon

Your own blueberry muffins, hot from the oven, just can't be beat. These are tender and fragrant, with great flavor from the orange zest and cinnamon.

1. Preheat oven to 350°F. Spray 12 muffin cups with nonstick baking spray containing flour and set aside. In a large bowl, combine flour, pastry flour, brown sugar, ⅓ cup sugar, oat bran, baking powder, baking soda, and salt.

2. In a medium bowl, combine applesauce, buttermilk, orange juice, egg whites, canola oil, orange zest, and vanilla and beat well. Add to dry ingredients and mix just until combined. Fold in both types of blueberries.

3. Divide mixture among muffin cups. In a small bowl, combine 2 tablespoons sugar and cinnamon; sprinkle over batter. Bake for 15 to 20 minutes or until muffins are golden brown and firm. Remove from cups and cool on wire rack.

Whole Wheat Pastry Flour

Whole wheat pastry flour is not the same as whole wheat flour. It's processed to look, act, and taste more like all-purpose flour. Look for it in specialty stores, in health food stores and co-ops, and online. Like most whole grain flours, it is quite perishable. Unless you use it a lot, store it, tightly covered, in the freezer.

Chapter 4
Beef

Thai Beef Salad 46

Hearty Meat Loaf 47

Pastitsio 48

Steak Stroganoff 49

Savory Pot Roast 50

Caribbean Beef 51

Spicy Beef and Cabbage 52

Beef Stew. 53

Beef Burgundy 54

Spicy Chinese Beef 55

Orange Beef and Broccoli Stir-Fry. .56

Hearty Bean Stew. 57

Ginger Peach Steak 58

Marinated Steak Kebabs 58

Surf and Turf Pasta 59

Beef and Snow Peas 60

Curried Beef Stir-Fry 61

Lean, Juicy Burgers. 62

Chimichangas. 63

Texan Rice 64

Thai Beef Salad

Toss the spaghetti with a tiny bit of oil when it's cooked so it won't stick together as it cools.

Calories: 323.70
Fat: 9.12 grams
Saturated Fat: 2.87 grams
Cholesterol: 103.70 mg
Sodium: 527.94 mg

3 tablespoons low-sodium soy sauce, divided
2 tablespoons brown sugar, divided
2 tablespoons water, divided
¾ pound top round steak
1 tablespoon vegetable oil
2 tablespoons seasoned rice vinegar
1 tablespoon lemon juice
3 cloves garlic, minced
1 teaspoon Asian sesame oil
¼ teaspoon crushed red pepper flakes
4 cups shredded Chinese or napa cabbage
1½ cups grated carrots
½ cup thinly sliced green onions
1 cup cooked, cooled spaghetti
¼ cup chopped cilantro

1. In shallow bowl, combine 1 tablespoon soy sauce, 1 tablespoon brown sugar, and 1 tablespoon water and mix well. Trim excess fat from beef and cut across the grain into ¼" × 4" strips. Add to soy sauce mixture and toss to coat. Let marinate for 30 minutes.

2. Drain beef, discarding marinade. In a large skillet or wok, heat 1 tablespoon vegetable oil and add beef. Stir-fry until browned, about 3 minutes, then remove from pan and set aside.

3. In a small bowl, combine remaining 2 tablespoons soy sauce, 1 tablespoon brown sugar, and 1 tablespoon water with the rice vinegar, lemon juice, garlic, sesame oil, and red pepper flakes; mix well.

4. In a large bowl, combine beef with cabbage, carrots, green onions, spaghetti, and cilantro. Pour lemon juice mixture over and toss to coat. Serve immediately.

Hearty Meat Loaf

Letting meat loaf stand after it's baked allows the juices to redistribute so it stays juicy and slices more easily.

Serves 4 to 6

Calories: 231.44
Fat: 8.06 grams
Saturated Fat: 2.73 grams
Cholesterol: 57.52 mg
Sodium: 554.87 mg

1 tablespoon olive oil
1 onion, chopped
½ cup chopped celery
    with leaves
½ cup seasoned dry
    bread crumbs
2 egg whites
1 teaspoon
    Worcestershire sauce
⅛ teaspoon pepper
1 pound lean top ground,
    ground
½ cup ketchup
2 tablespoons mustard

1. Preheat oven to 375°F. In a medium saucepan, heat olive oil over medium heat. Add onion and celery; cook and stir until tender, about 6 to 7 minutes. Remove from heat and place in medium bowl.

2. Add bread crumbs, egg whites, Worcestershire sauce, salt, and pepper and mix well. Add beef and mix gently until combined. Place mixture into nonstick 9" × 5" loaf pan.

3. In a small bowl, combine ketchup and mustard and mix well. Spread over top of loaf. Bake for 60 to 70 minutes or until internal temperature registers 160°F. Cover meat loaf with foil and let stand for 10 minutes before serving.

Ground Beef

If you grind your own beef, you can control the fat content. Trim excess fat from the beef and cut it into cubes. Place the cubes in a food processor and process using the pulse function until the beef is coarsely ground. You can also buy a steak and ask the butcher to grind it.

Pastitsio

This is a casserole to serve a crowd!
Make it ahead of time and store it, unbaked, in the fridge,
then add 10 to 15 minutes to the baking time.

Serves 10

Calories: 451.83
Fat: 7.99 grams
Saturated Fat: 3.68
grams
Cholesterol: 61.75 mg
Sodium: 528.49 mg

*1½ pounds lean ground
    beef*
1 onion, finely chopped
3 cloves garlic, minced
*2 cups fat-free beef broth,
    divided*
¾ cup dry white wine
*1 (6-ounce) can no-salt
    tomato paste*
½ cup bulgur wheat
1 teaspoon cinnamon
½ teaspoon nutmeg
½ teaspoon allspice
½ teaspoon salt
½ teaspoon pepper
2 tablespoons flour
*1 (13-ounce) can low-fat
    evaporated milk*
*¾ cup grated Parmesan
    cheese, divided*
*2 cups 1% cottage
    cheese, puréed*
1 pound elbow macaroni

1. Preheat oven to 350°F. In a large skillet, cook brown beef, stirring to break up beef, until partially cooked. Add onion and garlic; cook and stir until beef is done and vegetables are tender. Drain thoroughly.

2. Add 1 cup beef broth, wine, and tomato paste and stir until tomato paste is blended. Add bulgur, cinnamon, nutmeg, allspice, salt, and pepper and bring to a boil. Reduce heat and simmer for 20 minutes.

3. Bring a large pot of salted water to a boil. In a medium saucepan, combine flour and remaining 1 cup beef broth; stir to blend. Add evaporated milk and bring to a boil over medium heat. Cook and stir with wire whisk until thickened, about 5 to 6 minutes. Remove from heat and stir in ½ cup Parmesan cheese and the cottage cheese.

4. Cook pasta until al dente, drain and add to cheese mixture. Spray 9" × 13" glass baking dish with nonstick cooking spray. Layer half of the pasta mixture and half of the meat mixture in pan. Repeat layers, then sprinkle with remaining ¼ cup Parmesan cheese.

5. Bake for 45 to 50 minutes or until casserole is bubbling and cheese is melted and beginning to brown. Let stand for 10 minutes, then serve.

Steak Stroganoff

Stroganoff is the perfect recipe for entertaining.
Serve it with a spinach salad, some dinner rolls warm from the
oven, and an apple pie.

1. Trim off excess fat from the steak and slice against the grain into ¼-inch strips. In a large skillet, heat olive oil over medium heat. Add onion and mushrooms; cook and stir until tender, about 5 minutes.

2. Add beef and cook, stirring frequently, until browned, about 4 minutes longer.

3. Meanwhile, in small bowl combine tomato paste, water, basil, cornstarch, yogurt, and broth and mix with wire whisk until blended. Add to skillet and bring to a simmer. Simmer for 3 to 4 minutes or until sauce thickens. Serve immediately over hot cooked noodles.

Tomato Paste

Tomato paste is an excellent ingredient to add lots of flavor to a dish without extra fat. If you can find tomato paste in a tube, just store it in the refrigerator and use it as you need it. If you can only find it in a can, remove the paste from the can and freeze it in a small freezer bag. Cut off what you need when you need it.

Serves 6

Calories: 359.49
Fat: 11.33 grams
Saturated Fat: 3.19 grams
Cholesterol: 67.90 mg
Sodium: 91.66 mg

1 pound boneless round
  steak
2 tablespoons olive oil
1 onion, chopped
1 (8-ounce) package
  sliced mushrooms
3 tablespoons tomato
  paste
3 tablespoons water
½ teaspoon basil leaves
1 tablespoon cornstarch
1 cup plain low-fat yogurt
¼ cup fat-free beef broth
3 cups hot cooked
  noodles

Savory Pot Roast

Serves 8 to 10

Calories: 285.57
Fat: 10.04 grams
Saturated Fat: 3.10 grams
Cholesterol: 91.43 mg
Sodium: 402.63 mg

2 pounds beef bottom
    round roast
¼ cup flour
1 teaspoon salt
¼ teaspoon pepper
1 tablespoon vegetable oil
1 onion, chopped
3 celery stalks, chopped
2 carrots, sliced
½ cup dry red wine
½ cup low-sodium
    vegetable juice
    cocktail
1 teaspoon dried thyme
    leaves
1 teaspoon dried
    marjoram leaves
3 tablespoons honey
2 tablespoons apple cider
    vinegar
3 tablespoons ketchup

Pot roast is the perfect meal for a cold snowy day. You get all the preparation out of the way in the morning, and it will make your home smell fabulous as it cooks to perfection in the slow cooker.

1. Trim excess fat from beef and sprinkle with flour, salt, and pepper. Heat vegetable oil in large skillet. Brown beef on both sides over medium high heat, about 5 to 7 minutes total.

2. Meanwhile, in 4- to 5-quart slow cooker, combine onion, celery, and carrots. Place beef on vegetables.

3. Add wine and vegetable juice cocktail to skillet; cook and stir to remove pan drippings. Remove from heat and add remaining ingredients. Pour over beef in slow cooker.

4. Cover and cook on low for 9 to 10 hours or until beef and vegetables are very tender. Serve beef and vegetables with sauce.

Caribbean Beef

Ginger and pineapple combine with beef and vegetables to make an excellent and easy dinner perfect for entertaining.

1. In a large skillet, heat olive oil over medium heat. Add onion; cook and stir for 3 minutes. Then add cubes of beef; brown on all sides, about 5 minutes total.

2. Meanwhile, drain pineapple, reserving juice. Remove beef from skillet and add juice, water, vinegar, brown sugar, salt, and ginger root and bring to a simmer. Return beef to skillet, cover, and simmer over low heat until beef is tender, about 35 to 45 minutes.

3. In a small bowl mix cornstarch and soy sauce. Add to beef mixture along with bell pepper strips. Cook and stir for 8 to 10 minutes until sauce thickens, beef is very tender, and peppers are crisp-tender. Serve immediately over hot cooked rice.

Caribbean Ingredients

Ingredients from the tropics include pineapple, ginger, peppers, jicama, mango, and papaya. All of these ingredients add a lot of flavor with no fat—and they all have lots of vitamins, minerals, and fiber. Add more of these ingredients to your everyday cooking.

Serves 6

Calories: 292.17
Fat: 6.54 grams
Saturated Fat: 1.78 grams
Cholesterol: 93.50 mg
Sodium: 447.69 mg

1 tablespoon olive oil
1 onion, chopped
1½ pounds top round of beef, cubed
1 (13-ounce) can pineapple tidbits
½ cup water
⅓ cup apple cider vinegar
¼ cup brown sugar
½ teaspoon salt
1 tablespoon minced ginger root
2 tablespoons cornstarch
2 tablespoons low-sodium soy sauce
1 green bell pepper, cut into strips
1 red bell pepper, cut into strips

Spicy Beef and Cabbage

*Cabbage is delicious when lightly cooked. It adds color, crunch,
and fiber to this simple dish.*

Serves 4

Calories: 324.53
Fat: 9.08 grams
Saturated Fat: 2.34
grams
Cholesterol: 70.36 mg
Sodium: 236.14 mg

¾ pound top round beef
   steak
½ cup orange juice
2 tablespoons hoisin
   sauce
2 tablespoons rice
   vinegar
1 tablespoon cornstarch
⅛ teaspoon cayenne
   pepper
1 tablespoon vegetable oil
1 tablespoon minced
   ginger root
1 onion, chopped
1 (10-ounce) package
   shredded cabbage
1½ cups shredded carrots
3 green onions, julienned

1. Trim excess fat from steak and cut into ⅛" × 3" strips against the grain. In a small bowl, combine orange juice, hoisin sauce, rice vinegar, cornstarch, and pepper and mix well; set aside.

2. In a large skillet, heat vegetable oil over medium high heat. Add ginger root and onion; cook and stir for 3 to 4 minutes until onion is crisp-tender. Add beef and cook for 2 to 3 minutes or until browned. Remove beef and onion from skillet with slotted spoon and set aside.

3. Add cabbage, carrots, and green onion to skillet; stir-fry for 3 minutes. Stir orange juice mixture and add to skillet along with beef. Stir-fry until sauce thickens slightly and beef and vegetables are tender. Serve immediately over hot cooked rice.

Beef Stew

Stews simmer for a long time to tenderize the beef and blend ingredients. This easy recipe is a classic.

1. Trim excess fat from steak and cut into 1-inch cubes. Sprinkle cubes with salt, pepper, flour, and marjoram leaves. In a medium skillet, heat olive oil over medium heat. Add beef; cook and stir until browned, about 3 to 4 minutes.

2. Remove beef to 4-quart slow cooker. Add onion, potatoes, green beans, and tomatoes and mix well.

3. Add beef broth and water to skillet; bring to a boil, stirring to remove drippings. Pour into slow cooker. Cover and cook on low for 7 to 9 hours until beef and vegetables are tender.

Slow Cookers

Slow cookers are an excellent appliance for low-fat cooking. The meats used in slow cooker recipes are low in fat; because of this, moist heat cooks this type of meat to perfection. Slow cooked food is also lower in AGEs, those compounds that may play a part in heart disease and other inflammatory illnesses.

Serves 6

Calories: 337.54
Fat: 9.18 grams
Saturated Fat: 2.87 grams
Cholesterol: 59.50 mg
Sodium: 301.51 mg

1 pound lean top round steak
¼ teaspoon salt
⅛ teaspoon pepper
1 tablespoon flour
½ teaspoon dried marjoram leaves
1 tablespoon olive oil
1 onion, sliced
2 cups fat-free beef broth
6 new potatoes, cubed
1 cup green beans, chopped
1 cup chopped tomatoes
2 cups water

Beef Burgundy

Serves 8

Calories: 328.76
Fat: 12.67 grams
Saturated Fat: 3.78 grams
Cholesterol: 101.68 mg
Sodium: 253.53 mg

2 pounds round steak
½ teaspoon salt
¼ teaspoon pepper
3 onions, chopped,
    divided
6 cloves garlic, minced
1 teaspoon dried thyme
    leaves
1 bay leaf
1 cup burgundy wine
2 tablespoons flour
2 tablespoons olive oil
1 cup beef broth
1 (8-ounce) package
    sliced mushrooms
⅓ cup chopped flat-leaf
    parsley

This rich sauce is delicious served over hot cooked rice, pasta, or mashed potatoes. It's a classic—perfect for a holiday meal.

1.   Trim excess fat from steak and cut into 2-inch cubes. Sprinkle with salt and pepper and place in large glass bowl. Top with one of the onions, the garlic, thyme, bay leaf, and wine. Cover and refrigerate for 4 to 6 hours.

2.   Drain beef, reserving marinade, and dredge in flour. In a large skillet, heat oil over medium-high heat. Add remaining two onions and cook until crisp-tender, about 5 minutes, stirring frequently.

3.   Add the meat; cook and stir for 4 to 5 minutes until browned. Add reserved marinade and beef broth and bring to a simmer. Reduce heat, cover, and simmer for 1 hour or until beef is tender.

4.   Add mushrooms and parsley; simmer for another 10 to 15 minutes or until sauce is thickened and mushrooms are tender. Serve immediately.

Spicy Chinese Beef

You can use any quick-cooking vegetable in this super fast recipe. Mushrooms, eggplant, or summer squash are delicious.

1. In a small bowl, combine oyster sauce, chili paste, and beef broth; mix well. Prepare all ingredients.

2. In wok or large skillet, heat oil over high heat. Add onion, garlic, and ginger; stir-fry for 3 minutes. Add beef; stir-fry for 2 minutes until beef is browned.

3. Add tomatoes, bell peppers, and cabbage; stir-fry for 3 minutes longer. Stir oyster sauce mixture and add to skillet along with rice; stir-fry for 3 to 5 minutes or until hot.

4. Scoop onto serving plate, sprinkle with peanuts and green onions, and serve immediately.

Stir-Frying

It may take some time to prepare ingredients for stir-frying, but once the actual cooking starts, everything goes together quickly. It's easiest to have all of the ingredients prepared and ready before you start cooking. It's also important to use high heat and keep the food moving while it cooks.

Serves 8

Calories: 308.29
Fat: 9.61 grams
Saturated Fat: 2.50 grams
Cholesterol: 49.09 mg
Sodium: 333.81 mg

¼ cup oyster sauce
2 teaspoons chili paste
½ cup low-fat beef broth
1 tablespoon peanut oil
2 onions, chopped
4 cloves garlic, minced
1 tablespoon minced
    fresh ginger root
1 pound lean round steak,
    thinly sliced
2 tomatoes, cubed
2 green bell peppers,
    sliced
2 cups chopped Chinese
    cabbage
4 cups cold cooked
    brown rice
¼ cup chopped peanuts
¼ cup chopped green
    onions

Orange Beef and Broccoli Stir-Fry

Serves 6

Calories: 328.47
Fat: 6.93 grams
Saturated Fat: 1.90 grams
Cholesterol: 54.21 mg
Sodium: 513.29 mg

2 oranges
3 tablespoons low-sodium
    soy sauce
1 tablespoon rice wine
    vinegar
1 tablespoon cornstarch
1 teaspoon sugar
1 pound beef sirloin
1 tablespoon sesame oil
6 cloves garlic, minced
2 tablespoons minced
    ginger root
2 jalapeño peppers,
    minced
2 pounds broccoli, broken
    into small florets
⅓ cup water
1 red bell pepper, sliced
½ cup chopped green
    onion

The essential oils in citrus peels add lots of flavor with no fat. This recipe is very high in vitamin C as well as low in fat.

1. Thinly peel skin from oranges in wide strips, taking care not to include white pith. Julienne zest into thin strips. Squeeze orange juice and combine with soy sauce, vinegar, cornstarch, and sugar in small bowl.

2. Trim excess fat from beef and cut across the grain into ⅛" × 3" slices. Heat half of the sesame oil in large wok or skillet over medium high heat. Add garlic and ginger root; stir-fry for 2 minutes. Then add beef; stir-fry for 3 to 4 minutes until browned. Remove beef from wok with slotted spoon and set aside.

3. Add remaining oil to wok and add broccoli. Stir-fry for 1 minute, then add water. Cover and simmer, stirring occasionally, until water evaporates and broccoli is tender. Add bell pepper and onion to wok; stir-fry for 2 minutes.

4. Return beef to skillet along with orange juice mixture. Stir-fry until sauce has thickened, about 2 to 3 minutes. Serve immediately over hot cooked rice.

Hearty Bean Stew

This quick stew is scrumptiously filling and easy to make. Add any vegetable you like to the mixture to make it your own.

1. In a large saucepan, cook ground beef over medium heat, stirring to break up meat. Add celery and onion; cook and stir until crisp-tender, about 5 minutes. Add flour; cook and stir until bubbly. Add milk and broth; cook and stir until thickened.

2. Add remaining ingredients except the cheese and heat through. Sprinkle with cheese and serve immediately.

Canned Beans

Canned beans are an excellent addition to a low-fat diet. They are full of fiber and protein, but they can be high in sodium. Look for lower sodium varieties, especially in health food stores and co-ops. To reduce sodium content, you can thoroughly drain, then rinse the beans, then drain again before using in the recipe.

Serves 8

Calories: 462.24
Fat: 10.17 grams
Saturated Fat: 3.59 grams
Cholesterol: 47.10 mg
Sodium: 343.83 mg

1 pound lean ground beef
3 stalks celery, chopped
1 onion, diced
2 tablespoons flour
1 cup 1% milk
1 cup fat-free, low-sodium beef broth
2 (15-ounce) cans Great Northern Beans, drained
2 cups frozen corn, thawed
1 (14-ounce) can diced tomatoes, drained
⅛ teaspoon pepper
Dash Tabasco sauce
½ cup grated Cotija cheese

Ginger Peach Steak

Any steak can be prepared this way. The leaner cuts, including flank steak and the newest cut, flatiron steak, work best.

Serves 4

Calories: 410.64
Fat: 16.60 grams
Saturated Fat: 6.15 grams
Cholesterol: 70.41 mg
Sodium: 425.35 mg

*1 pound flank steak
1 (8-ounce) can peach
    slices in light syrup
1 tablespoon cornstarch
½ cup fat-free beef broth
2 tablespoons low-sodium
    soy sauce
1 tablespoon peanut oil
2 cloves garlic, minced
1 tablespoon minced
    fresh ginger root
½ cup sliced canned water
    chestnuts, drained
2 cups hot cooked rice*

1. Slice steak into ¼-inch strips against the grain. Drain peaches, reserving juice. In a small bowl, combine cornstarch, beef broth, soy sauce, and 2 tablespoons reserved peach juice.

2. In wok or large skillet, heat oil over medium high heat. Add garlic and ginger; stir-fry for 2 minutes. Add steak; stir-fry for 3 to 4 minutes until browned.

3. Add water chestnuts and stir-fry for 1 minute longer. Stir the broth mixture and add to wok along with peach slices. Stir-fry for 2 to 3 minutes or until sauce bubbles and thickens. Serve immediately over hot cooked rice.

Marinated Steak Kebabs

*You can marinate the beef for up to 4 hours in the refrigerator.
Don't marinate longer than that or the texture may soften too much.*

Serves 4

Calories: 218.90
Fat: 8.95 grams
Saturated Fat: 2.57 grams
Cholesterol: 73.38 mg
Sodium: 208.75 mg

*1 tablespoon lemon juice
1 tablespoon olive oil
½ teaspoon dried
    tarragon leaves
⅛ teaspoon Tabasco
    sauce
¼ teaspoon salt
⅛ teaspoon pepper
1 clove garlic, minced
1 pound round steak
1 red bell pepper, sliced
2 zucchini sliced*

1. In a medium bowl, combine lemon juice, olive oil, tarragon, Tabasco, salt, pepper, and garlic; mix well. Trim excess fat from steak and cut into 1-inch cubes. Add to lemon mixture and toss to coat; let stand for 20 minutes at room temperature.

2. Prepare and preheat grill. Thread marinated beef, bell pepper strips, and zucchini slices on metal skewers.

3. Cook 6 inches from medium coals for 6 to 8 minutes, turning once and brushing with any remaining lemon juice mixture, until beef is desired doneness and vegetables are tender. Serve immediately.

Surf and Turf Pasta

The combination of seafood and beef is classic; who knew you could have it in a low-fat recipe?

1. Bring a large pot of water to a boil. Trim excess fat from meat; cut into ¼-inch slices across the grain. Combine flour, salt, and pepper on plate; toss with shrimp and scallops.

2. Heat olive oil in large skillet over medium heat. Add beef; stir-fry for 2 to 3 minutes until browned; remove to bowl.

3. Add shrimp and scallops to skillet; stir-fry until cooked, about 4 to 5 minutes; remove to bowl with beef. Add garlic and chicken broth to skillet; bring to a simmer; simmer until thickened, about 5 minutes. Cook pasta according to package directions until al dente.

4. Return beef, shrimp, and scallops to skillet along with spinach, tomatoes, and basil leaves; bring to a simmer. Drain pasta and add to skillet; cook and stir until mixed. Serve immediately.

Serves 5

Calories: 434.35
Fat: 8.19 grams
Saturated Fat: 1.87 grams
Cholesterol: 73.92 mg
Sodium: 336.60 mg

½ pound sirloin steak
2 tablespoons flour
¼ teaspoon salt
Dash pepper
¼ pound medium shrimp, peeled
¼ pound scallops
1 tablespoon olive oil
4 cloves garlic, minced
1 cup fat-free chicken broth
1 (12-ounce) package radiatore pasta
1 cup chopped spinach leaves
6 dry-packed, sun-dried tomatoes, chopped
1 teaspoon dried basil leaves

Ginger root is a great ingredient to add flavor with absolutely no fat. You can substitute ½ teaspoon ground ginger for the fresh ginger in this recipe.

Calories: 305.09
Fat: 11.31 grams
Saturated Fat: 3.74 grams
Cholesterol: 48.86 mg
Sodium: 569.85 mg

⅔ cup fat-free beef broth
2 tablespoons low-sodium
    soy sauce
1 tablespoon sherry
1 teaspoon sugar
1 tablespoon cornstarch
2 tablespoons hoisin
    sauce
1 tablespoon peanut oil
1 onion, chopped
3 cloves garlic, minced
2 tablespoons minced
    fresh ginger root
½ teaspoon crushed red
    pepper flakes
¾ pound lean beef steak,
    cut into ¼-inch strips
2 cups snow peas

1. In a small bowl, combine broth, soy sauce, sherry, sugar, cornstarch, and hoisin sauce; mix well and set aside.

2. In wok or skillet, heat peanut oil over medium-high heat. Add onion, garlic, ginger root, and red pepper flakes; stir-fry for 3 minutes. Add beef; stir-fry until browned, about 3 to 4 minutes. Remove beef from skillet and set aside.

3. Add snow peas; stir-fry until crisp-tender, about 5 minutes. Stir beef broth mixture; add to skillet along with beef. Stir-fry until sauce thickens, about 2 to 3 minutes. Serve immediately over hot cooked rice.

Beef for Stir-Fry

For stir-frying, cut beef into ¼-inch strips that are about 3 inches long. Cut against the grain for the most tender results. Make sure you trim off any excess fat before you begin. Beef sliced this thin must be cooked quickly; do not over-brown in the first step.

Curried Beef Stir-Fry

Curry powder has a complex flavor that is the result of many spices blended together. It's delicious with the beef, fruit, and vegetables in this recipe.

1. In a medium bowl, combine cornstarch, sugar, soy sauce, plum sauce, vinegar, apple juice, and water and mix well to blend. Slice beef across the grain into ¼-inch slices and add to cornstarch mixture; let stand for 20 minutes.

2. Prepare remaining ingredients. In a large wok or skillet, heat olive oil over medium-high heat. Drain beef, reserving cornstarch mixture. Add beef to wok; stir-fry until browned, about 3 to 4 minutes. Remove beef from wok.

3. Add onions and garlic to wok; stir-fry for 3 minutes. Then add curry powder; stir-fry for 1 minute longer. Add celery and red bell pepper; stir-fry for 2 minutes.

4. Return beef to pan. Stir cornstarch mixture and add to the wok; stir-fry for 3 minutes or until sauce starts to bubble. Stir in grapes; stir-fry for 1 to 2 minutes until heated through. Serve over rice.

Serves 4

Calories: 407.62
Fat: 9.07 grams
Saturated Fat: 2.30 grams
Cholesterol: 53.55 mg
Sodium: 407.13 mg

2 tablespoons cornstarch
1 tablespoon sugar
2 tablespoons low-sodium soy sauce
2 tablespoons plum sauce
1 tablespoon vinegar
2 tablespoons apple juice
¼ cup water
1 pound round steak
1 tablespoon olive oil
1 onion, chopped
2 cloves garlic, minced
1 tablespoon curry powder
½ cup chopped celery
1 red bell pepper, chopped
1 cup red grapes
2 cups hot cooked rice

Lean, Juicy Burgers

Serves 6

Calories: 387.51
Fat: 13.45 grams
Saturated Fat: 3.41 grams
Cholesterol: 53.83 mg
Sodium: 600.99 mg

1 tablespoon canola oil
½ cup minced onion
½ cup minced celery
3 tablespoons dried
    bread crumbs
1 tablespoon
    Worcestershire sauce
¼ teaspoon salt
⅛ teaspoon pepper
1 pound 95% lean top
    round
6 hamburger buns
⅓ cup nonfat mayonnaise
3 tablespoons ketchup
6 tomato slices
6 red onion slices

Mixing these burgers like meat loaf keeps the meat tender and moist. Serve these at your next cookout.

1. Prepare and preheat grill or broiler. In a medium saucepan, combine the oil, onion, and celery; cook over medium heat for 5 minutes until tender. Add to bowl; add bread crumbs, Worcestershire sauce, and salt and pepper.

2. Add beef; gently mix to combine. Shape into six patties. Place the patties on a grill rack or broiler pan. Grill or broil, turn once, until well done 160°F, 7 to 8 minutes on each side.

3. When the burgers are almost ready, toast the buns on the grill or under the broiler until golden brown. Combine mayonnaise and ketchup and spread on the buns. Top with burgers, tomato and onion slices, and then the tops of the buns. Serve at once.

Grilling Hamburgers

Juicy hamburgers are easy to make—as long as you follow a few rules. First, handle the meat as little as possible. Keep it cold, and form it gently into patties. When you're cooking the burgers, do not press down on them with a spatula; that just squeezes out the juice you've worked so hard to keep in the burger!

Chimichangas

Chimichangas just sound like a party! Baking the chimichangas instead of frying them gives you less fat with just as much flavor.

1. Preheat oven to 400°F. In a large skillet, brown ground beef with onion and garlic until beef is cooked. Drain well. Add tomato, cilantro, chili powder, cumin, and jalapeño. Cook over medium heat for 10 more minutes, stirring frequently. Remove from the heat.

2. Stir cheese, sour cream, salt, and pepper into the beef mixture. Place two spoonfuls of meat filling in each tortilla; roll up and secure with toothpick. Place on baking sheet.

3. Repeat with remaining tortillas and filling. Brush filled tortillas with oil. Bake, uncovered, until crisp and brown, about 10 to 15 minutes. Serve with salsa.

Serves 6

Calories: 385.72
Fat: 13.79 grams
Saturated Fat: 3.62 grams
Cholesterol: 30.36 mg
Sodium: 796.87 mg

½ pound 95% lean ground beef
1 onion, chopped
3 cloves garlic, minced
1 tomato, chopped
2 tablespoons chopped cilantro
1 tablespoon chili powder
1 teaspoon cumin
¼ teaspoon salt
⅛ teaspoon cayenne pepper
1 jalapeño pepper, minced
1 cup shredded extra-sharp low-fat cheddar cheese
⅓ cup low-fat sour cream
6 (10-inch) flour tortillas, heated
2 tablespoons canola oil
½ cup Tomato Citrus Salsa (page 278)

Texan Rice

*This simple one-dish meal is a good choice for a
busy weeknight dinner.*

Serves 6

Calories: 248.85
Fat: 3.73 grams
Saturated Fat: 1.20 grams
Cholesterol: 25.12 mg
Sodium: 328.18 mg

*½ pound lean ground
    beef
1 onion, chopped
2 cloves garlic, minced
1 jalapeño pepper,
    minced
3 cups hot cooked brown
    rice
2 cups frozen corn,
    thawed
½ cup barbecue sauce
¼ cup ketchup
¼ teaspoon salt
⅛ teaspoon cayenne
    pepper*

1. In a large nonstick skillet, cook the beef over medium heat until browned, about 5 minutes. Drain off any fat. Add the onion, garlic, and jalapeño pepper and continue to cook until vegetables are tender, about 7 minutes longer. Drain again.

2. Add the rice, corn, barbecue sauce, ketchup, salt, and pepper and mix well. Cook over low heat, stirring frequently, until food is hot. Serve immediately.

Ground Beef

You can find several types of ground beef in the grocery store. The leanest is 95% ground beef, which means it contains 5% fat. If you're making a recipe that doesn't drain the beef after cooking, like meat loaf, the leanest beef is a good choice. Other percentages of lean to fat include 90%, 85%, and 75%.

Chapter 5
Pork

Tenderloin in BBQ Sauce 66

Curried Pork Chops 66

Split Pea Soup 67

Pork Medallions 68

Apricot Pork Pinwheels 69

Pork Chops Dijon 70

Raspberry Pork Chops 70

Sweet and Sour Pork 71

Baked Ziti 72

Pork Corn Dogs 73

Southwest Ham Succotash 74

Garlic Kasha with Pork 74

Pork and Garbanzo Bean Curry 75

Pork and Bean Salad 75

Pork and Veggie Casseroles 76

Tenderloin in BBQ Sauce

*Tenderloin is a lean, succulent cut of pork that's best cooked
fairly quickly. This sauce adds a lot of flavor.*

Serves 6

Calories: 228.20
Fat: 7.14 grams
Saturated Fat: 1.96 grams
Cholesterol: 59.69 mg
Sodium: 655.47 mg

1 tablespoon olive oil
1½ pound pork tenderloin
1 onion, chopped
¼ cup ketchup
2 tablespoons water
½ cup chili sauce
*3 tablespoons apple cider
     vinegar*
2 tablespoons brown sugar
*1 tablespoon
     Worcestershire sauce*
2 tablespoons mustard
1 tablespoon chili powder
⅛ teaspoon pepper

1. Preheat oven to 350°F. In a large ovenproof skillet, heat oil over medium heat. Brown tenderloin on all sides, about 6 minutes total. Remove from skillet and set aside.

2. Drain skillet, but do not wipe out. Add onion and sauté until translucent, about 5 minutes. Add ketchup, water, chili sauce, vinegar, brown sugar, Worcestershire sauce, mustard, chili powder, and pepper. Bring to a boil, reduce the heat to low; simmer for 15 minutes.

3. Return pork to the skillet and spoon sauce over. Cover, place in oven, and bake for 20 minutes. Uncover, turn tenderloin over, and bake until tender, about 5 to 10 minutes longer. Serve immediately.

Curried Pork Chops

*Pork is such a mild meat it can be seasoned many ways.
Curry powder, garlic, and onion make this dish special.*

Serves 6

Calories: 385.84
Fat: 11.08 grams
Saturated Fat: 3.35 grams
Cholesterol: 94.33 mg
Sodium: 467.43 mg

⅓ cup flour
¼ teaspoon salt
¼ teaspoon pepper
6 boneless loin pork chops
2 tablespoons olive oil
1 onion, chopped
*1 green bell pepper,
     chopped*
2 cloves garlic, minced
1 tablespoon curry powder
*1 (6-ounce) can tomato
     paste*
1½ cups water
½ cup raisins
½ cup mango chutney

1. In shallow bowl, combine flour, salt, and pepper, mixing well. Coat pork chops with the seasoned flour.

2. In a large skillet, heat oil over medium heat. Add chops and brown on both sides, about 5 minutes total. Remove chops from the skillet and set aside. Add onion, bell pepper, and garlic to skillet and cook until tender, about 7 minutes.

3. Drain off fat. Add curry powder, tomato paste, and water to skillet; bring to a simmer. Return pork to skillet and stir. Simmer, uncovered, over medium heat, until pork is tender, about 15 to 20 minutes. Add the raisins and chutney, heat through for another 5 minutes, and serve.

Split Pea Soup

*Split peas don't need to be soaked before
cooking like whole peas do.*

1. In soup pot, heat oil over medium heat. Add onion, carrots, celery, and garlic; cook and stir for 5 minutes. Add thyme, pepper, Worcestershire sauce, Tabasco, and bay leaves and stir well.

2. Add ham hocks, split peas, water, and potatoes; bring to a boil over medium-high heat. Reduce heat to low and simmer for 2 to 3 hours or until peas are tender.

3. Remove ham hocks and cut off meat. Return meat to pot along with potatoes; discard bones. Taste soup; if it needs salt, add more. Simmer for 20 to 30 minutes longer, or until potatoes are tender, then discard bay leaves and serve.

Ham Hocks

Ham hocks are usually available at the butcher's counter in your local grocery store, either cured or smoked. They give great flavor to soups and stews and are usually used when cooking greens in the southern United States. You can substitute cubed ham or cooked bacon for the hocks, but you won't get the same rich, smoky flavor.

Serves 8

Calories: 382.93
Fat: 10.04 grams
Saturated Fat: 2.64 grams
Cholesterol: 52.13 mg
Sodium: 218.10 mg

2 tablespoons olive oil
1 onion, chopped
2 carrots, sliced
2 celery stalks, sliced
4 cloves garlic, minced
½ teaspoon dried thyme
    leaves
¼ teaspoon pepper
1 teaspoon
    Worcestershire sauce
½ teaspoon Tabasco
    sauce
2 bay leaves
1 pound ham hocks
2 cups dried green split
    peas, rinsed
8 cups water
1 pound potatoes, peeled
    and diced
½ teaspoon salt

Pork Medallions

Serves 4

Calories: 241.20
Fat: 8.04 grams
Saturated Fat: 2.20 grams
Cholesterol: 45.80 mg
Sodium: 348.41 mg

4 (3-ounce) boneless lean
    pork chops
¼ teaspoon salt
⅛ teaspoon pepper
2 tablespoons olive oil,
    divided
1 cup sliced mushrooms
¼ cup shredded carrot
2 tablespoons sliced
    green onions
2 tablespoons diced
    celery
1 tablespoon lemon juice
½ teaspoon dried thyme
    leaves
1 tomato, chopped
2 tablespoons flour
1 cup fat-free chicken
    broth
1 tablespoon cornstarch
¼ cup skim milk

Medallions are simply thin pieces of tender, lean meat. They must be cooked quickly so they stay tender and juicy.

1. Place pork chops between two sheets of waxed paper. Gently pound with a meat mallet or rolling pin to a ⅛-inch thickness. Sprinkle with salt and pepper and set aside.

2. In a large saucepan, heat 1 tablespoon olive oil over medium heat. Add mushrooms, carrot, green onion, and celery; cook and stir until tender, about 5 minutes. Drain and remove to medium bowl; stir in lemon juice, thyme, and tomato.

3. Divide vegetable mixture among pork. Roll up, folding in sides, and secure with toothpicks or kitchen string. Sprinkle with flour.

4. In same skillet, heat remaining 1 tablespoon olive oil. Brown the pork bundles for 3 to 4 minutes. Pour chicken broth over pork, cover pan, and simmer until tender, about 10 to 15 minutes.

5. In a small bowl, combine cornstarch and milk, mix well. Remove pork from skillet and place on heated serving platter. Add cornstarch mixture to skillet; cook and stir over medium heat until thickened and bubbly, about 5 to 6 minutes.

6. Remove toothpicks or string; slice pork into 1-inch slices. Arrange on serving platter; pour sauce over medallions. Serve immediately.

Apricot Pork Pinwheels

This elegant dish is perfect for company. Serve with a spinach salad and cooked carrots.

Serves 6

Calories: 267.27
Fat: 7.24 grams
Saturated Fat: 1.94 grams
Cholesterol: 53.03 mg
Sodium: 146.79 mg

1 pound pork tenderloin
*⅓ cup chopped dried
    apricots*
*⅔ cup boiling fat-free
    chicken broth*
1 tablespoon olive oil
1 medium onion, chopped
*2 tablespoons chopped
    celery*
⅛ teaspoon cinnamon
*2 cups small whole wheat
    bread cubes*
2 tablespoons cornstarch
Dash nutmeg
1½ cups apricot nectar

1. Using a sharp knife, cut the tenderloin in half lengthwise; do not cut all the way through. Open the meat like a book, and pound with meat mallet to a 10" × 6" rectangle that is about ⅓ inch thick; set aside.

2. In a small bowl, combine apricots with chicken broth; let stand for 5 minutes. In a medium skillet, heat olive oil over medium heat. Add onion and celery; cook until tender, about 5 minutes. Remove pan from heat and add apricot mixture and cinnamon. Then add the bread crumbs, tossing to moisten.

3. Spread stuffing over pork. Roll up jelly-roll style, starting from the short edge. Secure with toothpicks or tie with kitchen string at 1-inch intervals. Cut into 6 slices.

4. Preheat broiler. Place meat slices on broiler pan. Broil 6 inches from heat for 10 minutes, then carefully turn and broil for 8 to 12 minutes longer until pork is cooked and tender. Remove string or toothpicks.

5. While meat is broiling, combine cornstarch, nutmeg, and nectar in medium skillet; bring to a boil over medium-high heat. Boil until thickened and reduced, about 6 to 7 minutes. Pour over meat and serve immediately.

Dried Apricots

Dried apricots are a great source of vitamin A, calcium, and iron. They are sweet and chewy and are good for snacking out of hand, in addition to being delicious when added to salads and sandwich spreads. The apricots are not peeled before drying; the peel helps hold in some of the moisture.

Pork Chops Dijon

We all need a quick and easy pork chop recipe in our repertoire.

Serves 4

Calories: 242.01
Fat: 9.08 grams
Saturated Fat: 3.70 grams
Cholesterol: 44.13 mg
Sodium: 473.03 mg

1 tablespoon olive oil
1 pound lean boneless pork chops
¼ teaspoon salt
⅛ teaspoon pepper
1 onion, chopped
2 carrots, sliced
3 tablespoons Dijon mustard
2 tablespoons Low-Fat Italian Salad Dressing (page 273)
¼ cup fat-free chicken broth
1 tablespoon cornstarch
⅛ teaspoon pepper

1. Heat olive oil in large skillet over medium heat. Sprinkle chops with salt and pepper and brown on both sides, turning once, about 4 to 5 minutes. Remove pork from skillet.

2. Add onion and carrots to skillet; cook and stir until tender. Remove onions and carrots from skillet. Remove skillet from heat. Return pork to pan and spoon onions and carrots on top.

3. In a small bowl, combine remaining ingredients and mix well. Spoon over the chops, cover the pan, and cook over medium-low heat until pork is tender and just pink in the center, about 12 to 14 minutes longer. Serve immediately.

Raspberry Pork Chops

Raspberries have a wonderful sweet and tart flavor that complement the meaty tenderness of the pork chops.

Serves 4

Calories: 283.69
Fat: 9.02 grams
Saturated Fat: 2.35 grams
Cholesterol: 65.09 mg
Sodium: 435.13 mg

4 boneless pork chops
¼ teaspoon salt
⅛ teaspoon pepper
1 tablespoon olive oil
¼ cup fat-free chicken broth
3 tablespoons raspberry vinegar
1 tablespoon low-sodium soy sauce
⅓ cup seedless raspberry jam
1 cup fresh raspberries

1. Sprinkle chops with salt and pepper. Heat olive oil in medium skillet over medium heat. Add chops; brown well on both sides, turning once, about 6 to 7 minutes total.

2. Add chicken broth, vinegar, and soy sauce to pan. Bring to a boil, then cover pan, reduce heat to low, and simmer for 10 minutes.

3. Uncover pan and remove pork. Add jam to sauce in pan and stir to blend. Return pork to pan and simmer for 2 to 4 minutes longer or until pork is just cooked and still slightly pink in center. Sprinkle with raspberries and serve immediately.

Sweet and Sour Pork

This is a healthy take on the classic combination of sweet and sour flavors found in Asian cuisine.

Serves 8

Calories: 381.51
Fat: 6.31 grams
Saturated Fat: 1.86 grams
Cholesterol: 66.44 mg
Sodium: 499.73 mg

1. Sprinkle pork with salt and pepper and cut into 1-inch cubes. Drain pineapple, reserving liquid. In a small bowl, combine 1 cup pineapple liquid with brown sugar, vinegar, soy sauce, ketchup, ginger, and cornstarch; mix well and set aside.

2. In a large skillet or wok, heat oil over medium heat and add pork; stir-fry until pork is browned, about 5 minutes; remove from skillet. Add celery, bell pepper, and onion; stir-fry until crisp-tender, about 5 minutes.

3. Return pork to skillet and stir-fry for 1 minute. Stir pineapple liquid mixture and add to skillet along with pineapple tidbits. Cook and stir until bubbly, then continue cooking, stirring frequently, until pork and vegetables are tender. Serve immediately with hot cooked brown rice.

2 pounds boneless pork loin chops
½ teaspoon salt
⅛ teaspoon pepper
1 (20-ounce) can pineapple tidbits
¼ cup brown sugar
½ cup apple cider vinegar
2 tablespoons reduced-sodium soy sauce
3 tablespoons ketchup
¼ teaspoon ground ginger
2 tablespoons cornstarch
1 tablespoon olive oil
1 cup sliced celery
1 red bell pepper, chopped
1 onion, chopped

Baked Ziti

Baked ziti is a classic Italian dish that is similar to lasagna but quicker and easier to make.

Serves 8

Calories: 454.70
Fat: 13.06 grams
Saturated Fat: 5.08 grams
Cholesterol: 42.06 mg
Sodium: 829.42 mg

1 pound spicy pork sausage
1 onion, chopped
4 cloves garlic, minced
½ cup dry white wine
2 (14-ounce) cans diced tomatoes, undrained
½ teaspoon dried basil leaves
½ teaspoon dried oregano leaves
¼ cup tomato paste
2 tablespoons flour
½ cup skim milk
¼ teaspoon salt
⅛ teaspoon pepper
1 (16-ounce) package ziti pastas
¾ cup shredded part-skim mozzarella cheese
¼ cup grated Romano cheese

1. Preheat oven to 400°F. Spray a 3-quart baking dish with nonstick cooking spray and set aside.

2. In a large skillet, cook sausage with onion and garlic, stirring to break up meat. When sausage is cooked, drain well. Add wine, tomatoes, basil, oregano, and tomato paste, stirring to blend; cook for 3 minutes.

3. In a small bowl combine flour, milk, salt, and pepper; stir well. Add to skillet. Cook, stirring occasionally, until slightly thickened, about 8 to 10 minutes.

4. Cook pasta as directed on package until not quite al dente. Drain and add to skillet, stirring to coat. Pour into prepared baking dish and top with cheeses.

5. Bake until casserole is bubbly and cheese begins to brown, about 25 to 35 minutes. Serve immediately.

Baking Pasta

When you're baking pasta that has been boiled, be sure to cook it less than al dente. The pasta should still have a firm center. The pasta will finish cooking in the sauce, whether it's being simmered or baked, and it will also absorb some of the flavors of the sauce.

Pork Corn Dogs

These taste just like corn dogs from the state fair, but they're better for you! Your kids will love them.

1. Preheat oven to 350°F. Spray a cookie sheet with nonstick cooking spray and set aside. In a medium bowl, sift together the flour, sugar, baking powder, and salt. Stir in the cornmeal.

2. Using a pastry blender or two knives, cut in the oil until the mixture resembles coarse meal. In a separate bowl, whisk together the egg and milk until blended and stir into the cornmeal mixture, mixing until blended.

3. Insert a wooden skewer into the end of each hot dog. Working in batches, coat the hot dogs evenly with the batter and arrange on prepared cookie sheet.

4. Bake for 15 to 25 minutes or until batter is lightly browned. Serve immediately with ketchup and mustard.

Serves 8

Calories: 244.94
Fat: 6.93 grams
Saturated Fat: 1.89 grams
Cholesterol: 63.03 mg
Sodium: 520.73 mg

1 cup flour
2 tablespoons sugar
1½ teaspoons baking powder
¼ teaspoon salt
⅔ cup cornmeal
3 tablespoons vegetable oil
1 egg
¾ cup skim milk
1 pound lower-fat frankfurters

Southwest Ham Succotash

Serves 4

Calories: 333.86
Fat: 10.39 grams
Saturated Fat: 2.24 grams
Cholesterol: 19.95 mg
Sodium: 620.81 mg

1 tablespoon olive oil
½ teaspoon cumin seeds
4 cloves garlic, minced
1 onion, chopped
1 red bell pepper, chopped
1 jalapeño pepper, minced
1 cup water
1 cup diced ham
3 tablespoons tomato paste
2 tablespoons adobo
    sauce
2 cups frozen corn
2 cups frozen baby lima
    beans
¼ cup chopped cilantro

*Succotash is a long-simmering mixture of lima beans and corn.
Adding ham elevates this humble side dish to a main dish.*

1. Heat the oil in a large skillet over medium-high heat. Add cumin seeds and let sizzle for 5 seconds. Add garlic and cook, stirring frequently for 1 minute longer. Add onions, bell pepper, and jalapeño; cook and stir for 4 minutes.

2. Add water, ham, tomato paste, and adobo sauce. Bring to a simmer, cover, reduce heat to low, and simmer for 10 minutes.

3. Add corn and lima beans and bring back to a simmer, stirring. Cover and cook for 7 to 10 minutes or until vegetables are tender and sauce is blended. Sprinkle with cilantro and serve immediately.

Adobo Sauce

Adobo sauce is a spicy Mexican condiment made from ground chilies, garlic, cumin, and oregano. It is often used to pack smoked jalapeño chilies, also called chipotles. The sauce adds a nice kick of flavor to soups and sauces. It keeps well for a long time when stored in the refrigerator.

Garlic Kasha with Pork

Serves 4

Calories: 221.75
Fat: 8.36 grams
Saturated Fat: 2.05 grams
Cholesterol: 94.55 mg
Sodium: 288.15 mg

1 tablespoon olive oil
1 cup kasha
1 egg, lightly beaten
1 cup boiling water
1 cup fat-free chicken broth
2 cloves garlic, minced
1 onion, finely chopped
1 tablespoon soy sauce
1½ cups cubed cooked pork

Kasha, or buckwheat groats, is the whole buckwheat kernel stripped of its hull. It's chewy even when cooked, making a great complement to the pork.

1. In a saucepan, heat oil over medium heat. Add the kasha and sauté for 5 minutes. Add the egg and stir until kasha is coated with the egg.

2. Pour in the boiling water, stir well, and cook, uncovered, for 3 minutes. Add the broth, garlic, onion, soy sauce, and pork, cover, and cook over low heat until kasha is tender, about 10 minutes. Remove from the heat and let stand, covered, for 5 minutes before serving.

Pork and Garbanzo Bean Curry

If you love curry, increase the curry powder to 1 tablespoon. You could also increase the amount of ginger you use.

1. In a large skillet, brown pork in olive oil over medium heat for 5 minutes. Add the garlic, onion, and ginger and cook for 2 minutes. Stir in the flour, curry powder, coriander, cumin, salt, and pepper.

2. Add carrots, potatoes, and water and bring to a boil. Reduce the heat to low, cover, and cook for 10 minutes, adding more water if the mixture begins to dry.

3. Add garbanzo beans, cover, and cook over medium heat until the vegetables are cooked through, about 10 minutes longer. Serve immediately.

Garbanzo Beans

Garbanzo beans, also called chick peas, are a wonderful source of high-quality protein and insoluble and soluble fiber. You need both types of fiber in your diet to help reduce cholesterol and prevent digestive diseases.

Serves 4

Calories: 456.27
Fat: 12.07 grams
Saturated Fat: 3.04 grams
Cholesterol: 85.45 mg
Sodium: 539.84 mg

1 pound pork tenderloin, cubed
1 tablespoon olive oil
2 cloves garlic, minced
1 onion, chopped
1 tablespoon minced ginger root
1 tablespoon flour
2 teaspoons curry powder
¼ teaspoon salt
⅛ teaspoon pepper
½ cup grated carrots
2 potatoes, peeled and cubed
½ cup water
1 (15-ounce) can garbanzo beans, drained

Pork and Bean Salad

This is a good recipe for using leftover pork, whether it's chops or tenderloin.

In a medium bowl, combine the beans, pork, bell pepper, garlic, and sage. Add the Salad Dressing and toss well. Chill for 30 minutes before serving.

Serves 4

Calories: 267.31
Fat: 4.86 grams
Saturated Fat: 1.29 grams
Cholesterol: 33.58 mg
Sodium: 105.15 mg

1 (15-ounce) can white beans, drained
1 cup cubed cooked pork
1 red bell pepper, chopped
1 green bell pepper, chopped
2 cloves garlic, chopped
2 teaspoons chopped fresh sage leaves
¼ cup Low-Fat Italian Salad Dressing (page 273)

Pork and Veggie Casseroles

It's fun to serve individual casseroles. You can't make this recipe ahead of time, however, because you can't partially cook meat and refrigerate it.

Serves 4

Calories: 388.79
Fat: 14.95 grams
Saturated Fat: 5.25 grams
Cholesterol: 74.78 mg
Sodium: 334.95 mg

1 tablespoon olive oil
4 boneless pork chops
¼ teaspoon salt
⅛ teaspoon pepper
1 cup sliced zucchini
2 carrots, sliced
1 onion, chopped
2 cloves garlic, minced
2 tomatoes, chopped
¼ cup sliced black olives
2 cups cooked rice
2 tablespoons minced flat-leaf parsley
1 tablespoon minced basil
1 tablespoon butter

1. Preheat oven to 350°F. In a medium skillet, heat olive oil over medium-high heat. Sprinkle pork with salt and pepper; brown on both sides in oil, about 5 to 6 minutes. Remove from skillet.

2. Add zucchini, carrot, onions, and garlic to skillet; cook and stir until crisp-tender, about 4 minutes. Add tomatoes, olives, rice, parsley, and basil; stir and remove from heat. Divide evenly between 4 individual baking dishes or gratin dishes.

3. Top each with a browned pork chop. Dot pork with the butter and cover with foil.

4. Bake until pork is tender and internal temperature reaches 155°F, about 35 to 40 minutes. Serve immediately.

Chapter 6
Chicken

Fruity Chicken Salad 78

Nutty Chicken Fingers 79

Easy BBQ Chicken 79

Cajun Chicken Strips 80

Yogurt Chicken Paprika 81

Skillet Chicken and Rice 82

Broiled Spicy Chicken in Yogurt 82

Quick Chicken Mozzarella 83

Chicken Salad Plate 84

Chicken Marsala 85

Poached Chicken 85

Very Lemon Chicken 86

Sesame Teriyaki Chicken 87

Crab-Stuffed Chicken 88

Chicken in Buttermilk 89

Chicken Breasts with Curried Stuffing 90

Cheesy Chicken Rolls 91

Garlicky Grilled Chicken 92

Fruity Chicken Salad

Serves 8

Calories: 178.77
Fat: 4.48 grams
Saturated Fat: 0.93 grams
Cholesterol: 45.24 mg
Sodium: 187.63 mg

*3 cups shredded cooked
    chicken*
*1½ cups peeled melon
    chunks*
*1½ cups peeled
    cucumber chunks*
2 cups green grapes
¼ cup nonfat mayonnaise
*1 cup strawberry low-fat
    yogurt*
*1 teaspoon apple cider
    vinegar*
⅛ teaspoon salt
⅛ teaspoon white pepper
¼ cup chopped cilantro
2 tablespoons lime juice

*This fresh salad is a nice choice for a quiet lunch on the porch or
for a packed lunch. You can add other fruits, too; strawberries or
blackberries are both nice.*

1. In serving bowl, combine chicken, melon, cucumber, and grapes; toss to mix.

2. In a small bowl, combine remaining ingredients and mix well with wire whisk. Add to chicken mixture and stir gently to coat. Cover and chill for 2 hours before serving.

Cucumbers
*Cucumbers belong to the watermelon family. They are about 95 percent
water and are very refreshing to eat. They contain vitamin C, as well as
potassium and magnesium. They are usually sold with a wax coating,
which is why they are peeled before use. Look for English cucumbers,
which are not waxed, to use the peel for more fiber.*

Nutty Chicken Fingers

These little sticks of chicken are great for kids. Serve them with a dipping sauce like Smoky Salsa (page 292 or Creamy Mustard Dip (page 280.

Serves 8

Calories: 117.39
Fat: 4.07 grams
Saturated Fat: 0.51 grams
Cholesterol: 34.51 mg
Sodium: 77.67 mg

¾ cup crushed cornflake
  crumbs
¼ cup finely chopped
  pecans
2 tablespoons chopped
  flat-leaf parsley
¼ teaspoon garlic salt
¼ teaspoon pepper
4 boneless, skinless
  chicken breasts
3 tablespoons 1% milk

1. Preheat oven to 400°F. In shallow dish, combine crumbs, pecans, parsley, garlic salt, and pepper and mix well.

2. Cut chicken into strips about 3 inches long and ½ inch wide. Dip the chicken in the milk, then roll in the crumb mixture to coat. Place in a 15" × 10" jelly roll pan.

3. Bake until chicken is tender and juices run clear when pierced with a fork, about 5 to 7 minutes. Serve at once with a dipping sauce.

Easy BBQ Chicken

Buttermilk adds a sweet tanginess to this easy barbecue sauce. Use it to cook pork chops and spareribs too.

Serves 8

Calories: 246.63
Fat: 5.64 grams
Saturated Fat: 1.46 grams
Cholesterol: 119.68 mg
Sodium: 571.85 mg

¼ cup buttermilk
⅓ cup ketchup
¼ cup chili sauce
3 tablespoons Dijon
  mustard
2 tablespoons honey
3 cloves garlic, minced
1 teaspoon dried oregano
  leaves
1 teaspoon dried basil
  leaves
1 teaspoon dried thyme
  leaves
½ teaspoon salt
¼ teaspoon pepper
3 pounds skinless chicken
  parts

1. In a large bowl, combine buttermilk, ketchup, chili sauce, mustard, honey, garlic, oregano, basil, thyme, salt, and pepper. Add chicken, turn to coat, cover, and refrigerate for 3 hours.

2. Prepare and preheat grill. Remove chicken from the marinade, reserving marinade. Place chicken on grill rack 6 inches over hot coals and grill, turning once, until the chicken is tender and thoroughly cooked, about 8 to 10 minutes on each side. Brush occasionally with reserved marinade. The chicken can be placed in a glass baking dish and topped with some of the marinade, then baked in a 325°F oven until done, about 40 to 50 minutes. Serve hot.

Cajun Chicken Strips

Serve these tender little strips of chicken with a variety of sauces, including barbecue sauce and Creamy Mustard Sauce (page 280.

Serves 6

Calories: 223.92
Fat: 4.04 grams
Saturated Fat: 0.77 grams
Cholesterol: 71.34 mg
Sodium: 271.13 mg

2 cloves garlic, minced
¾ cup dried bread
    crumbs
¼ cup grated Parmesan
    cheese
1 tablespoon dried
    parsley flakes
½ teaspoon paprika
½ teaspoon dried
    oregano leaves
⅛ teaspoon pepper
1½ pound boneless,
    skinless chicken
    breasts
1 cup buttermilk

1. Preheat oven to 425°F. Spray a cookie sheet with nonstick baking spray containing flour; set aside.

2. In shallow dish, combine garlic, bread crumbs, cheese, parsley, paprika, oregano, and pepper and mix well.

3. Cut chicken into ½-inch by 3-inch strips. Combine with buttermilk on plate, toss to coat, and let stand for 10 minutes.

4. Dip chicken into bread crumb mixture, then place in single layer on prepared cookie sheet. Bake for 5 minutes, then carefully turn with a spatula and bake for 5 to 6 minutes longer until chicken is thoroughly cooked. Serve immediately.

Yogurt Chicken Paprika

Yogurt and paprika are a classic combination when cooked with chicken. Serve this over hot cooked brown rice.

Serves 6

Calories: 272.99
Fat: 6.09 grams
Saturated Fat: 1.80 grams
Cholesterol: 90.95 mg
Sodium: 375.05 mg

3 boneless, skinless chicken thighs
3 boneless, skinless chicken breasts
⅛ teaspoon pepper
½ teaspoon salt
¼ cup flour
1 tablespoon olive oil
1 onion, diced
½ cup fat-free chicken broth
1 tablespoon lemon juice
2 tablespoons cornstarch
2 cups plain low-fat yogurt
2 teaspoons paprika

1. Season chicken with salt and pepper. Roll in the flour to coat. In a large skillet, heat oil over medium heat. Add chicken and brown on both sides, about 10 minutes total. Add onion, chicken broth, and lemon juice; bring to a simmer. Cover and simmer until tender and thoroughly cooked, about 12 to 17 minutes. Since the breasts will cook faster than the thighs, keep an eye on them and remove when cooked.

2. Meanwhile, combine cornstarch, yogurt, and paprika in a medium bowl. When chicken is cooked, remove from pan and drain off half of the liquid. Add yogurt mixture to pan drippings and bring to a simmer. Simmer over low heat for 5 minutes, then return chicken to the pan. Simmer for another 3 to 4 minutes until sauce is slightly thickened. Serve immediately.

Chicken Breasts and Thighs

The white meat and dark meat of chicken cook at different times, which is why it's difficult to roast a whole chicken to perfection. They are also done at different temperatures. White meat, or the breast, should be cooked to 170°F, while the dark meat, or thighs and wings, should be cooked to 180°F.

Skillet Chicken and Rice

*One-dish meals are a great time saver,
not only in preparation but also in cleanup.*

Serves 6

Calories: 320.74
Fat: 7.73 grams
Saturated Fat: 1.66 grams
Cholesterol: 100.68 mg
Sodium: 264.99 mg

*1 tablespoon olive oil
2 pounds chicken parts,
   skinned
¼ cup flour
3 cups sliced mushrooms
4 carrots, sliced ½-inch
   thick
¾ cup long-grain white rice
1 onion, chopped
2 cloves garlic, minced
2 cups fat-free chicken
   broth
1 teaspoon poultry
   seasoning
⅛ teaspoon white pepper*

1. Heat olive oil in large skillet over medium heat. Sprinkle chicken with flour. Brown chicken on both sides in hot oil, turning once, about 10 minutes. Remove chicken from skillet.

2. Add mushrooms, carrots, rice, onion, and garlic; cook and stir for 5 minutes. Add chicken broth, poultry seasoning, and pepper. Place chicken on top of rice mixture.

3. Bring to a simmer. Cover skillet and cook over low heat until rice is tender, liquid is absorbed, and chicken is thoroughly cooked, about 30 to 40 minutes. Serve immediately.

Broiled Spicy Chicken in Yogurt

Yogurt is a wonderful tenderizer, making chicken tender and juicy. You can use any combination of spices you'd like in this easy recipe.

Serves 6

Calories: 159.03
Fat: 2.10 grams
Saturated Fat: 0.80 grams
Cholesterol: 70.89 mg
Sodium: 202.48 mg

*1 cup plain low-fat yogurt
1 teaspoon cumin
1 teaspoon cayenne
   pepper
¼ teaspoon allspice
1 teaspoon paprika
1 teaspoon grated lemon
   zest
2 tablespoons lemon juice
3 cloves garlic, minced
¼ teaspoon salt
6 boneless, skinless
   chicken breasts*

1. In shallow dish, combine yogurt with the spices, lemon zest, lemon juice, garlic, and salt; mix well. Add chicken breasts and turn to coat. Cover and refrigerate for at least 8 hours or overnight.

2. When ready to eat, preheat broiler. Remove chicken from marinade and place on a broiler pan. Broil chicken 6 inches from heat, turning once, until golden brown and cooked through, about 8 to 11 minutes. Serve immediately.

Quick Chicken Mozzarella

When it's just the two of you, this super quick recipe is easy and delicious. It also works for a laid-back lunch with guests.

Serves 2

Calories: 274.05
Fat: 9.19 grams
Saturated Fat: 1.68 grams
Cholesterol: 73.17 mg
Sodium: 429.17 mg

*2 boneless, skinless
    chicken breast halves*
*2 tablespoons low-fat
    buttermilk*
*3 tablespoons seasoned
    dry bread crumbs*
1 tablespoon olive oil
*⅓ cup shredded nonfat
    mozzarella cheese*
2 (½-inch) tomato slices
*1 tablespoon chopped
    fresh basil*

1. Place chicken, smooth-side down, between waxed paper. Working from the center to the edges, pound gently with a meat mallet or rolling pin until meat is ⅛ inch thick. Brush chicken with buttermilk and dip into bread crumbs to coat both sides.

2. In a medium skillet, heat olive oil over medium heat. Add chicken and sauté, turning once, until golden brown and cooked through, about 7 to 8 minutes total.

3. Reduce heat to low. Top chicken with cheese, tomato, and basil. Cover pan and cook for 1 minute, then serve immediately.

Doubling Recipes

You can double most cooking recipes—that is, soups, broiled and grilled meats, and casseroles. Don't try to double baking recipes because they usually won't work. If you do double or even triple a recipe, be careful with seasonings. Use less than double and then add more if you think the recipe needs it.

Chicken Salad Plate

This salad has a lot of great taste and texture.
You could use any flavor of low-fat cheese you enjoy.

Serves 8

Calories: 381.27
Fat: 7.23 grams
Saturated Fat: 2.29 grams
Cholesterol: 50.58 mg
Sodium: 345.17 mg

3 cups cooked small white beans
3 cups cooked pink beans
3 cups cubed, cooked chicken breast
½ pound low-fat extra-sharp Cheddar cheese, cubed
½ teaspoon dried basil leaves
1 tablespoon sugar
¾ cup Low-Fat Italian Salad Dressing (page 273)
1 head iceberg lettuce
1 (6-ounce) can marinated artichoke hearts
1 lemon, cut into 8 wedges

1. In a bowl, combine beans, chicken, and cheese; toss to mix.

2. In a small bowl, combine basil, sugar, and salad dressing; stir to mix. Pour over bean mixture and toss well. Cover and chill for 2 to 3 hours.

3. Line eight salad plates with the lettuce leaves. Cut artichoke hearts into small pieces and scatter over the lettuce. Top with bean mixture and garnish with lemon wedges; serve immediately.

Cooking Beans

To cook beans, first pick over them to remove extraneous material, then rinse and drain. Cover with cold water and let stand overnight. The next day, drain beans and rinse again. Cover with cold water and bring to a simmer. Cover pan and simmer for 1½ to 2 hours until tender. Drain and store in refrigerator up to 3 days.

Chicken Marsala

Marsala wine is a sweet, rich wine with a deep amber color. It adds a complex flavor to this easy recipe.

1. Bring a large pot of water to a boil. Cut a small X in the bottom of each tomato; drop into the water for 10 seconds. Remove tomatoes and plunge into ice water. Remove skins, then cut tomatoes in half. Squeeze tomato halves to seed. Coarsely chop and set aside.

2. Sprinkle chicken with flour, salt, and pepper. Heat olive oil in large skillet over medium heat. Add chicken; cook until lightly browned, about 5 minutes, then remove from heat.

3. Add shallots, wine, chicken broth, and tomatoes to skillet; bring to a boil. Reduce heat and simmer for 10 minutes. Then return chicken to skillet, and simmer for 8 to 12 minutes longer until chicken is thoroughly cooked. Sprinkle with parsley and serve immediately.

Serves 4

Calories: 248.03
Fat: 5.63 grams
Saturated Fat: 1.05 grams
Cholesterol: 69.34 mg
Sodium: 276.89 mg

4 large tomatoes
4 boneless, skinless chicken breasts
2 tablespoons flour
¼ teaspoon salt
⅛ teaspoon pepper
1 tablespoon olive oil
2 tablespoons minced shallots
½ cup Marsala wine
½ cup fat-free chicken broth
¼ cup chopped flat-leaf parsley

Poached Chicken

Poaching, or cooking in liquid at a temperature just below simmer, results in very tender, moist chicken perfect for use in chicken salad or sandwiches.

1. In heavy large saucepan, heat olive oil over medium heat. Add onion, carrot, and celery; cook until crisp-tender, about 5 minutes. Add chicken, cover pan, and cook for 5 minutes longer.

2. Add broth, wine, and seasonings to the pan and bring to a simmer. Reduce heat to low and cook just below a simmer for about 25 to 30 minutes, or until chicken is thoroughly cooked. Use chicken meat in recipes, and save broth for use in soups.

Serves 8

Calories: 180.14
Fat: 5.53 grams
Saturated Fat: 1.19 grams
Cholesterol: 92.14 mg
Sodium: 106.91 mg

1 tablespoon olive oil
1 onion, sliced
3 carrots, sliced
3 celery stalks, sliced
2½ pounds chicken parts, skinned
3 cups fat-free chicken broth
¼ cup dry white wine, if desired
1 bay leaf
3 parsley sprigs
½ teaspoon dried thyme leaves
⅛ teaspoon pepper

Very Lemon Chicken

Lemon juice and lemon zest combine to make extremely tender chicken that is very well flavored.

Serves 4

Calories: 182.41
Fat: 3.86 grams
Saturated Fat: 0.96 grams
Cholesterol: 92.14 mg
Sodium: 253.28 mg

1¼ pounds chicken parts,
    skinned
½ cup lemon juice
2 tablespoons vinegar
½ cup slivered lemon zest
1 tablespoon chopped
    fresh oregano
1 onion, chopped
¼ teaspoon salt
⅛ teaspoon white pepper
½ teaspoon paprika

1. Place chicken in 9" × 13" glass baking dish. In a small bowl, combine lemon juice, vinegar, lemon zest, oregano, and onion; mix well. Pour over the chicken, cover, and refrigerate for 4 to 8 hours, turning chicken occasionally.

2. Preheat oven to 325°F. Sprinkle chicken with salt, pepper, and paprika. Cover dish with foil and bake for 30 minutes. Uncover and bake for 20 to 30 minutes longer or until chicken is thoroughly cooked. Serve immediately.

Lemon Zest
You can remove the zest from a lemon in several different ways. A lemon zester is a sharp tool with small holes that removes the zest in very thin strips. You can also use a sharp paring knife to peel the lemon, removing just the yellow skin and leaving the white pith, which can be bitter.

Sesame Teriyaki Chicken

This super quick dish can be served with hot cooked pasta or rice, a green salad, and steamed broccoli for a healthy dinner for two.

Serves 2

Calories: 176.15
Fat: 4.07 grams
Saturated Fat: 0.79 grams
Cholesterol: 68.66 mg
Sodium: 690.47 mg

2 tablespoons reduced-sodium teriyaki sauce
1 tablespoon chicken broth
2 cloves garlic, minced
1 teaspoon minced fresh ginger root
⅛ teaspoon pepper
2 boneless, skinless chicken breasts
1 tablespoon sesame seeds, toasted

1. In shallow bowl, combine teriyaki sauce, chicken broth, garlic, ginger, and pepper; mix well. Cut chicken into long ¾-inch-wide strips and add to teriyaki mixture, stirring to coat. Let stand for 20 minutes.

2. Preheat broiler. Drain chicken and thread onto two 10" metal skewers, accordion-style. Broil 6 inches from heat, turning once, until chicken is thoroughly cooked, about 5 to 6 minutes. Sprinkle with sesame seeds and serve immediately.

Toasting Seeds

Toasting seeds is just like toasting nuts, but you have to watch them more carefully. Because they are so small and high in fat, they can burn easily. Place on a cookie sheet and bake at 350°F for 4 to 7 minutes, shaking the pan once or twice during baking time. Let cool completely before you use in recipes.

Crab-Stuffed Chicken

Serves 6

Calories: 181.05
Fat: 3.51 grams
Saturated Fat: 0.67 grams
Cholesterol: 78.45 mg
Sodium: 396.39 mg

¼ pound cooked crabmeat
¼ cup diced water
   chestnuts
2 tablespoons fine dry
   bread crumbs
2 tablespoons low-fat
   mayonnaise
1 tablespoon minced flat-
   leaf parsley
1 teaspoon Dijon mustard
6 boneless, skinless
   chicken breasts
2 tablespoons white wine
   Worcestershire sauce
2 green onions, minced

Now this is a dish for entertaining! Make it ahead of time so all you have to do is bake it and eat with your guests.

1. Preheat oven to 375°F. Pick over crabmeat to remove any cartilage and bits of shell. In a small bowl, combine with water chestnuts, bread crumbs, mayonnaise, parsley, and mustard; mix well.

2. Place chicken, smooth-side down, between pieces of waxed paper. Pound with a meat mallet or rolling pin until ⅛ inch thick.

3. Divide crab mixture among chicken pieces. Roll up, folding in the sides, to make bundles. Place, seam-side down, into a 9" × 13" baking dish. Brush with the Worcestershire sauce.

4. Cover pan with foil and bake until chicken is thoroughly cooked and tender. Sprinkle with green onion and serve immediately.

Chicken in Buttermilk

Buttermilk is an excellent marinade ingredient. It is slightly acidic, so it tenderizes the meat and adds a cool tang to chicken.

1. Remove skin from chicken; sprinkle with flour. Heat olive oil in large skillet over medium heat. Add chicken and brown on both sides, turning once, about 10 minutes. Add half of the green onions to skillet; cook for 2 minutes longer.

2. In a food processor, combine tomatoes, buttermilk, dill, sugar, salt, and pepper; process until smooth. Pour over chicken and bring to a boil. Cover, reduce heat to low, and simmer until chicken is tender, about 20 to 25 minutes.

3. Add yogurt and cheese and stir well. Simmer for 10 minutes longer to blend flavors. Garnish with remaining green onions and serve immediately.

Coating Chicken

When you remove the skin from chicken, it's important to coat the exposed flesh with something when sautéing or pan frying. A thin coating of flour will help hold in the juices and will protect the flesh from the heat. You can leave the skin on chicken when you're cooking it, then remove the skin before you eat it to avoid most of the fat.

Serves 6

Calories: 409.38
Fat: 10.77 grams
Saturated Fat: 3.46 grams
Cholesterol: 133.46 mg
Sodium: 591.01 mg

1 tablespoon olive oil
2½ pound chicken, cut into serving pieces
¼ cup flour
6 green onions, chopped
3 (14-ounce) cans diced tomatoes, drained
2 cups low-fat buttermilk
1 teaspoon dried dill weed
1 teaspoon sugar
½ teaspoon salt
⅛ teaspoon white pepper
1 cup plain low-fat yogurt
⅓ cup grated Parmesan cheese

Chicken Breasts with Curried Stuffing

If you love curry powder, this is the recipe for you! Add curry powder to the yogurt topping as well for even more flavor.

Serves 4

Calories: 253.59
Fat: 5.22 grams
Saturated Fat: 2.53 grams
Cholesterol: 77.29 mg
Sodium: 322.59 mg

1 tablespoon butter
½ cup shredded carrot
¼ cup sliced green
   onions
2 teaspoons curry powder
½ cup fresh bread
   crumbs
3 tablespoons dried
   currants
1 tablespoon fat-free
   chicken broth
4 boneless, skinless
   chicken breasts
¼ teaspoon salt
⅛ teaspoon pepper
½ teaspoon paprika
⅓ cup plain low-fat yogurt
2 teaspoons flour
2 tablespoons orange
   marmalade

1. In a small saucepan, melt butter over medium heat. Add carrot, green onions, and curry powder, and cook, stirring, until tender, about 5 minutes. Remove from the heat and stir in the bread crumbs, raisins, and broth.

2. Preheat oven to 350°F. Place 1 chicken breast half, boned-side up, between two sheets of plastic wrap. Working from the center to the edges, pound lightly with a meat mallet or rolling pin until ¼-inch thick. Remove plastic wrap. Repeat with remaining chicken.

3. Sprinkle chicken pieces with salt and pepper. Place one-fourth of the stuffing mixture on each piece of chicken. Fold chicken breast over the filling and secure with a toothpick. Place chicken in an 8" square baking dish with 2" sides. Sprinkle with the paprika and cover with foil.

4. In a small bowl, combine yogurt, flour, and marmalade; spread over chicken. Bake until chicken is tender and the juices run clear when a piece is pierced, about 25 to 35 minutes.

Cheesy Chicken Rolls

This is another excellent make-ahead recipe that's good for entertaining. Serve with some scalloped potatoes and a spinach salad.

Serves 4

Calories: 218.47
Fat: 5.07 grams
Saturated Fat: 2.49 grams
Cholesterol: 77.37 mg
Sodium: 518.14 mg

½ cup shredded part-skim mozzarella cheese
1 (2½-ounce) jar sliced mushrooms, drained
⅓ cup plain low-fat yogurt, divided
1 tablespoon minced chives
1 tablespoon minced flat-leaf parsley
1 tablespoon chopped drained pimiento
4 boneless, skinless chicken breasts
¼ teaspoon salt
⅛ teaspoon white pepper
¼ cup dried seasoned bread crumbs
1 tablespoon paprika

1. Preheat oven to 350°F. In a small bowl, combine cheese, mushrooms, ¼ cup yogurt, chives, parsley, and pimiento and mix well.

2. Place one chicken breast, boned-side up, between two pieces of plastic wrap. Pound lightly with a meat mallet or rolling pin until ¼ inch thick. Remove the plastic wrap. Repeat with the remaining chicken and sprinkle with salt and pepper.

3. Divide filling among chicken breasts. Fold in the sides and roll up, then secure with toothpicks. Arrange rolls, seam-side down, in a glass baking dish.

4. In a small bowl, combine bread crumbs and paprika. Brush chicken with the remaining yogurt, then sprinkle with crumb mixture.

5. Bake until chicken is tender and juices run clear, about 20 to 30 minutes. Serve immediately.

Pounding Chicken

In recipes where chicken is rolled around a filling, the meat usually has to be pounded so it's thin enough to roll easily and contain the stuffing. Pound gently, being careful not to tear the meat. If you start from the center and pound to the edges, the meat will be more likely to stay intact.

Garlicky Grilled Chicken

Serves 8

Calories: 154.84
Fat: 3.18 grams
Saturated Fat: 0.63 grams
Cholesterol: 68.44 mg
Sodium: 223.85 mg

10 cloves garlic, chopped
1 tablespoon dried
    oregano leaves
1 red onion, chopped
⅓ cup olive oil
½ teaspoon salt
⅛ teaspoon pepper
1 cup fat-free chicken
    broth
8 boneless, skinless
    chicken breasts

This flavorful marinade adds a fabulous flavor to simple chicken breasts. You could also use it for pork chops or round steak.

1. In a large shallow dish, combine the garlic, oregano, onion, oil, salt, pepper, and broth. Mix well. Add chicken, turn to coat well, cover, and marinate in the refrigerator overnight.

2. Prepare and preheat grill. Remove chicken from marinade and place on grill rack. Grill 6 inches from medium coals, turning once and brushing several times with the marinade, until chicken is tender and the juices run clear when pierced, about 7 to 10 minutes on each side. Discard any remaining marinade. Serve hot or cold.

Grilling Chicken

When grilling chicken, make sure the coals are burned down enough that they have an even coating of gray ash. The heat should be medium so the outside of the chicken doesn't overcook before the inside is done. Control the heat by closing and opening the grill cover, and move the chicken around on the grill as it cooks.

Chapter 7
Turkey

Warm Chinese Turkey Salad 94

Mai Fun Turkey Salad 95

Turkey Shish Kebabs 95

Spicy Turkey Enchiladas 96

Curried Strawberry Turkey Salad 97

California Turkey Burgers 97

Fiesta Turkey 98

Indian Turkey Pilaf 99

Lime Turkey Tenderloin 100

Turkey with Couscous 100

Turkey Jerusalem 101

Turkey Tetrazzini 102

Pistachio Turkey Taco Salad 103

Sweet and Sour Turkey Burgers 104

Warm Chinese Turkey Salad

Ginger adds a fresh snap of flavor to tender
turkey in this delicious salad.

Serves 6

Calories: 379.39
Fat: 5.02 grams
Saturated Fat: 0.87 grams
Cholesterol: 73.95 mg
Sodium: 492.09 mg

*¾ cup Low-Fat Italian
Salad Dressing (page
273)*
*2 teaspoons low-sodium
soy sauce*
*2 teaspoons minced
ginger root*
2 turkey tenderloins
8 cups torn salad greens
¼ cup chopped cilantro
*¼ cup sliced green
onions*
5 peaches, peeled
*¼ cup sliced almonds,
toasted*
*2 tablespoons sesame
seeds, toasted*

1. In a large resealable food storage bag, combine the dressing, soy sauce, and ginger. Add turkey, seal the bag, and turn to coat well. Refrigerate for 30 minutes.

2. Prepare and preheat grill or broiler. Arrange greens on four salad plates. Sprinkle with cilantro and scallions. Pit and slice three of the peaches and arrange on the lettuce.

3. Remove turkey from the marinade, reserving the marinade. Grill or broil turkey, turning several times and basting occasionally with the marinade, until browned and cooked through, about 20 to 25 minutes. Set aside; keep warm.

4. Halve and pit the remaining two peaches. Baste with marinade and grill or broil, turning once, until browned and tender, about 5 minutes.

5. Slice turkey and arrange with grilled peach halves on the lettuce. In a small saucepan, bring the remaining marinade to a boil (this can be done on the grill, if desired). Add the almonds and sesame seeds. Pour over the salads and serve immediately.

Mai Fun Turkey Salad

This fresh salad is a good idea for using up leftovers after Thanksgiving.

Serves 6

Calories: 304.35
Fat: 8.03 grams
Saturated Fat: 1.85 grams
Cholesterol: 59.32 mg
Sodium: 230.95 mg

*6 large napa or savoy
    cabbage leaves
1 (8-ounce) package mai
    fun (rice sticks)
1 cup shredded carrots
2 cups cooked, cubed
    turkey breast
1 cup sugar snap peas
1 cucumber, peeled and
    chopped
½ cup Hoisin Dressing
    (page 273)*

1. Line salad plates with the cabbage leaves. Cook the mai fun as directed on package and place on cabbage.

2. Top with carrots, turkey, sugar snap peas, and cucumber. Drizzle with half of the dressing. Serve immediately, passing the rest of the dressing.

Turkey Shish Kebabs

You can make this excellent dish with cubed chicken if you'd like. Serve with a gelatin salad and some breadsticks.

Serves 6

Calories: 291.51
Fat: 10.34 grams
Saturated Fat: 2.51 grams
Cholesterol: 61.42 mg
Sodium: 281.65 mg

*1¼ pounds turkey
    tenderloin
⅓ cup chili sauce
2 tablespoons lemon juice
1 tablespoon brown sugar
12 mushrooms
12 cherry tomatoes
1 zucchini, sliced ½-inch
    thick
1 green bell pepper,
    sliced
2 red onions, quartered
2 tablespoons olive oil*

1. Cut turkey into 1½-inch cubes and place in a bowl. In a small bowl, stir together the chili sauce, lemon juice, and brown sugar. Pour over the turkey cubes and toss to coat. Cover and refrigerate for 4 to 8 hours, stirring occasionally.

2. When ready to eat, prepare and preheat grill. Remove turkey from marinade, reserving marinade. Thread turkey onto metal skewers alternately with mushrooms, cherry tomatoes, zucchini, bell pepper, and onions.

3. Brush lightly with oil and place on grill rack about 6 inches above medium-hot coals. Grill, turning occasionally, and basting frequently with the reserved marinade, until the turkey is cooked through and the vegetables are tender, about 9 to 10 minutes.

Spicy Turkey Enchiladas

*Using strongly flavored cheeses will let you use less,
keeping your food lower in fat.*

Serves 6

Calories: 406.93
Fat: 11.49 grams
Saturated Fat: 3.95
grams
Cholesterol: 75.93 mg
Sodium: 639.45 mg

1¼ pound turkey
  tenderloin
1 cup fat-free chicken
  broth
2 tablespoons olive oil
1 onion, chopped
3 cloves garlic, minced
1 green bell pepper,
  chopped
2 tablespoons flour
⅛ teaspoon pepper
1 (4-ounce) can diced
  green chilies, drained
2 (14-ounce) cans diced
  tomatoes, drained
3 tablespoons tomato
  juice
3 tablespoons tomato
  paste
1 tablespoon chili powder
12 corn tortillas
½ cup shredded Pepper
  Jack cheese
½ cup shredded Cotija
  cheese

1. Cut tenderloin into 1-inch cubes. Combine with the chicken broth in a medium skillet. Bring to a boil, then reduce heat, cover, and simmer until turkey is cooked, about 5 to 7 minutes. Remove from pan. Shred turkey and set aside in medium bowl. Reserve ½ cup of the broth.

2. In same skillet, heat olive oil over medium heat. Add onion, garlic, and bell pepper; cook and stir until tender, about 5 minutes. Sprinkle with flour and pepper; cook and stir until bubbly.

3. Add reserved ½ cup of the chicken broth; cook, stirring frequently, until mixture thickens. Add chilies, tomatoes, tomato paste, and chili powder; simmer for 10 minutes. Add ½ cup of this sauce to the shredded turkey; stir in Pepper Jack cheese and half of the Cotija cheese.

4. Preheat oven to 350°F. Dip tortillas into hot sauce, then place a few spoonfuls of the turkey mixture on each tortilla and roll up. Place, seam-side down, in 13" × 9" glass baking dish, and cover with remaining tomato sauce. Sprinkle with remaining Cotija cheese.

5. Bake for 20 to 25 minutes or until food is hot and sauce begins to bubble. Serve immediately.

Curried Turkey Strawberry Salad

Curry combined with fresh fruit, chutney, and turkey makes a spectacular salad perfect for picnics.

1. In a large bowl, combine mayonnaise, chutney, lemon juice, skim milk, salt, and curry powder; mix well.

2. Add turkey, celery, and red onion and mix well. Cover and chill for 2 to 3 hours to blend flavors. Just before serving, stir in strawberries. Garnish with mint sprigs.

Chutney

Chutney is a wonderful ingredient to keep on hand to add flavor without fat. The most common chutney flavor is mango, but you can also find fig chutney, apricot chutney, and blueberry chutney. Chutney will freeze well if it is properly packaged.

California Turkey Burgers

Avocado and tomato combine to add a California accent to these juicy low-fat burgers.

1. Prepare and preheat grill. In a large bowl, combine oatmeal, ketchup, egg, onion, salt, pepper, Worcestershire sauce, and Tabasco sauce and mix well.

2. Add turkey and mix gently but thoroughly until combined. Form into four patties. Place patties on grill rack and grill for about 6 minutes on each side, or internal temperature reaches 165°F.

3. Split hamburger buns and toast on grill. Make sandwiches with the burgers, avocado, tomato, and mustard.

Serves 4

Calories: 243.84
Fat: 9.28 grams
Saturated Fat: 2.10 grams
Cholesterol: 41.50 mg
Sodium: 410.34 mg

½ cup low-fat mayonnaise
3 tablespoons mango
   chutney
1 tablespoon lemon juice
1 tablespoon skim milk
¼ teaspoon salt
2 teaspoons curry powder
2 cups diced cooked
   turkey
1 cup sliced celery
¼ cup chopped red onion
2 cups strawberries, sliced
Fresh mint sprigs

Serves 4

Calories: 275.96
Fat: 3.97 grams
Saturated Fat: 1.02 grams
Cholesterol: 76.94 mg
Sodium: 528.02 mg

½ cup quick cooking oatmeal
¼ cup ketchup
1 egg, beaten
⅓ cup minced onion
½ teaspoon garlic salt
¼ teaspoon pepper
1 teaspoon
   Worcestershire sauce
⅛ teaspoon Tabasco sauce
1 pound ground turkey
   breast
6 hamburger buns
1 avocado, thinly sliced
1 tomato, sliced
2 tablespoons Dijon
   mustard

Fiesta Turkey

The combination of flavors and textures in this recipe is really good. If your family likes food spicy, triple the chili powder and double the amount of cayenne pepper.

Serves 6

Calories: 301.95
Fat: 1.96 grams
Saturated Fat: 0.59 grams
Cholesterol: 71.93 mg
Sodium: 302.49 mg

1 (8-ounce) can tomato sauce
½ cup orange juice
1 minced onion
¼ cup dried currants
2 tablespoons chopped pimiento
½ teaspoon dried oregano leaves
1 teaspoon chili powder
1 clove garlic, minced
¼ teaspoon salt
⅛ teaspoon cayenne pepper
1½ pounds turkey tenderloin, cubed
1 tablespoon cornstarch
2 tablespoons water
¼ cup chopped flat-leaf parsley
3 cups hot cooked rice

1. In a large skillet, combine tomato sauce, orange juice, onion, currants, pimiento, oregano, chili powder, garlic, salt, and pepper. Bring to a boil, cover, reduce the heat to low, and simmer for 5 minutes.

2. Add turkey to skillet and return to a simmer. Cover and simmer until internal temperature reaches 165°F, about 6 to 9 minutes.

3. Meanwhile, in small bowl, combine cornstarch and water. Stir into skillet; cook and stir until thickened and bubbly, about 3 to 4 minutes. Toss parsley into hot rice and spoon onto a platter or individual plates. Serve turkey mixture over rice.

Cayenne Pepper

The heat from cayenne peppers, or any hot peppers, comes from capsaicin, a molecule concentrated in the seeds and membranes of the peppers. It is a good source of vitamin A, a powerful antioxidant. Cayenne peppers also contain substance P, which researchers have found to be an anti-inflammatory agent that fights heart disease.

Indian Turkey Pilaf

*A pilaf is a spicy combination of rice and other ingredients.
Yogurt is added for a cooling contrast.*

1. In a medium saucepan, combine water, curry powder, turmeric, onion, garlic, and cinnamon. Bring to a boil, add the rice, cover, reduce the heat to low, and cook until the liquid is absorbed and the rice is tender, about 35 to 45 minutes.

2. Meanwhile, drain the beans thoroughly. Preheat oven to 375°F. When the rice is tender, spoon half into a 2½-quart baking dish. Top with beans, peaches, and turkey, then remaining rice mixture. Cover with foil.

3. Bake for 30 minutes, then uncover and top with yogurt. Bake for 10 to 15 minutes longer until food is hot. Serve immediately.

Serves 6

Calories: 277.46
Fat: 2.81 grams
Saturated Fat: 0.63 grams
Cholesterol: 63.94 mg
Sodium: 161.40 mg

2 cups water
1 tablespoon curry powder
½ teaspoon ground turmeric
1 onion, chopped
3 cloves garlic, minced
½ teaspoon cinnamon
1 cup long-grain brown rice
1 (9-ounce) package frozen green beans, thawed
2 peaches, peeled and chopped
3 cups diced cooked turkey breast
½ cup plain low-fat yogurt

Lime Turkey Tenderloin

Turkey tenderloins are quite low in fat and are also tender when properly cooked. Serve this dish with couscous or rice to soak up the sauce.

Serves 4

Calories: 201.95
Fat: 2.29 grams
Saturated Fat: 0.93 grams
Cholesterol: 67.34 mg
Sodium: 398.42 mg

1 tablespoon olive oil
2 shallots, minced
1 turkey tenderloin, cubed
½ teaspoon salt
⅛ teaspoon white pepper
2 tablespoons flour
½ teaspoon dried thyme
    leaves
3 tablespoons lime juice
1 cup apple juice
2 tablespoons cornstarch
½ cup fat-free chicken
    broth

1. Heat olive oil in large skillet over medium heat. Cook shallots for 2 to 3 minutes, stirring frequently. Sprinkle turkey with salt, pepper, and flour. Add turkey to skillet and cook, turning to brown evenly, until tender and juices run clear when a piece is pierced, about 8 to 10 minutes.

2. In a small bowl combine thyme, lime juice, apple juice, cornstarch, and broth. Add to skillet; cook and stir over medium heat until thickened and bubbly, about 3 to 4 minutes. Serve immediately.

Turkey with Couscous

This easy recipe can be doubled to serve 6. You could also add a chopped apple or some sliced mushrooms.

Serves 3

Calories: 493.95
Fat: 4.92 grams
Saturated Fat: 1.95 grams
Cholesterol: 53.92 mg
Sodium: 291.54 mg

1 (8-ounce) box instant
    couscous
½ teaspoon cinnamon
1 cup diced cooked
    turkey
1 (15-ounce) can
    garbanzo beans,
    drained
⅓ cup raisins
½ cup low-fat plain yogurt
⅛ teaspoon pepper

1. In a medium saucepan, cook the couscous according to package directions, adding the cinnamon at the start of cooking.

2. When it is done, stir in the turkey, garbanzos, raisins, yogurt, and pepper. Cook over low heat, stirring constantly, until hot, about 4 to 5 minutes. Serve immediately.

Turkey Jerusalem

This elegant dish is fancy enough for company. Serve with a spinach and strawberry salad, with Lemon Meringue Pie (page 261) for dessert.

1. Bring a large pot of water to a boil. Cut tenderloins into four pieces each. Take the end pieces and pair them up to form a piece about the same size as the center pieces. You'll have six pieces of turkey. Cut bacon in half. Stretch it out, and wrap each half around the turkey. This will hold the two pieces made of two parts together.

2. Dust turkey with paprika, flour, salt, and pepper. In a large skillet, melt butter over medium heat. Add turkey and brown on both sides, about 7 to 8 minutes. Remove from skillet and set aside.

3. Add green onions, wine, and broth to skillet and bring to a simmer. Add the mushrooms and artichoke hearts and cook for 5 minutes longer.

4. Cook the egg noodles until al dente according to package directions. While the pasta cooks, return turkey to skillet; simmer for 5 to 6 minutes until meat thermometer registers 165°F.

5. When pasta is done, drain and place on serving plate. Place turkey on pasta and pour sauce over all. Sprinkle with cheese and serve.

Serves 6

Calories: 563.92
Fat: 12.49 grams
Saturated Fat: 5.93 grams
Cholesterol: 104.94 mg
Sodium: 482.53 mg

2 turkey tenderloins
3 slices turkey bacon
1 teaspoon paprika
2 tablespoons flour
½ teaspoon salt
⅛ teaspoon pepper
3 tablespoons butter
2 green onions, chopped
¾ cup dry white wine
¾ cup fat-free chicken broth
1 (8-ounce) package sliced mushrooms
2 (14-ounce) cans artichoke hearts, drained, chopped
1 (16-ounce) package egg noodles
3 tablespoons grated Parmesan cheese

Turkey Tetrazzini

Tetrazzini is a classic dish that combines a flavorful cheese sauce with pasta and meat. Make it with leftover Thanksgiving turkey.

Serves 4

Calories: 539.23
Fat: 15.93 mg
Saturated Fat: 6.93 mg
Cholesterol: 85.94 mg
Sodium: 518.49 mg

1 tablespoon butter
1 (8-ounce) package
    sliced mushrooms
2 tablespoons flour
¼ teaspoon salt
⅛ teaspoon pepper
½ teaspoon dried thyme
    leaves
2 cups skim milk
1 tablespoon lemon juice
½ cup shredded low-fat
    Swiss cheese
1 green bell pepper,
    chopped
4 green onions, chopped
2 cups diced cooked
    turkey
1 (8-ounce) package
    spaghetti
⅓ cup grated Parmesan
    cheese

1. Preheat oven to 350°F. Spray a 2-quart baking dish with nonstick cooking spray and set aside. Bring a large pot of water to a boil over high heat.

2. In a large skillet, melt butter over medium heat. Add mushrooms and sauté, stirring occasionally, until tender, about 5 to 7 minutes. Add flour, salt, pepper, and thyme and stir until well blended. Slowly add milk, stirring constantly with a wire whisk. Add lemon juice, and simmer, stirring occasionally, until sauce thickens, about 5 minutes.

3. Cook spaghetti until almost al dente according to package directions. Meanwhile, add Swiss cheese, bell pepper, and scallions to the mushroom sauce and mix well.

4. Drain spaghetti, and add with turkey to mushroom sauce, mixing well. Transfer to prepared baking dish and sprinkle with Parmesan cheese. Bake casserole, uncovered, until hot and bubbly, about 25 to 35 minutes. Serve immediately.

Pistachio Turkey Taco Salad

Pistachios are an unusual and delicious ingredient in a taco salad. You could make this salad with shredded chicken or even cooked shrimp.

Serves 6

Calories: 286.94
Fat: 7.49 grams
Saturated Fat: 1.79 grams
Cholesterol: 64.95 mg
Sodium: 460.02 mg

1. In a medium bowl combine turkey, tomatoes, and bell pepper and toss. In a small bowl, combine sour cream, pistachios, salsa, and lime juice and mix well. Add to turkey mixture and stir gently to coat.

2. Tear lettuce into bite-sized pieces and divide among six plates. Heat taco shells as directed on package and coarsely crush. Sprinkle on the lettuce. Top with turkey mixture and serve immediately.

Taco Shells

Taco shells are made from corn or flour tortillas that have been curved and deep-fried to hold their shape. They come packaged in boxes, and are usually reheated in the oven before serving so they are crisp. In this recipe, you can substitute taco or tortilla chips, but they are more fragile than crushed taco shells.

3 cups shredded cooked turkey breast
4 tomatoes, chopped
1 green bell pepper, chopped
⅓ cup low-fat sour cream
¼ cup chopped pistachios
1 cup Smoky Salsa (page 292)
2 tablespoons lime juice
1 head green lettuce
1 head red lettuce
6 taco shells

Sweet and Sour Turkey Burgers

Sweet and sour is an excellent flavor combination to use in low-fat cooking because the main ingredients are fat-free. These tender and juicy burgers are really delicious.

Serves 4

Calories: 358.56
Fat: 9.35 grams
Saturated Fat: 2.27 grams
Cholesterol: 48.23 mg
Sodium: 403.93 mg

1 tablespoon soy sauce
1 tablespoon honey
1 tablespoon apple cider vinegar
¼ cup dried bread crumbs
1 pound ground turkey breast
¼ cup chopped green onions
6 slices canned pineapple, drained
6 hamburger buns, split
¼ cup chili sauce
6 butter lettuce leaves

1. In a medium bowl, combine soy sauce, honey, vinegar, and bread crumbs until blended. Add ground turkey and green onions and mix well. Shape into four patties.

2. In a nonstick skillet over medium heat, fry patties, turning once, until done, about 8 to 10 minutes. To serve, spread chili sauce on hamburger buns and top with a patty, pineapple ring, and lettuce. Top with half of the bun and serve immediately.

Ground Turkey

When you buy ground turkey, look for an evenly colored product that has very little liquid in the package. If there is a lot of liquid, the meat will be dry when cooked. Ground turkey freezes very well, so purchase a lot when there's a sale. You can also grind your own turkey in a food processor using the pulse function.

Chapter 8
Seafood

Louisiana Seafood 106

Scallop and Pepper Stir-Fry 106

French Country Mussels 107

Paella 108

Pad Thai 109

Jambalaya 110

Curried Shrimp and Vegetables 111

Shrimp Scampi 112

Citrus Shrimp and Scallops 113

Baked Sole Amandine 114

Baked Sole with Bread Crumbs 115

Stuffed Fillet of Sole 116

Microwave Sole Florentine 117

Baked Scrod 118

Crab Surprise 118

Curried Cod with Apricots 119

Poached Cod with Spicy Buttermilk Sauce 120

Lemon Tarragon Sole 120

Salmon with Fettuccine 121

Grilled Fish and Spinach Packets 122

Louisiana Seafood

*This combination of seafood is reminiscent of a
clam bake but is much easier to make.*

Serves 4

Calories: 359.54
Fat: 3.69 grams
Saturated Fat: 0.69 grams
Cholesterol: 128.28 mg
Sodium: 429.45 mg

2 shallots, chopped
3 cloves garlic, minced
¼ cup dry white wine
*½ teaspoon dried basil
   leaves*
*¼ teaspoon dried thyme
   leaves*
12 raw sea scallops
8 large raw shrimp
8 clams, scrubbed
8 mussels, debearded
*2 (6-ounce) frozen lobster
   tails, thawed, chopped*
2 tomatoes, chopped
*3 cups hot cooked brown
   rice*

1. In a large stock pot, combine shallots, garlic, and wine; bring to a simmer. Simmer until vegetables soften, about 5 minutes. Add basil and thyme.

2. Add seafood except lobster and tomatoes; cover and cook for 6 to 8 minutes, shaking pot frequently, until shrimp curl, scallops are opaque, and clams and mussels open. Discard any clams and mussels that do not open.

3. Remove cover and add lobster and tomato; cook and stir until lobster is hot, about 2 to 3 minutes longer. Serve over hot cooked rice.

Scallop and Pepper Stir-Fry

For a stir-fry, make sure that you have all of the ingredients prepared before you start cooking since the cooking time is so short.

Serves 4

Calories: 272.94
Fat: 4.64 grams
Saturated Fat: 0.67 grams
Cholesterol: 37.40 mg
Sodium: 333.95 mg

1 pound bay scallops
1 tablespoon cornstarch
¼ teaspoon salt
⅛ teaspoon cayenne pepper
1 tablespoon olive oil
1 red onion, chopped
2 cloves garlic, minced
*1 green bell pepper,
   chopped*
1 red bell pepper, chopped
*2 cups cold cooked white
   rice*
3 tablespoons apple juice
1 tablespoon lemon juice

1. In a medium bowl, combine scallops with cornstarch, salt, and pepper; toss to coat. In a large skillet or wok, heat olive oil over medium-high heat.

2. Add onion and garlic; stir-fry for 2 minutes. Add scallop mixture and bell peppers; stir-fry until scallops are just cooked, about 4 to 5 minutes.

3. Add rice, then sprinkle with apple juice and lemon juice. Stir-fry until rice is heated through, about 2 to 4 minutes. Serve immediately.

French Country Mussels

Purchase mussels from areliable fishmonger. They are beautiful and delicious, with shiny black shells and creamy beige flesh.

Serves 6

Calories: 373.93
Fat: 11.45 grams
Saturated Fat: 1.93 grams
Cholesterol: 84.67 mg
Carbs: 21.97 grams

2 tablespoons olive oil
1 onion, chopped
7 garlic cloves, minced
1 (14.5-ounce) can diced tomatoes, undrained
⅛ teaspoon white pepper
½ teaspoon dried thyme leaves
1 cup dry white wine
4 pounds mussels, scrubbed
½ cup minced flat-leaf parsley

1. In 8-quart stockpot, heat oil over medium heat. Add onion and garlic; cook and stir until tender and just beginning to brown, about 7 to 9 minutes. Carefully add tomatoes, pepper, thyme, and wine. Increase heat to high and bring to a boil.

2. Add mussels and cover pan. Cook, shaking pan frequently, over medium-high heat until the mussels open, about 5 to 6 minutes. Discard any mussels that do not open. Serve mussels immediately in soup bowls with the sauce; sprinkle with parsley.

Using Fresh Mussels

Fresh mussels have a small tangle of threads outside the shell, called the beard. Pull these threads off before cooking and scrub the shell under cold running water. Tap the mussels with your fingers; if any do not close before cooking, discard them. If any are not open after cooking, discard those because they are not safe to eat.

Paella

Paella is a dish for a celebration! This delicious recipe is a cross between a soup and a stew. Serve it with lots of garlic bread to soak up the juices.

Serves 6

Calories: 441.48
Fat: 9.99 grams
Saturated Fat: 1.97 grams
Cholesterol: 127.25 mg
Sodium: 468.81 mg

2 cups fat-free chicken broth
¼ teaspoon saffron threads
2 tablespoons olive oil
½ pound medium raw shrimp
1 pound boneless, skinless chicken breasts, chopped
½ teaspoon salt
⅛ teaspoon white pepper
1 onion, chopped
4 cloves garlic, minced
1 (14.5-ounce) can diced tomatoes, undrained
1 cup Arborio rice
1 (8-ounce) can artichoke hearts, chopped
1 cup frozen peas, thawed
½ cup chopped jarred roasted red pepper
12 whole mussels, debearded

1. In microwave-safe glass measuring cup, combine chicken broth and saffron. Microwave on high for 1 minute, then set aside.

2. In a large skillet, heat olive oil over medium heat. Add shrimp; cook and stir until shrimp curl and turn pink; remove from skillet. Add chicken to skillet and sprinkle with salt and pepper; cook and stir until chicken turns white; remove from skillet.

3. Add onion and garlic to drippings remaining in skillet; cook and stir for 3 minutes. Add tomatoes and rice; cook and stir for 2 to 3 minutes. Then add the chicken broth mixture. Bring to a simmer, then reduce heat to low, cover, and cook for 20 minutes.

4. Uncover skillet and add chicken, shrimp, artichoke hearts, peas, and red pepper to rice mixture; stir. Arrange mussels over all of the food and cover skillet. Cook, shaking skillet frequently, for 5 to 7 minutes or until mussels open. Serve immediately.

Pad Thai

This simple and quick dish uses the flavors and textures of Southeast Asia in a recipe perfect for a late-night dinner.

1. Place noodles in a large bowl and cover with warm water. Let soak until noodles are soft, about 20 minutes. Drain noodles well and set aside.

2. In a small bowl, combine rice vinegar, fish sauce, sugar, and chili paste and mix well; set aside. Have all ingredients ready.

3. In wok or large skillet, heat peanut oil over medium-high heat. Add garlic; cook until golden, about 15 seconds. Add egg; stir-fry until set, about 30 seconds. Add shrimp and stir-fry until pink, about 2 minutes.

4. Add noodles to the wok, tossing with tongs until they soften and curl, about 1 minute. Add bean sprouts and green onions; stir-fry for 1 minute. Stir vinegar mixture and add to wok; stir-fry until mixture is hot, about 1 to 2 minutes longer. Sprinkle with peanuts and serve immediately.

Bean Sprouts

You can grow your own bean sprouts; there are books and lots of information online on the subject. You can also find them in the grocery store, either fresh in the produce aisle or canned. They are very perishable. If you buy them fresh, use them within 2 days or they may start to spoil.

Serves 4

Calories: 321.18
Fat: 10.44 grams
Saturated Fat: 1.85 grams
Cholesterol: 139.01 mg
Sodium: 720.71 mg

¼ pound dried rice noodles
3 tablespoons rice vinegar
1 tablespoon fish sauce
2 tablespoons sugar
1 teaspoon Chinese chili paste with garlic
1 tablespoon peanut oil
3 cloves garlic, minced
1 egg, beaten
½ pound medium shrimp, peeled
2 cups mung bean sprouts
½ cup sliced green onions
¼ cup chopped peanuts

Jambalaya

Serves 10

Jambalaya is a party in a pot! Serve this excellent recipe with lots of toasted bread rubbed with garlic to soak up all the juices.

Calories: 464.49
Fat: 10.29 grams
Saturated Fat: 3.38 grams
Cholesterol: 124.32 mg
Sodium: 577.19 mg

1 tablespoon butter
1 tablespoon olive oil
2 large onions, chopped
4 cloves garlic, minced
2 cups chopped celery
1 green bell pepper, chopped
1 red bell pepper, chopped
¼ pound chorizo, diced
1½ pounds skinless, boneless chicken breasts, cubed
2 bay leaves
1 teaspoon dried oregano leaves
1 teaspoon dried thyme leaves
1 teaspoon salt
½ teaspoon cayenne pepper
1 teaspoon black pepper
2 (14-ounce) cans diced tomatoes, undrained
1 (8-ounce) can tomato sauce
4 cups fat-free chicken broth
2½ cups long-grain white rice
1 pound medium raw shrimp, peeled
½ cup chopped flat-leaf parsley

1. In a large soup pot, combine olive oil and butter over medium heat. Add onion, garlic, celery, and bell peppers; cook and stir for 3 minutes. Add chorizo, chicken, bay leaves, oregano, thyme, salt, cayenne pepper, and black pepper; cook and stir for 5 minutes.

2. Add tomatoes, tomato sauce, and chicken broth and bring to a boil. Add rice and reduce heat to low; simmer until rice is tender, about 20 to 25 minutes.

3. Add the shrimp; cook until shrimp turn pink, stirring frequently, about 5 to 6 minutes longer. Sprinkle with parsley and serve immediately.

Curried Shrimp and Vegetables

Adding lots of vegetables to seafood not only enhances the flavor, it increases the nutrition of a dish and lowers the fat and cholesterol content.

1. In a large skillet, heat oil over medium heat. Add onion and garlic; cook and stir until crisp-tender, about 4 minutes. Add curry powder and cinnamon; cook and stir for 1 minute longer.

2. Add water, carrots, and potatoes; bring to a simmer. Then reduce the heat to low, cover, and cook for 8 to 10 minutes or until carrots are crisp-tender. Add zucchini, tomatoes, and shrimp, cover again, and simmer for 5 to 8 minutes longer or until shrimp are pink.

3. Spoon rice onto individual plates and top with shrimp and vegetables; serve immediately.

Cooking with Curry

The flavors in curry powder are enhanced when they are heated, which is why the powder is often cooked in the first step of many Indian recipes. It's still good when uncooked. You can buy curry powder in many blends, from hot to mild. Curry powder is a blend of spices, and each blend is usually unique to a particular area of India.

Serves 6

Calories: 372.23
Fat: 5.24 grams
Saturated Fat: 0.88 grams
Cholesterol: 114.84 mg
Sodium: 164.31 mg

1 tablespoon olive oil
1 onion, chopped
3 cloves garlic, minced
1 tablespoon curry powder
½ teaspoon cinnamon
1½ cups water
2 carrots, sliced
2 russet potatoes, peeled and cubed
1 zucchini, sliced
1 (14.5-ounce) can diced tomatoes
1 pound raw shrimp
4 cups hot cooked brown rice

Shrimp Scampi

Scampi is usually made with lots of butter. This version adds more vegetables and dry white wine and serves the mixture over lots of pasta to help reduce the fat.

Serves 6 to 8

Calories: 381.56
Fat: 6.96 grams
Saturated Fat: 2.51 grams
Cholesterol: 136.83 mg
Sodium: 150.62 mg

*1½ pounds medium raw
   shrimp*
*3 tablespoons lemon
   juice, divided*
1 tablespoon olive oil
2 tablespoons butter
1 onion, chopped
4 cloves garlic, minced
*1 green bell pepper,
   chopped*
1 cup dry white wine
*1 teaspoon dried basil
   leaves*
*½ teaspoon dried
   oregano leaves*
*1 (16-ounce) package
   fettuccine pasta*

1. Bring a large pot of water to a boil. Shell and devein shrimp, if necessary, and sprinkle with 1 tablespoon lemon juice; set aside.

2. In a large saucepan, combine olive oil and butter and heat over medium heat. Add onion and garlic; cook and stir for 3 minutes. Then add green bell pepper; cook and stir for 2 minutes longer.

3. Cook fettuccine until al dente according to package directions. Add wine, basil, and oregano to onion mixture and bring to a boil. Add shrimp; cook and stir until shrimp just turn pink, about 5 minutes.

4. Drain fettuccine when done, reserving ¼ cup of the pasta cooking water. Add fettuccine to shrimp mixture; toss to coat, adding reserved pasta cooking water if necessary. Add remaining 2 tablespoons lemon juice and serve immediately.

Cleaning Shrimp

To clean shrimp, remove the legs and carefully peel off the shell. Then make a shallow cut into the curled back of the shrimp and rinse to remove the vein. If you are serving the shrimp in a dish like Shrimp Scampi, remove the tails too. If you are serving the shrimp as an appetizer, leave the tails on.

Citrus Shrimp and Scallops

*Nothing enhances the flavor of seafood more than citrus fruits.
Serve these delicious kebabs over a brown rice pilaf.*

1. Remove the small muscle from the side of scallops, if necessary. Cut scallops in half. Place scallops and shrimp in large, resealable plastic bag. Add orange zest, orange juice, lemon juice, ginger root, cayenne pepper, garlic, and salt. Seal bag and knead to combine. Marinate in refrigerator for 30 minutes.

2. Prepare and preheat grill. Drain seafood, reserving marinade.

3. Thread seafood, snow peas, and mushrooms on 10" metal skewers. Grill 6 inches from heat, brushing occasionally with marinade, for 9 to 12 minutes until shrimp turn pink and scallops are just opaque. Discard remaining marinade.

Serves 4

Calories: 173.02
Fat: 2.19 grams
Saturated Fat: 0.34 grams
Cholesterol: 116.18 mg
Sodium: 385.11 mg

½ pound sea scallops
½ pound large raw
  shrimp, peeled
1 teaspoon orange zest
⅓ cup orange juice
2 tablespoons lemon juice
2 teaspoons minced fresh
  ginger root
⅛ teaspoon cayenne
  pepper
1 clove garlic, minced
¼ teaspoon salt
½ pound snow peas
½ pound small button
  mushrooms

Baked Sole Amandine

Almonds contain lots of healthy monounsaturated fat. Just a few add great flavor and crunch to this classic recipe.

Serves 4

Calories: 299.89
Fat: 12.43 grams
Saturated Fat: 3.23 grams
Cholesterol: 133.06 mg
Sodium: 403.63 mg

1 egg
¼ cup skim milk
½ cup dried bread crumbs
¼ cup ground almonds
1 teaspoon dried basil leaves
¼ teaspoon salt
½ teaspoon dried thyme leaves
1 pound sole fillets
2 tablespoons lemon juice
1 tablespoon water
1 tablespoon butter, melted
¼ cup sliced almonds
3 green onions, chopped

1. Preheat oven to 425°F. Line a baking sheet with parchment paper and set aside.

2. In shallow dish, combine egg and milk; beat until combined. On plate, combine bread crumbs, ground almonds, basil, salt, and thyme and mix well.

3. Dip the fish into the egg mixture, then in the crumb mixture to coat. Place on prepared baking sheet.

4. In a small bowl, combine lemon juice, water, and melted butter. Sprinkle over the fish. Sprinkle with sliced almonds. Bake for 8 to 10 minutes or until fish flakes easily when tested with fork. Sprinkle with green onions and serve immediately.

Almonds

Almonds come in several types. Plain whole almonds come with the skin attached. Blanched almonds have had their skins removed. Sliced almonds are thinly sliced unblanched whole almonds. Slivered almonds are blanched almonds cut into little sticks. If a recipe calls for ground almonds, slivered almonds are the best choice; grind them in a food processor.

Baked Sole with Bread Crumbs

The tomato juices soak into the flavorful bread mixture to make a delicious topping on delicate, light fish for an excellent main dish.

1. Preheat oven to 400°F. Spray a 2-quart baking dish with nonstick cooking spray and set aside.

2. Arrange fillets in single layer in baking dish. In a large skillet, heat butter and olive oil over medium heat. Add onion and garlic; cook and stir until softened but not brown, about 4 to 5 minutes.

3. In a large bowl, combine onion mixture, bread crumbs, lemon juice, wine, marjoram, salt, and pepper and mix well.

4. Spoon bread crumb mixture over fish in baking dish. Top with tomatoes and Parmesan cheese.

5. Bake for 15 to 20 minutes or until fish is opaque and flakes easily when tested with a fork, and topping is browned. Serve immediately.

Making Bread Crumbs

There are several ways you can make your own bread crumbs. Tear the bread into tiny pieces with your fingers or cut the bread into cubes and process in a food processor with a bit of flour to prevent sticking. You can also let bread dry for a day or two, then grate it on a food grater.

Serves 4 to 6

Calories: 342.71
Fat: 10.62 grams
Saturated Fat: 3.72 grams
Cholesterol: 85.72 mg
Sodium: 525.53 mg

1½ pounds sole fillets
1 tablespoon butter, melted
1 tablespoon olive oil
1 onion, minced
2 cloves garlic, minced
3 cups fresh soft bread crumbs
2 tablespoons lemon juice
¼ cup dry white wine
½ teaspoon dried marjoram leaves
¼ teaspoon salt
⅛ teaspoon white pepper
2 large tomatoes, chopped
3 tablespoons grated Parmesan cheese

Stuffed Fillet of Sole

You could substitute small cooked shrimp or lobster tail for the crabmeat if you'd like. This elegant recipe is perfect for entertaining.

Serves 4

Calories: 301.23
Fat: 4.58 grams
Saturated Fat: 1.17 grams
Cholesterol: 153.97 mg
Sodium: 832.14 mg

¾ cup plain dried
  breadcrumbs
½ cup dry sherry or apple
  juice
1 egg, beaten
2 tablespoons lemon
  juice, divided
8 ounces frozen lump
  crabmeat, thawed and
  drained
4 (4-ounce) sole fillets
⅛ teaspoon salt
⅛ teaspoon white pepper
½ teaspoon paprika

1. Preheat oven to 350°F. Grease a small baking dish and set aside.

2. In a medium bowl, combine breadcrumbs, sherry, egg, and 1 tablespoon lemon juice and mix well. Pick over crabmeat, removing any cartilage or shell. Add crabmeat to breadcrumbs mixture and mix gently.

3. Pat stuffing onto 1 side of each fillet. Roll up fillet and secure with toothpicks. Place in prepared baking dish, seam-side down. Sprinkle with salt, pepper, and paprika, then drizzle with remaining lemon juice.

4. Bake for 20 to 30 minutes or until fish flakes easily in center when tested with a fork. Serve immediately.

Stretching Seafood

You can save money as well as calories by stretching rich seafood like shrimp or crabmeat and combining it with low-fat fish fillets. Just make sure the seafood will be done at the same time; fillets cook for 10 minutes per inch of thickness, while shrimp usually takes only about 5 minutes to cook, unless it's in a filling.

Microwave Sole Florentine

In the food world, florentine means served with spinach. This fresh and light dish is easy and quick to make.

Serves 4

Calories: 158.55
Fat: 5.06 grams
Saturated Fat: 0.86 grams
Cholesterol: 72.25 mg
Sodium: 268.86 mg

1 pound sole fillets
¼ teaspoon salt
⅛ teaspoon white pepper
1 tablespoon lemon juice
1 tablespoon olive oil
2 cups coarsely chopped baby spinach
¼ teaspoon nutmeg

1. In microwave-safe glass baking dish, arrange the fillets. Sprinkle with salt, pepper, lemon juice, and olive oil. Cover with microwave-safe plastic wrap and vent 1 corner.

2. Microwave on high, rotating dish once during cooking time, for 4 minutes. Remove plastic wrap and arrange spinach leaves on top; sprinkle with nutmeg.

3. Return to microwave oven and microwave on high for 1 to 2 minutes longer, or until fish flakes easily when tested with fork and spinach wilts slightly. Let stand on solid surface for 3 minutes before serving.

Cooking in the Microwave

Follow recipe directions carefully when cooking in the microwave. Most recipes ask you to turn or rearrange food halfway through cooking time so the food cooks evenly. And if the recipe calls for standing time, let the dish stand on a solid surface (not a wire rack) for the specified time before serving so the food finishes cooking.

Baked Scrod

Scrod isn't a specific species or variety of fish; it's a generic term for haddock or cod, especially when it weighs less than 2 pounds when harvested.

Serves 4

Calories: 233.84
Fat: 2.24 grams
Saturated Fat: 0.50 grams
Cholesterol: 73.30 mg
Sodium: 589.02 mg

4 (6-ounce) scrod fillets
¼ teaspoon salt
⅛ teaspoon pepper
¾ teaspoon marjoram
2 tablespoons lemon juice
1 cup dry white wine
⅔ cup seasoned dry
*   bread crumbs*

1. Preheat oven to 350°F. Line a roasting pan with foil. Place scrod on the pan and sprinkle with salt, pepper, and marjoram. Sprinkle with the lemon juice.

2. Pour wine around the fish. Bake for 10 minutes, until fish is just opaque.

3. Preheat the broiler. Sprinkle fish with the bread crumbs. Broil 6 inches from heat source for 2 to 3 minutes or until bread crumbs are just browned. Serve immediately.

Crab Surprise

Ketchup is a low-fat product that adds lots of flavor to this takeoff on Crab Louis. Surprisingly, it contains a lot of vitamin A!

Serves 4

Calories: 341.45
Fat: 9.81 grams
Saturated Fat: 1.40 grams
Cholesterol: 60.88 mg
Carbs: 35.02 grams

2 tablespoons olive oil
¼ cup minced onion
3 tablespoons flour
⅔ cup low-sodium, fat-
*   free chicken broth*
⅔ cup skim milk
¼ cup ketchup
1 teaspoon
*   Worcestershire sauce*
1 teaspoon paprika
⅛ teaspoon Tabasco
*   sauce*
2 tablespoons lemon juice
1 pound lump crabmeat
2 cups hot cooked brown
*   basmati rice*

1. In a large saucepan, heat oil over medium-low heat. Add onion; cook and stir until crisp-tender, about 4 minutes. Add the flour and cook, stirring constantly, for 2 minutes until mixture bubbles. Whisk in the broth and milk and simmer until slightly thickened, stirring frequently, about 8 minutes.

2. Add ketchup, Worcestershire sauce, paprika, Tabasco sauce, and lemon juice and cook 2 minutes longer. Add crabmeat and simmer just until crab is hot, about 8 to 10 minutes longer.

3. Spoon rice onto serving plate, top with crab mixture, and serve immediately.

Curried Cod with Apricots

Cod, like other white fish, is very mild and adapts well to almost any flavoring. Curry and apricots are a marvelous combination with this fish.

Serves 4

Calories: 228.82
Fat: 4.26 grams
Saturated Fat: 0.63 grams
Cholesterol: 48.73 mg
Sodium: 209.74 mg

1 tablespoon olive oil
1 onion, chopped
3 cloves garlic, minced
*1 tablespoon curry
    powder*
1 cup dry white wine
*½ teaspoon dried thyme
    leaves*
¼ teaspoon salt
⅛ teaspoon white pepper
1 pound cod fillets
*½ cup dried apricots,
    thinly sliced*

1. Heat olive oil in large skillet over medium heat. Add onion and garlic; cook and stir for 3 minutes. Add curry powder; cook and stir for 3 minutes longer until onion is tender. Add wine and thyme and bring to a boil.

2. Reduce heat to medium. Sprinkle cod with salt and pepper and add to skillet with sauce. Simmer for 5 minutes, then turn and simmer for 5 to 6 minutes longer until fish flakes when tested with fork.

3. Remove fish to serving platter and cover to keep warm. Add apricots to skillet and cook over high heat until they plump, about 2 to 3 minutes. Spoon apricots and sauce over fish and serve immediately.

White Wine

Adding wine to recipes is a wonderful way to reduce fat and add lots of flavor. You really should use a wine that you would enjoy drinking; don't try to save money by using a cheap variety. Alcohol, like fat, is a flavor carrier, so wine spreads the flavors throughout the dish.

Poached Cod with Spicy Buttermilk Sauce

Buttermilk just tastes rich; in reality it's low in fat and calories. It makes an excellent marinade for both fish and chicken.

Serves 6

Calories: 135.04
Fat: 1.66 grams
Saturated Fat: 0.71 grams
Cholesterol: 52.82 mg
Sodium: 362.23 mg

1½ pounds cod fillets
1 teaspoon ground
   turmeric
⅛ teaspoon pepper
2½ cups buttermilk
2 tablespoons lemon juice
½ teaspoon salt
2 teaspoons ground
   cumin
⅛ teaspoon crushed red
   pepper flakes

1. Sprinkle cod with turmeric and pepper. Pour the buttermilk into a large skillet and bring to a simmer over medium heat.

2. Carefully slip the fish into the skillet, cover, and poach for 5 to 6 minutes, until fish is almost cooked.

3. Using a spatula, remove fish from the skillet. Add lemon juice, salt, and cumin to the buttermilk in the skillet and bring to a boil over high heat. Boil for 5 minutes to reduce buttermilk by half.

4. When buttermilk is reduced, stir in red pepper flakes, and return the fish to the skillet. Turn heat to low. Simmer until the fish flakes easily when tested with a fork, about 1 to 2 minutes longer. Spoon sauce over fish to serve.

Lemon Tarragon Sole

This simple recipe and technique can be used with any mild white fish. Serve with a dark green salad and some bakery breadsticks.

Serves 4

Calories: 109.29
Fat: 1.77 grams
Saturated Fat: 0.62 grams
Cholesterol: 52.99 mg
Sodium: 101.41 mg

¼ cup plain yogurt
1 teaspoon flour
1 teaspoon dried tarragon
   leaves
1 tablespoon lemon juice
1 teaspoon grated lemon
   zest
1 pound sole fillets

1. Preheat broiler. In a small bowl, combine all ingredients except the fish and mix well.

2. Place fish on broiler pan. Spread yogurt mixture evenly onto fish. Broil fish 8 inches from heat source for 5 to 8 minutes, or until fish flakes when tested with fork. Serve immediately.

Salmon with Fettuccine

Salmon is a rich, nutritious fish that is easy to cook. It's tossed in a light tomato sauce in this simple main dish recipe.

1. Bring a large pot of water to a boil. Meanwhile, in large skillet combine broth and wine and bring to a boil. Reduce heat to low so the mixture simmers. Add salmon, cover, and simmer until the fish is opaque, about 5 to 6 minutes. Remove fish from skillet with slotted spoon and set aside.

2. Turn heat to high and reduce liquid to ½ cup.

3. In another large skillet, heat oil over medium heat. Add the shallots and garlic; cook and stir until tender, about 5 minutes. Add tomatoes, tomato paste, milk, reduced liquid, and the pepper and bring to a boil. Simmer until the sauce thickens slightly, about 10 minutes.

4. Meanwhile, cook pasta until al dente. Add the salmon to the tomato sauce and heat through. Drain pasta and add to the salmon mixture; toss gently over low heat. Serve sprinkled with Parmesan cheese.

Serves 6

Calories: 376.44
Fat: 12.90 grams
Saturated Fat: 3.00 grams
Cholesterol: 49.34 mg
Sodium: 224.78 mg

1 cup low-sodium, fat-free chicken broth
½ cup dry white wine or chicken broth
1 pound salmon fillets, cubed
1 tablespoon olive oil
3 shallots, minced
3 cloves garlic, minced
1 (14-ounce) can diced tomatoes, undrained
3 tablespoons tomato paste
½ cup nonfat evaporated milk
⅛ teaspoon white pepper
¼ cup fresh dill weed, minced
1 (12-ounce) package no-egg fettuccine
⅓ cup grated Parmesan cheese

Grilled Fish and Spinach Packets

This beautiful method of cooking delicate fish is perfect for entertaining. The packets make a gorgeous presentation.

Serves 4

Calories: 171.73
Fat: 4.55 grams
Saturated Fat: 0.56 grams
Cholesterol: 68.00 mg
Sodium: 286.52 mg

1 tablespoon olive oil
1 onion, chopped
2 cloves garlic, minced
¼ cup dry white wine
¼ teaspoon salt
⅛ teaspoon white pepper
1 tablespoon chopped fresh tarragon
1 (10-ounce) package fresh baby spinach
1 pound fish fillets
1 green bell pepper, julienned

1. Prepare and preheat grill. In a small skillet, heat oil over medium heat. Add onion and garlic; cook and stir until tender, about 6 to 7 minutes. Remove from heat and stir in wine, salt, and pepper.

2. Return to high heat and boil until reduced by half, about 5 minutes. Remove from heat and stir in tarragon. Set aside.

3. Tear off four 12" × 18" pieces of heavy duty foil and place on work surface. Divide spinach into quarters and place on foil. Cut fish into four pieces and place on top of spinach. Spoon onion mixture on fish and top with green bell pepper strips.

4. Bring up long edges of foil and, leaving some space for steam expansion, seal with a double fold, then fold in short ends to seal. Place on grill rack 6 inches from medium coals. Grill, turning packets twice and rearranging on grill, until fish flakes easily when tested with fork, about 15 to 20 minutes. Serve immediately.

En papillote

Food cooked in foil or parchment paper is called en papillote. *This method of cooking keeps food moist and is an excellent way to cook delicate foods like greens and fish. The food steams in the packet, sealing in juices and flavor. Warn your guests to be careful opening these packets because steam will billow out.*

Chapter 9
Vegetarian Entrees

Wintertime Chili. 124

Italian Bean Soup 125

Italian Vegetable Bake 126

Potato Corn Chowder 127

Lentil Stew 128

Slow-Cooker Chili Tortilla Bake 129

Apple Squash Soup 130

Cheese Egg Casserole 131

Potato Vegetable Soup 131

John Barleycorn Casserole 132

Cream of Mushroom Soup 133

Portobello Sandwiches 134

Potato Cheese Casserole 135

Lima Bean Casserole 136

Wonderful Risotto. 137

Welsh Rarebit. 137

Soulful Black-Eyed Peas 138

Wintertime Chili

Serves 6

Calories: 174.93
Fat: 1.89 grams
Saturated Fat: 0.04 grams
Cholesterol: 0.0 mg
Sodium: 400.98 mg

*1 green bell pepper,
    chopped*
1 red bell pepper, chopped
1 onion, chopped
2 cloves garlic, minced
1 teaspoon cumin
*2 to 3 tablespoons chili
    powder*
1 jalapeño pepper, minced
½ teaspoon cocoa powder
½ teaspoon brown sugar
*1 (8-ounce) can tomato
    sauce*
*2 (15-ounce) cans kidney
    beans, drained*
*2½ cups water or tomato
    juice*
¼ teaspoon salt
¼ teaspoon pepper

*Serve this spicy and rich-tasting chili with Spicy Corn Bread
(page 38) for a wintertime treat.*

In a large saucepan, combine all ingredients. Bring to a boil, cover, and reduce heat to low. Simmer, stirring occasionally, until chili is hot and vegetables are tender, about 45 to 50 minutes. Serve immediately.

Italian Bean Soup

*This delicious soup is really a meal in one
for a cold winter day. Pair it with some nice crusty bread
and all you need is a glass of wine.*

1. Sort over the dried beans, rinse them well, drain, then place in large bowl. Cover with cold water, cover, and let stand overnight. The next day, drain beans.

2. In soup pot, heat oil over medium heat. Add onion and garlic; cook and stir until crisp-tender, about 5 minutes. Add beans to pot along with vegetable broth and oregano leaves. Bring to a simmer, cover, reduce heat to low, and cook until beans are tender, about 45 minutes.

3. Add tomatoes, carrots, celery, and pasta. Simmer for 15 minutes until pasta is tender. Add spinach and pepper; heat through. Sprinkle with cheese and serve immediately.

Tomatoes and Beans

Dried beans won't soften as they cook if there is too much salt or too many acidic ingredients in the liquid. Tomatoes and lemon juice are two culprits, as is broth that is too salty. Cook beans without these ingredients, then add the acidic or salty ingredients once the beans are tender.

Serves 8

Calories: 340.93
Fat: 3.98 grams
Saturated Fat: 1.24 grams
Cholesterol: 4.03 mg
Sodium: 241.04 mg

3 cups mixed dried beans
1 tablespoon olive oil
1 onion, chopped
3 cloves garlic, minced
*2 quarts fat-free vegetable
  broth*
*1 teaspoon dried oregano
  leaves*
*1 (14-ounce) can diced
  tomatoes, undrained*
1 cup sliced carrots
1 cup sliced celery
1 cup small pasta shells
*2 cups torn spinach
  leaves*
⅛ teaspoon pepper
*½ cup grated Romano
  cheese*

Italian Vegetable Bake

Serves 6

Basil and oregano are the classic Italian herbs that give unmistakable flavor to this healthy and colorful dish.

Calories: 119.84
Fat: 1.83 grams
Saturated Fat: 0.52 grams
Cholesterol: 4.92 mg
Sodium: 320.93 mg

2 (14-ounce) cans diced
    tomatoes
1 onion, chopped
½ pound green beans,
    sliced
½ pound okra, cut into ½-
    inch lengths
1 chopped green bell
    pepper
2 tablespoons lemon juice
1 tablespoon chopped
    fresh basil
1½ teaspoons fresh
    oregano leaves
3 medium zucchini
1 eggplant
2 tablespoons grated
    Parmesan cheese

1. Preheat oven to 325°F. In a large baking dish, combine tomatoes and their liquid, onion, green beans, okra, bell pepper, lemon juice, basil, and oregano. Cover with foil or a lid.

2. Bake for 15 minutes. Meanwhile, cut zucchini into 1-inch chunks. Peel eggplant and cut into 1-inch cubes. Add zucchini and eggplant to baking dish, cover, and continue to bake, stirring occasionally, until vegetables are tender, about 1 hour.

3. Sprinkle with Parmesan cheese and bake, uncovered, for 10 minutes longer or until cheese melts and casserole is bubbly. Serve immediately.

Potato Corn Chowder

This simple recipe is full of rich ingredients that are good for you. You can also use white corn in this recipe, but yellow corn is prettier.

1. Chop the potatoes and combine in large pot with the onion and garlic. Add water to just cover the vegetables, bring to a boil, then reduce heat to a simmer and cook for 10 minutes. Using a potato masher, mash half of the vegetables; stir in corn and bring back to a simmer.

2. In a small saucepan, heat olive oil over medium heat. Add green bell pepper; cook and stir until crisp-tender, about 4 minutes. Sprinkle flour over mixture; cook and stir until bubbly.

3. Add milk, salt, pepper, and tarragon to the flour mixture; cook and stir until thickened. Add to the soup mixture; cook and stir until soup thickens and almost comes to a boil. Serve immediately.

Chowders

Chowders are usually thick soups with a milk base and potatoes and flour added for thickening. They can be made vegetarian or with any meat, including chicken, ham, beef, and seafood. Most chowders are mild in flavor, relying on the ingredients to provide seasoning. You can make your chowder as thick or thin as you like.

Serves 6

Calories: 346.31
Fat: 3.41 grams
Saturated Fat: 0.57 grams
Cholesterol: 2.76 mg
Sodium: 299.74 mg

4 russet potatoes, peeled
1 onion, chopped
3 cloves garlic, minced
3 cups frozen corn
1 tablespoon olive oil
1 green bell pepper, chopped
1 tablespoon flour
1 (13-ounce) can nonfat evaporated milk
½ teaspoon salt
½ teaspoon dried tarragon leaves

Lentil Stew

Lentils are small and tender and have a wonderful meaty, nutty taste. Serve this soup with some cheese bread.

Serves 10

Calories: 210.94
Fat: 3.98 grams
Saturated Fat: 0.81 grams
Cholesterol: 13.93 mg
Sodium: 429.93 mg

2 tablespoons olive oil
3 onions, chopped
3 cloves garlic, minced
3 carrots, sliced
1 teaspoon dried
   marjoram leaves
1 teaspoon dried thyme
   leaves
2 (14-ounce) cans diced
   tomatoes, undrained
2 quarts fat-free vegetable
   broth
1½ cups brown lentils
½ teaspoon salt
¼ teaspoon pepper
½ cup dry white wine
¼ cup chopped flat-leaf
   parsley
¼ cup grated Parmesan
   cheese

1. In a large soup pot, heat olive oil over medium heat. Add onions and garlic; cook and stir for 5 minutes. Add carrots, marjoram, and thyme; cook and stir for 3 minutes longer.

2. Add tomatoes, broth, and lentils. Bring to a boil over high heat, then reduce heat to low, cover, and simmer for 1 to 1½ hours, until lentils are tender.

3. Add salt, pepper, wine, and parsley; cook for 10 minutes longer. Serve garnished with Parmesan cheese.

Slow-Cooker Chili Tortilla Bake

Beans and corn combine to make complete protein in this satisfying and savory dish.

1. In a medium saucepan, heat olive oil over medium heat. Add onion and jalapeños; cook and stir until crisp-tender, about 4 minutes. Add tomato sauce, juice, black beans, and seasonings. Simmer for 10 minutes.

2. Place ½ cup of sauce in bottom of 4-quart slow cooker. Top with 1 tortilla and 2 tablespoons cheese. Repeat layers, ending with cheese.

3. Cover slow cooker and cook on low for 6 to 8 hours. Serve with sour cream, if desired.

Serves 6

Calories: 219.94
Fat: 3.91 grams
Saturated Fat: 0.49 grams
Cholesterol: 18.93 mg
Sodium: 594.89 mg

1 tablespoon olive oil
1 onion, chopped
2 to 3 jalapeño peppers, minced
1 (8-ounce) can tomato sauce
1½ cups tomato juice
2 (15-ounce) cans black beans, drained
1 tablespoon chili powder
½ teaspoon salt
⅛ teaspoon pepper
1 tablespoon steak sauce
6 corn tortillas
1 cup low-fat extra-sharp grated Cheddar cheese
½ cup nonfat sour cream

Apple Squash Soup

Serves 8

Calories: 178.35
Fat: 4.32 grams
Saturated Fat: 0.64 grams
Cholesterol: 0.0 mg
Sodium: 154.66 mg

2 tablespoons olive oil
2 onions, chopped
3 cloves garlic, minced
6 cups water
3 pounds butternut
   squash, peeled and
   cubed
3 Granny Smith apples,
   peeled and cubed
⅓ cup old-fashioned
   rolled oats, ground
2 tablespoons minced
   fresh ginger root
2 tablespoons curry
   powder
½ teaspoon salt
⅛ teaspoon white pepper

This sweet soup is packed full of vitamin A and fiber. It's smooth and silky without any cream.

1. Heat oil in large soup pot over medium heat. Add onion and garlic; cook and stir until tender, about 6 to 7 minutes. Add water and squash and bring to a simmer. Simmer for 15 to 20 minutes or until squash is almost tender.

2. Stir in apples and remaining ingredients. Bring back to a simmer and cook for 10 to 15 minutes or until apples and squash are tender.

3. Using an immersion blender, blend the soup until it's smooth and creamy. Serve immediately.

Apples and Squash

Apples and squash come into season around the same time, so they are natural partners. They are both sweet, but using an apple that is also tart will result in the most balanced flavor. Apples are easy to prepare, but squash can be tricky. Hold the knife with both hands when you chop the squash so you won't cut yourself.

Cheese Egg Casserole

This is a strata, or a casserole made of bread, cheese, and vegetables baked in an egg custard until puffed and golden.

1. Arrange bread slices in a single layer in a shallow baking dish so they fit snugly. In a small bowl, combine eggs, egg whites, milk, mustard, salt, and pepper and beat well. Pour over bread.

2. In a small skillet, cook onion and garlic in olive oil until tender, about 5 to 6 minutes. Sprinkle onion mixture and cheese over the bread in casserole. Cover and refrigerate overnight.

3. The next day, preheat oven to 350°F. Bake casserole, uncovered, until golden brown and puffed, 25 to 35 minutes. Cut into squares and serve immediately.

Serves 4

Calories: 305.93
Fat: 11.94 grams
Saturated Fat: 3.92 grams
Cholesterol: 90.89 mg
Sodium: 502.93 mg

*6 slices stale Oat Bran
  French Bread (page 37)
2 eggs
6 egg whites
1 cup 1% milk
⅛ teaspoon dry mustard
½ teaspoon salt
⅛ teaspoon pepper
1 tablespoon olive oil
2 onions, chopped
3 cloves garlic, minced
1 cup shredded low-fat
  sharp Cheddar cheese*

Potato Vegetable Soup

A hearty soup is always welcome on a cold day. This is a good one to put in a thermos and tuck into a lunchbox.

1. In a sauté pan, melt the butter over medium heat. Add the garlic and onion and sauté for 4 minutes, or until the onion is soft. Add the broth, potatoes, carrots, celery, and zucchini and bring to a boil. Reduce the heat to low and cook, covered, until the potatoes are tender, about 20 minutes.

2. Add the dill, parsley, salt, pepper, and cornstarch-water mixture, stir well, and continue to cook for about 15 minutes or until soup is slightly thickened. Ladle into bowls to serve.

Serves 6

Calories: 243.73
Fat: 4.19 grams
Saturated Fat: 1.58 grams
Cholesterol: 5.09 mg
Sodium: 594.02 mg

*1 tablespoon butter
2 cloves garlic, minced
1 onion, chopped
6 cups fat-free vegetable
  broth
3 potatoes, peeled and
  diced
3 carrots, sliced
2 stalks celery, sliced
1 zucchini, sliced
1 teaspoon dried dill weed
1 bunch flat-leaf parsley,
  minced
½ teaspoon salt
⅛ teaspoon pepper
2 tablespoons cornstarch
3 tablespoons water*

John Barleycorn Casserole

Serves 4

Calories: 320.93
Fat: 5.03 grams
Saturated Fat: 0.84 grams
Cholesterol: 0.0 mg
Sodium: 402.94 mg

1 tablespoon olive oil
1 onion, chopped
3 cloves garlic, minced
1 cup shredded carrots
½ teaspoon salt
⅛ teaspoon white pepper
½ teaspoon dried marjoram leaves
1 cup pearl barley
3 cups fat-free vegetable broth
2 cups frozen corn kernels, thawed
¼ cup chopped flat-leaf parsley

If you aren't a vegetarian, you can make this dish with chicken broth and stir in some chopped chicken at the beginning.

1. Preheat oven to 350°F. In a flameproof baking dish, heat oil over medium high heat. Add the onion, garlic, and carrots and sauté until the onion is translucent, 5 to 7 minutes.

2. Sprinkle with salt, pepper, and marjoram leaves. Add the barley and broth and cover with foil or a lid.

3. Bake until the barley is tender, about 1 hour. Uncover and add the corn and parsley, mixing well. Cover and continue to bake until heated through, about 10 to 15 minutes, then serve.

Barley

Barley is incredibly good for you. It contains a lot of soluble fiber, which helps remove cholesterol from your body. It is also rich in B vitamins, folic acid, and vitamin E. It is tender, nutty, and slightly chewy when cooked al dente. Barley combines well with many styles of cuisine—and it's a fat-free food!

Cream of Mushroom Soup

If the only cream of mushroom soup you've ever eaten was out of a can, you're in for a treat. This rich and creamy soup is a homemade classic.

Serves 4

Calories: 238.29
Fat: 2.46 grams
Saturated Fat: 1.36 grams
Cholesterol: 12.84 mg
Sodium: 510.21 mg

1. In a large soup pot, combine mushrooms, onion, garlic, and celery with the wine over medium heat. Bring to a simmer and cook until vegetables are soft, about 5 to 6 minutes, stirring frequently.

2. Add the 1% milk and nutmeg and bring back to a simmer. Cover pan, reduce heat to very low, and simmer for 20 minutes.

3. In a small bowl, combine evaporated milk with flour, cornstarch, salt, and pepper and mix well. Add to soup and increase heat to medium. Cook, stirring frequently, until the soup thickens

4. Add lemon juice and stir. Serve topped with the parsley.

*2 (8-ounce) packages
   sliced mushrooms
1 onion, chopped
2 cloves garlic, minced
2 stalks celery, chopped
¼ cup dry white wine
3 cups 1% milk
¼ teaspoon nutmeg
1 (13-ounce) can
   evaporated skim milk
2 tablespoons flour
2 tablespoons cornstarch
½ teaspoon salt
⅛ teaspoon white pepper
2 teaspoons lemon juice
⅓ cup chopped flat-leaf
   parsley*

Cleaning Mushrooms

Commercially produced mushrooms are grown in sterile soil. Still, they need to be cleaned. Use a soft slightly dampened cloth to wipe off the mushrooms; do not rinse them or soak to clean because they'll soak up the water. You may want to trim off the bottoms of the stems because they can be slightly tough.

Portobello Sandwiches

Serves 4

Calories: 295.93
Fat: 5.03 grams
Saturated Fat: 0.66 grams
Cholesterol: 5.02 mg
Sodium: 298.34 mg

2 tablespoons low-fat
  mayonnaise
2 tablespoons mustard
1 teaspoon lemon juice
6 cloves Roasted Garlic
  (page 23)
2 tomatoes, chopped
¼ cup chopped fresh
  basil leaves
4 large portobello
  mushrooms
1 tablespoon olive oil
4 kaiser rolls, split and
  toasted
4 butter lettuce leaves

*Grilled meaty portobello mushrooms are filled with a fragrant
tomato mixture, then encased in toasted rolls. Yum!*

1. Preheat broiler. In a small bowl, combine mayonnaise, mustard, lemon juice, and garlic; set aside. In another small bowl, combine tomato and basil; set aside. Brush mushrooms with the oil and place on a broiler pan, gill-side up. Broil until tender, about 5 to 7 minutes.

2. Spoon tomato mixture into mushroom caps. Spread mayonnaise mixture over the bottom halves of the rolls and top each with a mushroom cap, tomato-side up. Top with lettuce. Spread top halves of rolls with remaining mayonnaise mixture and place on lettuce. Serve immediately.

Potato Cheese Casserole

Potatoes and cheese are natural partners; in a low-fat recipe, they're even more delicious together!

1. Place potatoes in large saucepan with water to cover. Bring to a boil, reduce the heat to medium, and simmer until tender, about 25 minutes. Drain potatoes and set aside.

2. Preheat oven to 350°F. Spray a 2½-quart baking dish with nonstick cooking spray. In a medium bowl, beat cottage cheese until smooth.

3. In a small pan, heat olive oil; add onion and garlic and cook until tender, about 5 minutes. Add to cottage cheese along with flour, thyme, salt, and pepper.

4. Layer one-third of the sliced potatoes in prepared baking dish. Cover with half of the cottage cheese mixture. Repeat layers, ending with potatoes. Pour milk evenly over the potato-cheese layers.

5. In a small bowl, mix bread crumbs with Parmesan cheese and sprinkle over the potatoes; dot with butter. Bake until cheese is lightly browned, about 35 to 40 minutes.

Potato Types

You can choose from several kinds of potatoes, including russet, red, white, and colored. For boiling, russet and red potatoes are the best choice because they hold their shape and don't become soggy. The Yukon Gold potato, while buttery, doesn't boil as well. Test potatoes with a fork; when they are tender, drain immediately.

Serves 6

Calories: 314.60
Fat: 8.12 grams
Saturated Fat: 3.70 grams
Cholesterol: 15.66 mg
Sodium: 527.94 mg

6 potatoes, peeled and sliced
2 cups 1% cottage cheese
1 tablespoon olive oil
1 onion, chopped
3 cloves garlic, minced
2 tablespoons flour
1 teaspoon dried thyme leaves
¼ teaspoon salt
⅛ teaspoon white pepper
⅓ cup skim milk
⅓ cup fine dry bread crumbs
3 tablespoons grated Parmesan cheese
2 tablespoons butter

Lima Bean Casserole

Lima beans are delicious—nutty, soft, and buttery. They're a satisfying meat substitute in this easy casserole.

Serves 6

Calories: 196.93
Fat: 2.98 grams
Saturated Fat: 0.42 grams
Cholesterol: 0.0 mg
Sodium: 127.76 mg

1 tablespoon olive oil
1 onion, chopped
3 cloves garlic, minced
1 Granny Smith apple,
  peeled and chopped
¼ cup tomato paste
⅓ cup tomato juice
2 tablespoons mustard
3 tablespoons red wine
  vinegar
1 teaspoon dried oregano
  leaves
3 tablespoons honey
⅛ teaspoon pepper
2 (10-ounce) packages
  frozen lima beans,
  thawed

1. Preheat oven to 350°F. Spray a 2-quart baking dish with nonstick cooking spray and set aside.

2. In a large skillet, heat oil over medium heat. Add the onion, garlic, and apple and sauté until the onion is translucent, about 5 minutes. Add tomato paste, juice, mustard, vinegar, oregano, honey, and pepper and remove from heat.

3. Stir gently to combine, then mix in the lima beans. Transfer to prepared dish and cover with foil. Bake until beans are tender, about 30 to 40 minutes. Serve hot with rice.

Wonderful Risotto

Risotto has a reputation for being difficult to make, but it isn't. Just add the broth gradually and keep stirring!

Serves 6

Calories: 348.93
Fat: 9.18 grams
Saturated Fat: 2.39 grams
Cholesterol: 19.93 mg
Sodium: 472.94 mg

5 cups fat-free vegetable broth
1 tablespoon olive oil
1 onion, diced
1 shallot, diced
2 cloves garlic, minced
2 cups medium-grain rice
¼ cup sherry
¼ cup grated Parmesan cheese
1 tablespoon butter

1. In a medium saucepan, place broth over low heat. In a large saucepan, melt butter over medium heat. Add onion, shallot, and garlic and sauté until tender, about 7 minutes. Add rice; cook and stir for 3 minutes longer.

2. Start adding the broth, a cup at a time, stirring frequently until broth is absorbed. When all the broth is added, rice is al dente, and the sauce is creamy, stir in sherry, cheese, and butter. Cover and remove from heat; let stand for 5 minutes. Stir and serve immediately.

Welsh Rarebit

Adding some vegetables to traditional rarebit adds color, flavor, and nutrition.

Serves 4

Calories: 249.05
Fat: 2.40 grams
Saturated Fat: 0.49 grams
Cholesterol: 4.02 mg
Sodium: 350.93 mg

1 tablespoon olive oli
½ cup shredded cabbage
½ cup shredded carrot
1 green bell pepper, chopped
2 stalks celery, sliced
1 onion, chopped
4 slices whole wheat bread, toasted
1 cup shredded low-fat extra-sharp Cheddar cheese
1 tablespoon cornstarch
2 tablespoons skim milk
½ teaspoon paprika

1. Preheat broiler. In a medium saucepan, heat olive oil. Add cabbage, carrot, bell pepper, celery, and onion; cook and stir until tender, about 6 minutes.

2. Top each slice of toast with an equal amount of the vegetable mixture. Place slices on a baking sheet.

3. In a small saucepan, combine the cheese and cornstarch and toss to coat. Add milk and paprika and stir gently. Place over low heat and stir until the cheese melts. Spoon cheese mixture over the sandwiches, dividing evenly.

4. Broil sandwiches about 6 inches from heat source until the cheese sauce is bubbly and begins to brown, about 5 minutes. Serve immediately.

Serves 6

Calories: 256.07
Fat: 4.57 grams
Saturated Fat: 0.70 grams
Cholesterol: 0.0 mg
Sodium: 439.95 mg

*1 pound dried black-eyed
    peas*
1 tablespoon olive oil
1 onion, chopped
3 cloves garlic, minced
*2 cups fat-free vegetable
    broth*
2 cups water
½ teaspoon salt
*1 teaspoon dried thyme
    leaves*
1 bay leaf
*¼ teaspoon cayenne
    pepper*
3 cups hot cooked rice

Soulful Black-Eyed Peas

*Eating black-eyed peas on New Year's Day is supposed to bring
you good luck for the coming year. Served with rice, they make a
hearty meal.*

1. Pick over the peas, rinse, and drain. Cover with cold water and let stand
    overnight.

2. The next day, drain the peas and set aside. In a large, heavy saucepan,
    heat oil over medium heat. Add onion and garlic and sauté until tender,
    about 5 minutes. Stir in broth, water, salt, thyme, bay leaf, and pepper.

3. Bring to a boil, then add drained peas, and return to a boil. Cover,
    reduce the heat to low, and cook until peas are tender, about 45 min-
    utes to 1 hour. Remove bay leaf and serve over rice.

Black-Eyed Peas

*Black-eyed peas literally do have a tiny black spot on one side of the
pea. For complete protein, black-eyed peas and other legumes must be
served with another complementary grain. Rice is a traditional—and
ideal—accompaniment.*

Chapter 10
Sandwiches and Pizza

Grilled Vegetable Sandwich 140

Roast Beef Pitas 141

Chicken Pocket Sandwiches 141

Curried Turkey Pockets 142

Grilled Tarragon Chicken Sandwich 143

Peach Pita Sandwiches 144

California Vegetable Pizza 144

Beef and Veggie Pitas 145

A Year in Provence Sandwiches 146

Steak Subs 147

Greek Lamb Pizza 147

French Bread Pizza 148

Chicken Pizza 149

Rosie's Pizza Sauce 150

California French Bread Pizza 151

Top Hat Pizza 152

Grilled Vegetable Sandwich

Serves 6

Calories: 298.45
Fat: 2.78 grams
Saturated Fat: 0.62 grams
Cholesterol: 0.50 mg
Sodium: 588.32 mg

*1 small eggplant, sliced
 ¼-inch thick*
*1 summer squash, sliced
 ¼-inch thick*
*1 zucchini, sliced ¼-inch
 thick*
1 onion, sliced
*1 teaspoon dried Italian
 seasoning*
*¼ teaspoon cayenne
 pepper*
*2 baguettes, sliced
 lengthwise*
2 tomatoes, sliced
⅛ teaspoon pepper
*2 jalapeño peppers,
 minced*
8 fresh basil leaves
8 arugula leaves
*1 (7-ounce) jar roasted
 red peppers, drained*
*¾ cup Creamy Mustard
 Sauce (page 280)*

*You can also grill these vegetables on a charcoal grill; place
them in a grill basket for easiest handling.*

1. Preheat broiler. Spray a baking sheet with nonstick cooking spray. Arrange the eggplant, yellow squash, zucchini, and onion in a single layer on the baking sheet. Sprinkle the Italian dressing and cayenne pepper over all. Broil, turning once, for about 5 minutes on each side, or until browned. Remove the baking sheet, but leave the broiler on.

2. Scoop out the soft inner bread from the halved baguettes. Place in the broiler and toast for 2 minutes on each side. Put a few slices of tomato into each baguette half. Sprinkle with black pepper and jalapeño pepper.

3. Place 4 basil leaves, 4 arugula leaves, and 4 pieces of roasted pepper onto the bottom half of each baguette. Layer slices of eggplant, yellow squash, zucchini, and onion on top. Coat the inside of the remaining half of each baguette with the Mustard Sauce and place it on top of the vegetables. Cut each baguette crosswise into 3 equal pieces and serve immediately.

Roast Beef Pitas

Fresh basil adds a lemony, peppery scent and taste to these simple sandwiches.

1. In a large bowl, stir together the basil, horseradish, yogurt, and pepper. Spread the horseradish-yogurt mixture on the beef slices.

2. Separate lettuce into individual leaves and wrap each beef slice in a lettuce leaf. Put the lettuce-wrapped beef and 2 slices of tomato into each pita bread half. Serve immediately.

Serves 6

Calories: 201.48
Fat: 3.04 grams
Saturated Fat: 1.10 grams
Cholesterol: 39.52 mg
Sodium: 830.86 mg

½ cup chopped fresh basil
2 tablespoons prepared horseradish
½ cup plain nonfat yogurt
⅛ teaspoon pepper
1 pound deli-sliced lean roast beef
1 head butter lettuce
3 whole wheat pita breads, halved
2 tomatoes, sliced

Chicken Pocket Sandwiches

Fruits and nuts are a great way to add flavor and some good fats to sandwiches and other recipes. You can also use hazelnuts or walnuts in this easy recipe.

.   In a medium bowl, combine all ingredients except pita breads and lettuce. Cut pita breads in halves and open pockets. Line each with a lettuce leaf and spoon in chicken mixture. Serve immediately.

Serves 4

Calories: 589.32
Fat: 12.99 grams
Saturated Fat: 3.01 grams
Cholesterol: 68.43 mg
Sodium: 530.82 mg

2 cups cubed cooked chicken
¾ cup plain low-fat yogurt
½ cup sliced almonds, toasted
½ cup chopped nectarine
⅓ cup chopped green onions
2 tablespoons lemon juice
⅛ teaspoon pepper
½ teaspoon dried dill weed
4 whole wheat pita breads
8 lettuce leaves

Curried Turkey Pockets

Curry powder adds great flavor to this complex sandwich. Vary the amount to suit your taste buds.

Serves 4

Calories: 538.93
Fat: 12.48 grams
Saturated Fat: 3.01 grams
Cholesterol: 52.38 mg
Sodium: 529.31 mg

¾ cup plain low-fat yogurt
2 teaspoons curry powder
⅛ teaspoon ground mace
2 cups cubed, cooked
    turkey
½ cup Low-Fat Italian
    Salad Dressing
    (page 273)
1 green apple, cubed
½ cup sliced celery
¼ cup sliced almonds,
    toasted
¼ cup raisins
4 pita breads
8 curly lettuce leaves

1. In a small bowl, stir the yogurt with curry powder and mace and mix well. Cover and refrigerate for at least 4 hours or up to 24 hours to blend the flavors. Meanwhile, in a medium bowl, combine turkey and Italian dressing. Cover and marinate in the refrigerator for at least 4 hours or up to 8 hours.

2. Add the apple, celery, almonds, and raisins to the turkey. Stir the curry-yogurt dressing into turkey mixture. Cut the pita breads in half, forming 8 pockets. Line each pocket with 1 lettuce leaf, then spoon in the turkey mixture, dividing it evenly. Serve immediately.

Pita Breads

Pita breads come from the Middle East. They are usually quite low in fat. They are made by baking a moist dough at very high temperatures, so the air inside the dough expands rapidly, forming a pocket of air. You can find whole wheat and whole grain varieties in most grocery stores.

Grilled Tarragon Chicken Sandwich

The tarragon dressing can be kept in the refrigerator and used as a sandwich spread or an appetizer dip.

Serves 6

Calories: 378.87
Fat: 12.38 grams
Saturated Fat: 4.08 grams
Cholesterol: 81.39 mg
Sodium: 528.73 mg

1. Prepare and preheat grill. Meanwhile, in a small saucepan, combine the vinegar and tarragon, and bring to a boil. Cook until reduced by half and set aside.

2. In a small skillet, melt butter over medium heat. Add shallots and sauté for 5 minutes, or until tender. Transfer to a small bowl and add the mayonnaise, vinegar reduction, and white pepper. Mix well and refrigerate.

3. Pound the chicken breasts lightly with meat mallet or rolling pin. Season with salt and pepper.

4. Place the chicken on the grill on medium fire and cook, turning once and basting each side with 1 tablespoon of the mayonnaise mixture, for about 7 minutes on each side, or until done. Just before the chicken is ready, place the buns, cut-sides down, on the grill rack to warm.

5. Spread the cut sides of the buns generously with the flavored mayonnaise. Place 1 chicken piece on the bottom of each bun. Top with lettuce and tomato and then the bun top. Serve immediately.

2 tablespoons red wine vinegar
1 tablespoon dried tarragon leaves
2 tablespoons butter
1 shallot, minced
¾ cup low-fat mayonnaise
¼ teaspoon white pepper
6 boneless, skinless chicken breasts
½ teaspoon salt
⅛ teaspoon pepper
6 hoagie sandwich buns, split and toasted
6 lettuce leaves
2 tomatoes, sliced

Peach Pita Sandwiches

Peaches and ham are a natural combination. The sweet peaches contrast beautifully with the salty ham.

Serves 4

Calories: 450.38
Fat: 6.37 grams
Saturated Fat: 1.88 grams
Cholesterol: 53.92 mg
Sodium: 893.14 mg

4 pita breads, halved
8 curly lettuce leaves
2 cups 1% low-sodium cottage cheese
8 tomato slices
6 extra-lean ham slices, chopped
1 (16-ounce) can sliced cling peaches, drained

Cut pita breads in half, forming 8 pockets. Line with the lettuce leaves. Add cottage cheese, tomato slices, ham, and drained peaches. Serve immediately.

Pita Breads
You can find pita breads in most bakeries and large grocery stores. Cut the breads in half to make two half-moons. You may need to slightly cut between the layers to form the pocket. These breads are baked at a very high temperature so the gas inside expands quickly, forming the pocket as the structure sets.

California Vegetable Pizza

The artichoke hearts and olives add the distinct Californian accent to this easy pizza.

Serves 8

Calories: 259.84
Fat: 8.49 grams
Saturated Fat: 3.84 grams
Cholesterol: 7.38 mg
Sodium: 829.35 mg

1 recipe Rosie's Pizza Dough (page 39), prebaked
1 recipe Rosie's Pizza Sauce (page 150)
1 cup chopped frozen broccoli, thawed
1 cup chopped canned artichoke hearts, drained
¼ cup sliced black olives
6 green bell pepper rings
1 cup part-skim shredded mozzarella cheese

1. Preheat oven to 425°F. Place crust on 12" pizza pan and spread sauce on the dough to within 1 inch of edge. Arrange all the vegetables in layers on the sauce, ending with the tomatoes and pepper rings. Sprinkle with cheese.

2. Bake until the crust is brown and crisp, about 15 to 25 minutes. Remove from the oven and let cool for 5 minutes, then cut into wedges to serve.

Beef and Veggie Pitas

This recipe is a good example of using beef primarily for flavor; you get less than two ounces per serving, but the sandwiches taste very meaty.

1. Thinly slice the beef into bite-sized strips and combine in medium bowl with soy sauce, water, cornstarch, and pepper. Let stand for 10 minutes.

2. Heat olive oil in wok or large skillet. Drain beef, reserving marinade. Stir-fry beef until browned, about 2 to 3 minutes. Remove from wok with slotted spoon and set aside.

3. Stir-fry broccoli, carrot, and bell pepper until crisp-tender, about 4 minutes. Add mushrooms and tomato; stir-fry for 2 minutes. Return beef to skillet along with marinade; bring to a boil. Boil until thickened, about 2 to 3 minutes.

4. Make sandwiches with the beef filling and the pita breads; serve immediately.

Serves 4

Calories: 358.32
Fat: 10.28 grams
Saturated Fat: 2.87 grams
Cholesterol: 41.39 mg
Sodium: 693.25 mg

½ pound top round steak
2 tablespoons low-sodium soy sauce
¼ cup water
1½ teaspoons cornstarch
⅛ teaspoon pepper
1 tablespoon olive oil
1½ cups chopped broccoli florets
4 baby carrots, diced
½ green bell pepper, chopped
8 mushrooms, sliced
1 tomato, chopped
4 whole wheat pita breads, halved

A Year in Provence Sandwiches

These fresh sandwiches are a wonderful choice for lunch or a picnic. You can add slices of cooked chicken or ham if you like.

Serves 4

Calories: 369.32
Fat: 8.20 grams
Saturated Fat: 2.09 grams
Cholesterol: 10.63 mg
Sodium: 693.89 mg

1 tablespoon olive oil
1 onion, sliced
1 teaspoon dried oregano leaves
1 teaspoon dried basil leaves
1 tablespoon water
¼ cup sliced black olives
¼ cup grated Parmesan cheese
12 to 18 baby spinach leaves
4 French bread rolls, split and toasted
4 (1-ounce) slices part-skim mozzarella cheese
4 plum tomatoes, sliced
3 tablespoons Dijon mustard

1. Heat oil in large skillet over medium heat. Add onion; cook and stir until crisp-tender, about 5 minutes. Add oregano and basil along with water. Bring to a simmer; cook for 5 minutes until liquid evaporates. Remove from heat and stir in olives and cheese.

2. Arrange half of the spinach leaves on bottom half of each roll. Top with warm onion mixture, then cheese slices and plum tomatoes. Spread mustard on top half of each roll; place mustard-side down on tomatoes to make sandwiches. Serve immediately.

Taming Onions

Onion tastes very sharp and can overwhelm a recipe. By simmering an onion in water with a bit of sugar, the sulfur compounds escape into the air, and the onion tastes very mild, almost sweet. You can do this with any onion, but it works especially well with sliced onions used in sandwiches.

Steak Subs

This hearty sandwich stretches a pound of meat to serve 6, but it's so flavorful you won't feel like you're being short-changed.

1. Prepare and preheat grill. Trim excess fat from steaks and sprinkle with salt and pepper. Grill steak on both sides, turning once, until desired doneness, about 8 to 15 minutes. Remove from grill, cover, and let stand.

2. Cut French Bread in half lengthwise. Place, cut-side down, on grill to toast for 1 to 2 minutes until brown. Remove from grill, set cut-side up, and sprinkle cheese on 1 of the halves.

3. Cut steak into thin slices against the grain. Layer on the cheese; top with red peppers and lettuce. Spread top half of bread with mustard; place mustard-side down on lettuce to make sandwich. Slice into 6 sections and serve immediately.

Greek Lamb Pizza

The combination of lamb, oregano, and feta cheese is inspired by Greek cuisine.

1. Preheat oven to 425°F. In a large nonstick skillet, combine lamb, onion, garlic, and celery over medium heat. Sauté until the vegetables are tender and lamb is browned, about 5 minutes. Drain thoroughly.

2. Drain spinach by pressing between paper towels. Add spinach, oregano, salt, and pepper, to skillet. Cook, stirring, for 5 minutes until heated through.

3. Remove from heat and add the yogurt. Place pita breads on a cookie sheet. Divide spinach mixture among the breads. Sprinkle with feta and Parmesan cheese. Bake for 15 to 25 minutes or until pita is toasted and cheese melted. Serve immediately.

Serves 6

Calories: 439.25
Fat: 7.93 grams
Saturated Fat: 3.84 grams
Cholesterol: 69.46 mg
Sodium: 493.25 mg

1 pound boneless sirloin
    steak
½ teaspoon salt
⅛ teaspoon pepper
1 loaf Oat Bran French
    Bread (page 37)
1 cup shredded low-fat
    extra-sharp Cheddar
    cheese
1 (7-ounce) jar roasted
    red peppers, drained
shredded lettuce
3 tablespoons Dijon
    mustard

Serves 6

Calories: 275.40
Fat: 10.08 grams
Saturated Fat: 4.96 grams
Cholesterol: 41.62 mg
Sodium: 559.05 mg

½ pound lean ground lamb
1 onion, minced
3 cloves garlic, minced
1 stalk celery, chopped
1 (10-ounce) package
    frozen spinach, thawed
1 teaspoon oregano leaves
¼ teaspoon salt
⅛ teaspoon pepper
⅓ cup plain low-fat yogurt
4 pita breads
1 tomato, chopped
½ cup crumbled feta
    cheese
3 tablespoons grated
    Parmesan cheese

French Bread Pizza

French bread makes an excellent crust for pizza. Instead of buying the frozen kind, make your own!

Calories: 402.39
Fat: 12.38 grams
Saturated Fat: 4.39 grams
Cholesterol: 10.34 mg
Sodium: 793.23 mg

1 loaf Oat Bran French Bread (page 37)
3 tablespoons olive oil, divided
1 onion, chopped
1 green bell pepper, chopped
1 red bell pepper, chopped
3 garlic cloves, minced
2 teaspoons dried basil leaves
1 teaspoon dried oregano leaves
2 cups Rosie's Pizza Sauce (page 150)
3 tomatoes, sliced
½ cup sliced black olives
2 cups shredded carrots
1 cup shredded part-skim mozzarella cheese
½ cup grated Parmesan cheese

1. Preheat oven to 450°F. Slice the bread in half lengthwise. Drizzle cut sides of both halves with 2 tablespoons oil and place on a baking sheet.

2. In a large skillet, heat the remaining 1 tablespoon oil over medium heat. Add onion, bell peppers, garlic, basil, and oregano and cook for 5 minutes, or until tender. Remove from heat.

3. Spoon 1 cup spaghetti sauce on each piece of bread. Top evenly with the onion-pepper mixture, tomatoes, and black olives. Then sprinkle evenly with the carrots, mozzarella cheese, and Parmesan cheese.

4. Bake for 14 to 18 minutes or until cheese is melted and bubbly and the bread is lightly browned. Cut each loaf into 4 pieces to serve.

Shredded Carrots

Shredded carrots are a surprise ingredient on this pizza, and they also sneak their way into many recipes for spaghetti sauce. Not only is it a good way to get your kids to eat vegetables, but it helps thicken the sauce and adds a slight sweetness. If you want them to melt into the sauce, it's best to shred the carrots yourself; preshredded carrots can be dry.

Chicken Pizza

Red currant preserves add a tartness that complements chicken, shrimp, avocado, and cheese.

1. Preheat oven to 450°F. Soak the tomatoes in hot water for 30 minutes. Drain and set aside.

2. In a skillet, heat 2 tablespoons oil over medium heat. Add the chicken, oregano, basil, thyme, salt, and pepper and cook, stirring often, until the chicken is tender and thoroughly cooked, about 8 to 10 minutes. Drain and set aside.

3. Place crust on cookie sheet and prebake the pizza for 5 minutes. Spoon preserves over crust and spread in an even layer. Spoon chicken mixture over dough. Sprinkle with rehydrated tomatoes, shrimp, avocado, jalapeño, and cheeses.

4. Bake until the crust is golden brown and topping is hot, about 15 to 20 minutes. Cut into wedges to serve.

Preparing Avocados

It's not difficult to prepare an avocado; it just takes some practice. Cut the avocado in half lengthwise around the pit. Twist the halves to pull apart, then hit the pit with a chef's knife, twist, and pull out. Scoop the flesh out of the skin with a large spoon, then slice or dice as recipe directs.

Serves 8

Calories: 549.36
Fat: 17.49 grams
Saturated Fat: 3.08 grams
Cholesterol: 94.39 mg
Sodium: 420.35 mg

½ cup julienned dry-packed sun-dried tomatoes
2 tablespoons olive oil
1 pound boneless, skinless chicken breasts, diced
½ teaspoon dried oregano leaves
½ teaspoon dried basil leaves
½ teaspoon dried thyme leaves
½ teaspoon salt
¼ teaspoon pepper
1 recipe Chewy Pizza Crust (page 40)
½ cup red currant preserves
1 cup cooked, diced shrimp
1 avocado, diced
1 jalapeño pepper, minced
1 cup shredded part-skim mozzarella cheese
¼ cup grated Parmesan cheese

Rosie's Pizza Sauce

Your own homemade pizza sauce is delicious, and it's nice to be able to control what goes on your pizza!

**Yields 1½ cups;
8 servings**

Calories: 31.45
Fat: 1.83 grams
Saturated Fat: 0.19 grams
Cholesterol: 0.0 mg
Sodium: 320.89 mg

1 tablespoon olive oil
½ cup chopped onion
3 tablespoons tomato paste
1 cup tomato purée
1 tablespoon Dijon mustard
½ teaspoon salt
*¼ teaspoon crushed red
    pepper flakes*
*1 teaspoon dried basil
    leaves*
*1 teaspoon dried thyme
    leaves*
*1 teaspoon dried oregano
    leaves*
¼ teaspoon pepper

1. In a small saucepan, combine olive oil and onion; cook and stir until tender, about 5 minutes.

2. Add all remaining ingredients and cook, stirring frequently, over low heat until thickened, about 15 minutes. Use as directed in a pizza recipe, or store, covered, in refrigerator up to 5 days.

California French Bread Pizza

You can, of course, use a loaf of bakery French bread for your pizza, but try it with your own homemade bread for a spectacular recipe.

Serves 8

Calories: 328.46
Fat: 4.39 grams
Saturated Fat: 1.93 grams
Cholesterol: 8.39 mg
Sodium: 580.35 mg

*1 loaf Oat Bran French
    Bread (page 37)*
*3 tablespoons olive oil,
    divided*
2 onions, chopped
4 cloves garlic, minced
*2 green bell peppers,
    chopped*
*2 (4-ounce) jars sliced
    mushrooms, drained*
*1½ cups Rosie's Pizza
    Sauce (page 150)*
½ cup sliced green olives
*1 cup shredded part-skim
    mozzarella cheese*
*3 tablespoons grated
    Romano cheese*

1. Preheat oven to 425°F. Slice the bread in half lengthwise. Drizzle cut sides of both halves with 2 tablespoons oil and place on a baking sheet.

2. In a medium saucepan, cook 1 tablespoon olive oil, onions, and garlic over medium heat until crisp-tender, about 5 minutes.

3. In bowl, combine onion, garlic, bell pepper, and mushrooms with Pizza Sauce. Spread sauce mixture over the bread halves and sprinkle with olives and cheeses.

4. Bake until cheese is slightly browned and bubbly and topping is hot, about 20 to 30 minutes. To serve, slice each half into 4 pieces.

Romano Cheese

Romano cheese is similar to Parmesan cheese, but it's often saltier and tangier. Pecorino Romano is made from sheep's milk, while Caprino Romano is made from goat's milk. For a milder version, look for Vacchino Romano, made from cow's milk or a combination of all 3 milks.

Serves 8

Calories: 397.45
Fat: 11.38 grams
Saturated Fat: 2.04 grams
Cholesterol: 10.52 mg
Sodium 649.32 mg

1 recipe Rosie's Pizza Dough (page 39)
2 cups shredded part-skim mozzarella cheese
1 red bell pepper, thinly sliced
1 green bell pepper, thinly sliced
1 (4-ounce) can chopped green chilies, drained
½ cup sliced black olives
2 green onions, sliced
1 avocado, sliced
1 tablespoon lemon juice
½ teaspoon seasoned salt
⅛ teaspoon pepper
⅛ teaspoon hot pepper sauce
12 plum tomatoes, sliced

Top Hat Pizza

This unusual pizza doesn't have any sauce; instead, cheese forms the base. The vegetables bake down into the cheese, and the whole thing is topped with cold avocados and tomatoes.

1. Preheat oven to 425°F. Prebake Pizza Dough for 5 minutes; remove from oven. Let cool for 10 minutes.

2. Sprinkle cooled crust with mozzarella cheese, red and green bell peppers, chilies, olives, and green onions. Bake until toppings are hot and cheese is melted, 15 to 20 minutes.

3. Meanwhile, prepare avocados, sprinkling with lemon juice. In a small bowl, combine salt, pepper, plum tomatoes, and hot pepper sauce; toss to coat.

4. When pizza comes out of oven, top with avocados and tomato mixture; serve immediately.

Chapter 11
Rice

Herbed Rice Pilaf 154

Citrus Rice Salad 154

Seafood Rice 155

Chinese Rice Salad 156

Black Bean and Rice Salad 157

Cuban Black Beans and Rice 158

Curried Beans and Rice Salad 159

Rice with Black Beans and Ginger 160

Risotto with Winter Squash 161

Pineapple Rice 162

Risotto with Vegetables 163

Vegetable Fried Rice 163

Indian Rice 164

Wild Rice Pilaf 165

California Rice 166

Wild Rice Casserole 167

Orange Pilaf 168

Herbed Rice Pilaf

*The tiny thyme leaves will drop off the stem as the pilaf cooks,
adding a lemony-mint flavor to this easy recipe.*

Serves 4

Calories: 230.43
Fat: 3.89 grams
Saturated Fat: 0.61 mg
Cholesterol: 0.0 mg
Sodium: 210.94 mg

1 tablespoon olive oil
1 onion, chopped
2 stalks celery, chopped
2 cloves garlic, minced
1 fresh thyme sprig
½ teaspoon salt
⅛ teaspoon pepper
1 bay leaf
2½ cups water
1 cup long-grain brown
    rice

1. In a large saucepan, heat oil over medium heat. Add onion, celery, garlic, and thyme and sauté until onion is translucent, about 5 minutes. Add salt, pepper, bay leaf, and water, and bring to a boil.

2. Add rice, bring to a simmer, then cover, reduce heat to low, and simmer until all the water is absorbed and rice is tender, about 20 minutes. Remove and discard the bay leaf and the thyme stem; stir gently. Serve immediately.

Citrus Rice Salad

*A flavorful creamy dressing coats a blend of rice, fruit, and vegetables
in this satisfying salad. Serve it with a grilled steak for a summer meal.*

Serves 4

Calories: 274.85
Fat: 5.95 grams
Saturated Fat: 1.49 grams
Cholesterol: 5.93 mg
Sodium: 293.84 mg

2 stalks celery, sliced
4 green onions, sliced
1 (8-ounce) can mandarin
    oranges, drained
½ cup sliced cucumber
¼ cup golden raisins
2 cups cooked rice
¾ cup plain low-fat yogurt
2 tablespoons orange
    juice
1 tablespoon lemon juice
1 teaspoon orange zest
2 tablespoons honey
½ teaspoon ground
    ginger
¼ teaspoon salt
⅛ teaspoon white pepper

1. In a large bowl, combine the celery, green onions, oranges, cucumber, and raisins. Gently stir in the rice to combine.

2. In a small bowl, stir together the yogurt, orange juice, lemon juice, orange zest, honey, ginger, salt, and pepper, mixing well. Pour over the salad and toss gently to coat. Cover and chill for 2 to 3 hours before serving.

Seafood Rice

The tomato paste adds a slight pink tint to this excellent recipe.
Serve it with a green salad and some toasted garlic bread.

Serves 8

Calories: 329.35
Fat: 8.02 grams
Saturated Fat: 1.40 grams
Cholesterol: 88.49 mg
Sodium: 295.36 mg

1. In a large saucepan, heat the oil over medium heat for 1 minute. Add the green onion, onion, and garlic and sauté until soft, about 5 minutes. Transfer to a bowl.

2. In the same pan, add the scallops and shrimp and cook, stirring for a few minutes until the shrimp turn pink. Transfer the seafood to same bowl.

3. Add the wine, clam juice, water, and tomato paste to the pan over medium heat. Add the rice, stir, and bring to a boil. Cover, reduce the heat to low, and cook until all the liquid is absorbed and the rice is tender, about 30 minutes.

4. Add the seafood mixture, parsley, pepper, and lemon juice to the cooked rice. Cook over medium-low heat for 4 to 5 minutes until hot, then serve.

2 tablespoons olive oil
6 green onions, sliced
1 onion, minced
2 cloves garlic, minced
1 pound bay scallops
1 pound raw deveined shrimp
2 cups wine
½ cup clam juice
½ cup water
2 tablespoons tomato paste
1½ cups brown rice
½ cup minced flat-leaf parsley
⅛ teaspoon white pepper
2 tablespoons lemon juice

Brown Rice

Brown rice has a heartier taste than white, and it is better for you. Brown rice is made by removing just the outer covering, or hull, from the rice so it can absorb water as it cooks. White rice has the bran and most of the germ removed along with the hull. Brown rice also has more B vitamins, iron, and fiber than white.

Chinese Rice Salad

This delicious salad is nice served on some shredded Chinese or napa cabbage; eat it with chopsticks!

Serves 6

Calories: 179.37
Fat: 5.63 grams
Saturated Fat: 0.93 grams
Cholesterol: 0.0 mg
Sodium: 197.95 mg

2 tablespoons low-sodium
    soy sauce
1 tablespoon rice vinegar
1 tablespoon toasted
    sesame oil
1 tablespoon peanut oil
1 tablespoon minced
    fresh ginger root
3 cloves garlic, minced
¼ teaspoon white pepper
¼ teaspoon dry mustard
4 cups cooked brown
    basmati rice
1 red bell pepper,
    chopped
1 cup sliced celery
½ cup sliced green
    onions
½ pound snow peas

1. In a medium bowl, stir together soy sauce, vinegar, sesame oil, peanut oil, ginger root, garlic, pepper, and dry mustard. Add the rice and toss gently; cover and chill for 1 hour.

2. Add red pepper, celery, green onions, and snow peas and stir gently to coat. Serve immediately or cover and chill for up to 8 hours before serving.

Basmati Rice

Basmati rice is a long-grain rice that cooks up fluffy and dry. It is grown in India; some varieties, like Texmati, are grown in the United States. The rice is very fragrant; some varieties smell like popcorn when cooking. The brown basmati rice is more tender than regular long-grain brown rice.

Black Bean and Rice Salad

Rice and beans are a healthy combination; together, they provide complete protein. Choose a smooth red wine to serve with it.

1. Cook brown rice according to package directions until tender. When cooked, place in serving bowl and add beans, bell peppers, and red onion; toss to mix.

2. In a small bowl, combine remaining ingredients and mix well with wire whisk. Pour over rice mixture and stir gently to coat. Cover and chill for 2 to 4 hours before serving.

Serves 8

Calories: 167.34
Fat: 4.37 grams
Saturated Fat: 0.69 grams
Cholesterol: 0.0 mg
Sodium: 320.04 mg

1 cup long-grain brown rice
1 (15-ounce) can black beans, rinsed and drained
1 red bell pepper, chopped
1 green bell pepper, chopped
½ cup diced red onion
2 tablespoons olive oil
3 tablespoons orange juice
1 tablespoon apple cider vinegar
2 tablespoons chopped flat-leaf parsley
1 teaspoon ground cumin
½ teaspoon garlic salt
1 teaspoon chili powder

Cuban Black Beans and Rice

If you like it spicy, add a jalapeño or two to this classic dish of healthy carbohydrates. Serve with a fruit salad for a cooling contrast.

Serves 6 to 8

Calories: 341.98
Fat: 3.82 grams
Saturated Fat: 1.99 grams
Cholesterol: 23.95 mg
Sodium: 389.29 mg

*1 pound dried black
   beans*
1 tablespoon butter
1 onion, chopped
4 cloves garlic, minced
3 cups water
2 cups beef broth
2 bay leaves
*½ teaspoon dried thyme
   leaves*
*½ teaspoon dried
   oregano leaves*
½ teaspoon salt
*1 red bell pepper,
   chopped*
*1 green bell pepper,
   chopped*
*2 tablespoons apple cider
   vinegar*
*4 cups hot cooked white
   rice*

1. Pick over the beans, rinse well, drain, and place in large bowl. Cover with water and let soak overnight. The next day, drain the beans.

2. In a large pot, melt butter over medium heat. Add onion and garlic; cook and stir until translucent, about 6 minutes. Add drained beans, water, broth, bay leaves, thyme, oregano, and salt and mix well. Bring to a boil, then cover pot, reduce heat to low, and simmer until beans are tender, 1 to 1½ hours.

3. Add red and green bell pepper to beans along with vinegar; cook for 20 to 30 minutes longer until tender. Serve over hot cooked rice.

Black Beans

Black beans are a wonderful source of fiber, which helps lower cholesterol. The fiber also stabilizes blood sugars, which help keep you feeling full longer. Combined with rice, they provide complete protein. The little beans are also a great source of antioxidants, up to ten times the amount in oranges and equal to the amount in grapes and wine.

Curried Beans and Rice Salad

Curry powder can be mild or hot; the choice is yours. Try several brands to see which is your favorite.

1. In a small saucepan, heat olive oil over medium heat. Add curry powder and sauté for several seconds. Stir in broth and bring to a boil. Stir in rice, cover, reduce heat to low, and cook for 15 to 20 minutes or until rice is tender.

2. Remove from heat and combine in large bowl with celery, green onion, bell pepper, kidney beans, almonds, and tomatoes.

3. In a small bowl, combine lime juice, yogurt, salt, and pepper and mix well. Add to rice mixture and stir to coat. Cover and chill for 3 to 4 hours before serving.

Serves 6

Calories: 238.55
Fat: 5.93 grams
Saturated Fat: 1.96 grams
Cholesterol: 6.39 mg
Sodium: 305.83 mg

1 tablespoon olive oil
1 tablespoon curry
 powder
1 cup fat-free vegetable
 broth
⅓ cup long-grain rice
⅓ cup chopped celery
2 tablespoons chopped
 green onions
1 green bell pepper,
 chopped
1 (15-ounce) can kidney
 beans, rinsed and
 drained
2 tablespoons toasted
 slivered almonds
1 cup grape tomatoes
1 tablespoon lime juice
½ cup plain nonfat yogurt
¼ teaspoon salt
⅛ teaspoon pepper

Rice with Black Beans and Ginger

Rice and black beans contain complementary proteins, so this hearty dish is an excellent choice for vegetarians.

Serves 4

Calories: 256.83
Fat: 4.72 grams
Saturated Fat: 2.35 grams
Cholesterol: 0.0 mg
Sodium: 278.93 mg

1 tablespoon olive oil
2 cloves garlic, minced
1 onion, chopped
1 tablespoon minced
    fresh ginger root
1 cup brown rice
2 cups fat-free vegetable
    broth
1 (15-ounce) can black
    beans
⅛ teaspoon pepper

1. In a large skillet, heat oil over medium heat. Add garlic, onion, and ginger; cook and stir for 4 minutes. Add rice; cook and stir for 3 minutes.

2. Stir in broth and bring to a boil. Lower heat, cover pan, and simmer for 30 to 40 minutes or until rice is tender and liquid is absorbed.

3. Drain black beans, rinse well, and drain again. Add along with pepper to the rice mixture; cook and stir over medium heat for 5 to 6 minutes until hot. Serve immediately.

Cooking Rice

Some people have a hard time cooking rice so it ends up fluffy and separate. If you have this problem, try these tips. Rinse the rice before cooking to remove surface starch. Use double the amount of liquid than rice when cooking, and don't lift the lid when the rice is cooking. Finally, let it stand, off heat, for 5 minutes, covered, then fluff and serve.

Risotto with Winter Squash

Sweet and tender squash combines wonderfully with sage, onion, and leek in this creamy risotto. This could be the main dish for a vegetarian dinner.

1. Place broth in medium saucepan; place over low heat. In a large saucepan, heat oil over medium heat. Add squash; cook and stir until squash begins to brown, about 6 to 7 minutes. Add onion, garlic, and leek; cook and stir for 4 to 5 minutes longer until onion is translucent.

2. Stir in sage, salt, pepper, and rice; cook and stir for 3 minutes longer. Slowly add warm broth, ½ cup at a time, stirring frequently. When rice is al dente and squash is tender, add the cheese, butter, and parsley, cover, and remove from heat.

3. Let stand for 5 minutes, then stir and serve immediately.

Serves 6

Calories: 296.23
Fat: 5.73 grams
Saturated Fat: 3.53 grams
Cholesterol: 46.03 mg
Sodium: 418.89 mg

4 cups fat-free vegetable broth
1 tablespoon olive oil
3 cups cubed butternut squash
1 onion, chopped
3 cloves garlic, minced
1 cup chopped leek
1 teaspoon dried sage leaves
½ teaspoon salt
⅛ teaspoon white pepper
1½ cups Arborio rice
¼ cup grated Parmesan cheese
1 tablespoon butter
¼ cup chopped flat-leaf parsley

Pineapple Rice

Serves 4

Calories: 305.93
Fat: 7.49 grams
Saturated Fat: 2.97 grams
Cholesterol: 7.84 mg
Sodium: 284.95 mg

*1 (8-ounce) can crushed
    pineapple*
¼ teaspoon salt
*1 cup long-grain brown
    rice*
1 tablespoon butter
½ cup minced onion
2 cloves garlic, minced
1 cup sliced mushrooms
*1 tablespoon low-sodium
    soy sauce*
*½ teaspoon ground
    ginger*
¼ cup chopped cashews

This can be served as a side dish, but you can stir in some chopped ham along with the mushrooms and make it a main course.

1. Drain pineapple, reserving liquid. Pour liquid into a measuring cup and add enough water to measure 2½ cups. Pour into medium saucepan, add salt, and bring to a boil. Stir in rice. Cover, bring to a simmer, reduce heat to low, and cook until liquid is absorbed and the rice is tender, about 35 minutes.

2. Meanwhile, about 10 minutes before rice is done, melt butter in a skillet over medium heat. Add onion, garlic, and mushrooms and sauté until tender, about 6 minutes.

3. When rice is done, add to skillet along with soy sauce, ginger, and pineapple, mixing well. Cook and stir for 2 minutes. Add cashews, then serve immediately.

Cashews

Cashews are seeds—not nuts—which come from the cashew tree, originally found in Brazil. They contain heart-healthy monounsaturated fats and they have a lower overall total fat content than most nuts. Most of the monounsaturated fat is oleic acid, the same found in olive oil. The bottom line: snack on cashews for a low-fat, good fat treat.

Risotto with Vegetables

Arborio rice is a short-grain rice. It has more starch than long-grain, which is why it's used in risotto.

1. In a medium saucepan, place broth and heat over low heat. Melt 1 tablespoon butter in large skillet over medium heat. Add onion and garlic and sauté until softened, about 6 minutes. Add rice, salt, and pepper and stir to coat.

2. Reduce heat to low and add ½ cup broth at a time, stirring frequently, until absorbed. Continue adding broth, ½ cup at a time, cooking and stirring until absorbed.

3. When last ½ cup of broth is added, stir in zucchini and green beans; cook and stir for 6 minutes. Risotto is done when rice is still slightly firm in the center and mixture is creamy. Add the parsley, Parmesan, and remaining 1 tablespoon butter and stir gently; serve immediately.

Serves 4

Calories: 276.84
Fat: 7.93 grams
Saturated Fat: 4.89 grams
Cholesterol: 20.96 mg
Sodium: 540.25 mg

4 cups fat-free vegetable broth
2 tablespoons butter, divided
1 onion, chopped
3 cloves garlic, minced
1 cup Arborio rice
¼ teaspoon salt
⅛ teaspoon white pepper
1 cup chopped zucchini
1 cup chopped green beans
⅓ cup minced flat-leaf parsley
¼ cup grated Parmesan cheese

Vegetable Fried Rice

Oyster sauce is literally made of oysters, reduced down to a thick brown sauce. It's very savory, with lots of umami.

1. In a large skillet, heat oil over medium heat. Add onion and garlic; stir-fry for 3 minutes. Add bell pepper, zucchini, and celery; stir-fry for 3 minutes more. Add rice; stir-fry for 1 minute longer.

2. Stir in the eggs and stir-fry for 2 to 3 minute until cooked. Add bean sprouts; stir-fry for 1 minute until hot. Add oyster sauce and mix gently, then serve immediately.

Serves 6

Calories: 230.93
Fat: 5.30 grams
Saturated Fat: 1.98 grams
Cholesterol: 72.93 mg
Sodium: 549.37 mg

1 tablespoon peanut oil
1 onion, chopped
2 cloves garlic, minced
2 red bell peppers, diced
2 cups sliced zucchini
1 cup celery, sliced
4 cups cooked cold rice
2 eggs, beaten
1 cup bean sprouts
¼ cup oyster sauce

Indian Rice

Use any of your favorite vegetables in this easy recipe. Baby peas or grated carrots would be a nice addition.

Serves 8

Calories: 279.45
Fat: 3.70 grams
Saturated Fat: 1.89 grams
Cholesterol: 22.94 mg
Sodium: 306.49 mg

1 tablespoon butter
2 onions, chopped
4 cloves garlic, minced
½ teaspoon salt
⅛ teaspoon white pepper
4 cups fat-free vegetable broth
1 (8-ounce) package sliced mushrooms
1½ cups long-grain white rice
1 cup green lentils, rinsed
1 tablespoon minced ginger root
1 tablespoon curry powder
⅓ cup chopped flat-leaf parsley

1. In a large skillet, melt butter over low heat. Add onions and garlic and cook, stirring occasionally, until tender, about 10 minutes.

2. Meanwhile, in another large saucepan, combine broth, salt, pepper, mushrooms, rice, lentils, ginger, and curry powder. Bring to a boil, reduce heat to low, cover, and cook until the rice and lentils are tender and the liquid is absorbed, about 25 to 30 minutes.

3. Uncover and stir onion mixture into rice mixture. Then add parsley and stir gently. Serve immediately.

Curry Powder Recipe

It's fun to make your own curry powder. For a basic blend, combine 1 tablespoon turmeric, 2 teaspoons ground cumin, 1 tablespoon cinnamon, ½ teaspoon cardamom, 2 teaspoons ground ginger, 1 teaspoon ground white pepper, ½ teaspoon dry mustard powder, and ½ teaspoon ground nutmeg. Store in an airtight container in a cool place.

Wild Rice Pilaf

Wild rice and brown rice take the same amount of time to cook,
so they work well together in this recipe.

1. In a large skillet, heat oil over medium heat. Add onion and garlic; cook until crisp-tender, about 4 minutes. Add salt and pepper and stir. Add broth and bring to a simmer.

2. Stir in wild rice and brown rice and bring to a simmer. Cover, reduce heat to low, and simmer for 35 to 45 minutes or until rices are tender but still chewy. Stir in parsley and basil and serve immediately.

Wild Rice

Wild rice isn't really a rice but rather a grass seed. It's native to the upper Midwest and used to be harvested by Native Americans gliding through marshlands in canoes. Some is still produced that way, but the development of sturdier varieties has led to commercial production. Look for long, whole grains with an even dark color.

Serves 6

Calories: 237.45
Fat: 2.74 grams
Saturated Fat: 0.41 grams
Cholesterol: 0.0 mg
Sodium: 277.94 mg

1 tablespoon olive oil
1 onion, diced
2 cloves garlic, minced
½ teaspoon salt
⅛ teaspoon pepper
3 cups fat-free vegetable broth
1 cup wild rice
½ cup brown rice
¼ cup chopped flat-leaf parsley
½ teaspoon dried basil leaves

California Rice

Serves 6

Calories: 369.46
Fat: 11.49 grams
Saturated Fat: 6.39 grams
Cholesterol: 42.95 mg
Sodium: 732.53 mg

2 tablespoons butter
2 onions, chopped
4 cups cooked brown rice
1 cup low-fat sour cream
1 cup 1% cottage cheese
½ teaspoon dried
  oregano leaves
½ teaspoon dried basil
  leaves
½ teaspoon dried
  marjoram leaves
2 (4-ounce) cans
  chopped green
  chilies, drained
1 cup shredded low-fat
  extra-sharp Cheddar
  cheese
2 tablespoons grated
  Parmesan cheese

If you like your food really spicy, use two cans of chopped jalapeño peppers instead of the green chilies. Chopped green chilies are made from poblano peppers, which are quite mild. For more spice, use canned jalapeño or habanero peppers instead.

1. Preheat oven to 375°F. Grease a 2-quart baking dish. In a large skillet, melt butter over medium heat. Add onions; cook until crisp-tender, about 5 minutes. Remove from heat.

2. Stir in rice, sour cream, cottage cheese, and herbs and mix well. Layer one-third of the rice mixture in prepared dish. Top with half of the chilies, then half of the Cheddar cheese. Repeat layers, ending with a layer of rice.

3. Sprinkle with Parmesan cheese. Bake for 30 to 40 minutes or until casserole is bubbling and cheese melts and begins to brown. Serve immediately.

Wild Rice Casserole

This deliciously elegant dish pairs well with grilled or broiled chicken and a fruit salad.

1. Preheat oven to 325°F. In a medium skillet, heat oil over medium heat. Add onions and garlic and sauté until tender, about 5 minutes. Add mushrooms and celery; cook and stir for 3 minutes longer.

2. Transfer to 2-quart baking dish and add rice, seasoned salt, boiling broth, and pepper. Cover tightly with foil. Bake until the rice is tender, about 55 to 65 minutes. Stir gently, then serve immediately.

Shiitake Mushrooms

Shiitake mushrooms contain a substance that lowers blood cholesterol levels, no matter what type of fat you eat. They also have a good amount of antioxidants, which help reduce inflammation in your arteries. These mushrooms have a deep, smoky flavor that adds a lot to recipes without adding any fat.

Serves 6

Calories: 244.35
Fat: 2.54 grams
Saturated Fat: 0.36 grams
Cholesterol: 0.0 mg
Sodium: 305.93 mg

1 tablespoon olive oil
1 onion, chopped
2 cloves garlic, minced
1 (8-ounce) package shiitake mushrooms
3 stalks celery, chopped
1½ cups wild rice
½ teaspoon seasoned salt
4 cups boiling fat-free vegetable broth
⅛ teaspoon pepper

Orange Pilaf

Orange and raisins add flavor and wonderful aroma to this simple pilaf. Serve it alongside grilled salmon.

Serves 4

Calories: 287.54
Fat: 9.03 grams
Saturated Fat: 1.94 grams
Cholesterol: 0.0 mg
Sodium: 239.85 mg

⅓ cup slivered almonds
⅓ cup orange juice
1 teaspoon grated orange zest
1 teaspoon Asian sesame oil
1 tablespoon olive oil
1 cup long-grain brown rice
1 onion, chopped
2 cups water
¼ teaspoon salt
½ teaspoon dried tarragon leaves
⅛ teaspoon white pepper
½ cup raisins

1. Combine almonds, orange juice, zest, and sesame oil in a blender or food processor. Blend or process until smooth, about 10 to 15 seconds.

2. In a large saucepan, heat olive oil over medium heat. Add rice and onion and sauté for 3 minutes. Add salt, tarragon, pepper, and raisins and stir.

3. Add orange mixture and water. Bring to a simmer, then reduce heat to low, cover, and cook until rice is tender, about 18 to 23 minutes. Fluff with a fork before serving.

Chapter 12
Pasta

Chunky Pasta Sauce 170

Creamy Tomato Sauce 171

Marinara Sauce 171

Shells with Scallops 172

Seafood Linguine Fra Diavolo 173

Vermicelli with Tuna and Anchovies 174

Tuna Tomato Sauce 175

Broccoli Pasta Toss 176

Pasta Shells with Zucchini 177

Fusilli and Ricotta 177

Italian Pistachio Pasta 178

Angry Ziti 179

Garden Pasta 180

Macaroni and Cheese 181

Pasta with Summer Squash 182

Chunky Pasta Sauce

**Yields 1 quart;
serving size ½ cup**

Calories: 62.39
Fat: 1.39 grams
Saturated Fat: 0.38
grams
Cholesterol: 0.0 mg
Sodium: 239.23 mg

1 tablespoon olive oil
1 onion, chopped
3 cloves garlic, minced
*1 (8-ounce) package
    sliced mushrooms*
*1 green bell pepper,
    chopped*
2 celery stalks, chopped
*2 (14-ounce) cans diced
    tomatoes, undrained*
*1 (6-ounce) can tomato
    paste*
*1 (8-ounce) can tomato
    sauce*
½ cup red wine or water
1 teaspoon brown sugar
*1 teaspoon dried oregano
    leaves*
*2 tablespoons dried basil
    leaves*
*1 tablespoon chopped
    flat-leaf parsley*
*⅛ teaspoon red pepper
    flakes*
½ teaspoon salt

*Vegetables add flavor and nutrition to a classic pasta sauce; they
also help reduce the fat content. Serve this over hot cooked
whole wheat pasta.*

1. In a nonstick skillet over low heat, heat olive oil and add onion and garlic. Cook and stir until tender, about 5 minutes. Add mushrooms, bell pepper, and celery; cook and stir for 3 minutes longer.

2. Add all remaining ingredients and stir well to combine. Bring to a simmer, then cover skillet, reduce heat to low, and simmer for 15 to 20 minutes to blend flavors.

Creamy Tomato Sauce

Yogurt helps temper the acidity of tomato sauce, and fresh basil leaves add amazing flavor.

In a medium saucepan, combine all ingredients and stir well. Place over low heat and cook until the sauce almost comes to a simmer. Toss with hot pasta and serve immediately.

Cooking with Yogurt

Low-fat yogurt works better than nonfat yogurt in most recipes. Nonfat yogurt can have a sour taste. When you're cooking with yogurt, be careful not to bring it to a boil. If the yogurt does break down or separate, combine 1 teaspoon cornstarch with 1 tablespoon water and stir into mixture. This may help it bind together.

Marinara Sauce

Marinara sauce is a basic Italian tomato sauce made with onions and herbs.

1. In a large saucepan, heat olive oil over medium heat. Add onion and garlic; cook and stir for 5 minutes. Add all remaining ingredients except basil and bring to a simmer.

2. Reduce heat, partially cover pan, and simmer for 10 to 15 minutes or until slightly thickened. Stir in basil and serve with hot cooked pasta.

Yields 2 cups

Calories: 42.39
Fat: 1.39 grams
Saturated Fat: 1.29 grams
Cholesterol: 3.52 mg
Sodium: 240.14 mg

1 cup tomato sauce
1 cup plain low-fat yogurt
1 teaspoon sugar
¼ cup grated Parmesan cheese
½ cup torn fresh basil leaves
⅛ teaspoon pepper

Serves 8

Calories: 51.29
Fat: 1.29 grams
Saturated Fat: 0.05 grams
Cholesterol: 0.0 mg
Sodium: 198.23 mg

1 tablespoon olive oil
1 onion, minced
4 cloves garlic, minced
1 (14-ounce) can diced tomatoes, undrained
1 (8-ounce) can tomato sauce
1 (6-ounce) can tomato paste
1 teaspoon dried oregano leaves
⅛ teaspoon salt
1 teaspoon sugar
⅛ teaspoon pepper
¼ cup minced fresh basil

Shells with Scallops

Serves 6

This pesto can be used in many other ways as well; toss it with plain pasta, use it as a sandwich spread, or combine it with plain yogurt for an appetizer dip.

Calories: 380.03
Fat: 8.95 grams
Saturated Fat: 1.50 grams
Cholesterol: 27.15 mg
Sodium: 366.40 mg

1 cup water
½ cup dry-pack sun-dried
   tomatoes
2 cloves garlic, chopped
2 tablespoons pine nuts
3 tablespoons grated
   Parmesan cheese
2 tablespoons olive oil,
   divided
¼ teaspoon salt
¼ cup dry white wine
1 tablespoon cornstarch
1 pound bay scallops
1 cup fat-free chicken
   broth
1 (16-ounce) package
   medium shell pasta
2 tablespoons chopped
   fresh flat-leaf parsley

1. Bring a large pot of water to a boil. Meanwhile, in a small saucepan, bring water to a boil over high heat. Add sun-dried tomatoes and garlic; reduce heat to low and simmer for 8 to 10 minutes until tomatoes are soft.

2. For pasta; drain tomato mixture, reserving ⅓ cup liquid. Place tomato mixture in food processor. Add pine nuts, cheese, 1 tablespoon olive oil, and salt along with ¼ cup of reserved liquid. Process until smooth, adding more liquid if necessary. Set aside. In a small bowl, combine wine and cornstarch and set aside.

3. In a large saucepan, heat remaining 1 tablespoon olive oil over medium heat. Add scallops and cook for 4 minutes, stirring frequently.

4. Cook pasta until al dente according to package directions. While the pasta cooks, add broth and wine mixture to scallops along with pesto; cook, stirring frequently, until sauce thickens slightly, about 2 to 3 minutes.

5. Drain pasta and add to scallop mixture; toss over medium heat for 1 to 2 minutes. Sprinkle with parsley and serve immediately.

Seafood Linguine Fra Diavolo

Fra Diavolo *is an Italian term that refers to a spicy tomato sauce;
the term literally means "the devil's brother."*

Serves 6

Calories: 420.64
Fat: 8.09 grams
Saturated Fat: 1.23 grams
Cholesterol: 102.62 mg
Sodium: 363.41 mg

*2 tablespoons olive oil
1 onion, chopped
3 cloves garlic, minced
½ teaspoon crushed red
    pepper flakes
1 pound tomatoes, peeled
1 cup chopped fresh basil
½ teaspoon salt
⅛ teaspoon cayenne
    pepper
1 (12-ounce) package
    linguine
½ pound sea scallops
½ pound raw medium
    shrimp
½ pound haddock fillet
12 mussels, scrubbed
    and debearded*

1. Bring a large pot of water to a boil. Meanwhile, in large skillet, heat olive oil over medium heat. Add onion and garlic; cook and stir until tender, about 5 minutes. Add red pepper flakes; cook and stir for 1 minute longer.

2. Add tomatoes, basil, salt, and cayenne pepper to onion mixture; bring to a boil, then reduce heat to low and simmer.

3. At this point, add the linguine to the boiling water; cook until al dente according to package directions.

4. While the pasta cooks, add scallops, shrimp, haddock, and mussels to the tomato mixture; cover and cook for 3 to 4 minutes, shaking pan occasionally, until scallops and shrimp are opaque and mussels open.

5. Drain linguine and add to seafood mixture; cook and stir over medium heat for 1 to 2 minutes, then serve immediately.

Seafood Doneness

Usually, seafood is considered done when the flesh turns opaque. Fish usually cooks for 10 minutes per inch of thickness. Shrimp are done when they curl and turn pink. Scallops turn opaque, and mussels and other shellfish open. Another test for seafood doneness is to insert a fork into the flesh and twist; the flesh should flake easily.

Vermicelli with Tuna and Anchovies

Vermicelli is thinner than spaghetti and is a good choice for light sauces that won't weigh it down.

Calories: 475.51
Fat: 7.11 grams
Saturated Fat: 1.94 grams
Cholesterol: 16.98 mg
Sodium: 349.38 mg

1 tablespoon olive oil
1 onion, chopped
3 cloves garlic, minced
1 (14-ounce) can diced
    tomatoes, undrained
½ teaspoon dried
    oregano leaves
1 (12-ounce) package
    vermicelli pasta
1 anchovy fillet, finely
    chopped
2 tablespoons capers,
    rinsed
1 (6-ounce) can white
    chunk tuna, drained
¼ cup grated Parmesan
    cheese
2 tablespoons chopped
    flat-leaf parsley

1. Bring a large pot of water to a boil. In a large skillet, heat oil over medium heat. Add onion and garlic; cook and stir until tender, about 6 minutes. Add tomatoes carefully along with oregano and stir; simmer for 5 minutes.

2. Cook pasta in boiling water until al dente according to package directions. Drain, reserving ½ cup pasta cooking water.

3. Add pasta to tomato mixture along with anchovies, capers, and tuna; cook and stir over medium heat for 2 to 3 minutes, adding reserved cooking water as necessary, until sauce thickens slightly. Sprinkle with cheese and parsley and serve immediately.

Cooking Pasta

Pasta should be cooked in a large quantity of rapidly boiling, salted water. When you add the pasta to the water, stir gently so the pasta doesn't stick together. Do not add oil to the pasta water; control the boiling and foaming by stirring and slightly reducing the heat. Drain pasta when al dente, or still slightly firm in the center, and use immediately.

Tuna Tomato Sauce

Tuna is a nice change from beef or pork in this flavorful pasta dish. Serve it with a green salad and some fresh fruit for dessert.

1. Bring a large pot of water to a boil. Meanwhile, in large saucepan, heat olive oil over medium heat. Add garlic; cook and stir for 2 minutes. Then add anchovy paste and red pepper flakes; cook for 1 minute.

2. Add tomato purée and pepper; bring to a boil over medium-high heat. Reduce heat to low and simmer for 15 minutes.

3. Cook pasta according to package directions until al dente. Drain well. Stir tuna and parsley into tomato sauce. Add pasta; toss over medium heat for 2 minutes. Serve immediately.

Tuna

You can buy processed tuna in several forms—canned in water, canned in oil, and in pouches. The one you use is up to you. Tuna in oil doesn't have many more calories than tuna packed in water if it's well drained, and it is more flavorful. The pouch type, which is aseptic packaging, is packed in less liquid and has more flavor.

Serves 4

Calories: 59.25
Fat: 1.60 grams
Saturated Fat: 0.23 grams
Cholesterol: 8.39 mg
Sodium: 295.25 mg

1 tablespoon olive oil
2 cloves garlic, minced
1 teaspoon anchovy paste
½ teaspoon red pepper flakes
1 (28-ounce) can tomato purée
½ teaspoon pepper
1 (12-ounce) package spaghetti pasta
1 (7-ounce) can tuna in water, drained
⅓ cup minced fresh parsley

Broccoli Pasta Toss

This easy recipe is good for a last minute dinner. You can use bell peppers, mushrooms, or carrots instead of the broccoli.

Serves 4

Calories: 193.24
Fat: 3.92 grams
Saturated Fat: 1.01 grams
Cholesterol: 2.39 mg
Sodium: 192.84 mg

*2 cups small broccoli
    florets
1 (12-ounce) package
    fettuccine pasta
2 tablespoons olive oil
2 tablespoons lemon juice
½ teaspoon garlic salt
⅛ teaspoon white pepper
3 tablespoons grated
    Parmesan cheese
1 tablespoon toasted
    sesame seeds*

1. In a large saucepan, cook broccoli and pasta in boiling salted water until the pasta is al dente, stirring once or twice. Drain and place in a bowl.

2. In a small bowl, combine oil, lemon juice, garlic salt, and pepper and mix well. Add to pasta mixture and toss well. Add cheese and sesame seeds and toss to coat Serve immediately.

Toasting Seeds

Toasting seeds helps increase flavor because it intensifies the oils. Be careful when you toast seeds because they can burn easily. To toast, place seeds in a dry pan and cook over low heat, shaking the pan frequently until seeds are fragrant and turn light golden brown. Cool completely before using in recipes.

Pasta Shells with Zucchini

Rosemary adds a rich depth of flavor to this simple summer pasta recipe, and the Parmesan cheese topping adds just the right texture and taste.

1. Bring a large pot of water to a boil. In a large skillet, melt butter over medium heat. Add garlic and zucchini and cook until crisp-tender, about 5 to 6 minutes. Add rosemary and season with salt and pepper. Cook for 2 to 3 minutes to blend flavors. Remove from heat.

2. Meanwhile, cook pasta in boiling salted water until al dente. Drain and add to zucchini mixture. Return to the heat and toss until the shells are coated with sauce, 2 to 3 minutes. Add the parsley and cheese and toss again. Serve immediately.

Serves 4

Calories: 329.59
Fat: 4.30 grams
Saturated Fat: 2.91 grams
Cholesterol: 14.92 mg
Sodium: 420.32 mg

1 tablespoon butter
2 cloves garlic, minced
3 zucchini, sliced
2 teaspoons fresh rosemary leaves, minced
¼ teaspoon salt
⅛ teaspoon white pepper
1 (12-ounce) package medium pasta shells
3 tablespoons chopped flat-leaf parsley
¼ cup grated Parmesan cheese

Fusilli and Ricotta

Ricotta is a soft cheese similar to cottage cheese, but it is made from whey instead of milk. It has a creamy texture and rich flavor.

1. In a food processor or blender, combine ricotta cheese, milk, salt, pepper, and Parmesan. Process or blend until smooth.

2. In a large skillet, heat oil over medium heat. Add onion and sauté until nearly browned, about 10 minutes. Add garlic and cook until softened.

3. Add ricotta mixture and stir in basil, chives, and parsley. Cook over low heat, stirring frequently, until hot and blended.

4. Meanwhile, cook pasta in boiling water until al dente. Drain and add to skillet. Toss well so pasta is coated with sauce. Transfer to a warm serving bowl and serve.

Serves 6

Calories: 429.24
Fat: 9.24 grams
Saturated Fat: 3.29 grams
Cholesterol: 29.41 mg
Sodium: 402.14 mg

1 (15-ounce) container part-skim ricotta cheese
⅔ cup skim milk
¼ teaspoon salt
⅛ teaspoon white pepper
¼ cup grated Parmesan cheese
1 tablespoon olive oil
1 onion, chopped
4 cloves garlic, minced
½ cup chopped basil leaves
¼ cup chopped chives
¼ cup chopped flat-leaf parsley
1 (16-ounce) package fusilli pasta

Italian Pistachio Pasta

Serves 6

Calories: 520.35
Fat: 21.94 grams
Saturated Fat: 3.52 grams
Cholesterol: 30.29 mg
Sodium: 792.32 mg

1 tablespoon butter
1 tablespoon olive oil
1 onion, chopped
4 cloves garlic, minced
1 red bell pepper, chopped
1 green bell pepper, chopped
¼ pound prosciutto
1 cup pistachios, chopped
1 tablespoon fresh rosemary leaves, minced
1 (16-ounce) package penne pasta

Colorful and delicious, this easy pasta recipe is also satisfying because of the pistachios and prosciutto.

1. Bring a large pot of water to a boil. In a large skillet, melt butter and oil over low heat. Add onion and garlic and sauté until crisp-tender, about 5 minutes. Add bell peppers and cook for 3 to 4 minutes longer.

2. Trim visible fat from prosciutto, then dice. Stir prosciutto, pistachios, and rosemary into onion mixture. Continue to cook over low heat, stirring, until thoroughly heated.

3. Meanwhile, cook penne in boiling salted water until al dente. Drain, reserving ¼ cup cooking water. Add penne, cooking water, and Parmesan cheese to saucepan; cook and stir to form a sauce. Serve immediately.

Pistachios

Pistachios are high in monounsaturated fats, which are heart-healthy. Adding pistachios to your diet can help reduce cholesterol levels and improve the ratio of HDL to LDL cholesterol. And they're delicious. Look for pistachios that have not been dyed, and use unsalted varieties for cooking.

Angry Ziti

The spiciness of this ziti makes it "angry." If you like it hotter, use habanero peppers and increase the cayenne amount.

1. Bring a large pot of water to a boil. Meanwhile, in large skillet, heat oil over medium heat. Add onions and garlic and sauté until crisp-tender, about 5 minutes. Add jalapeños and mushrooms and sauté for 2 minutes.

2. Add plum tomatoes, basil, canned tomatoes, white wine, tomato paste, salt, and pepper and sauté until blended, stirring frequently, about 5 minutes.

3. Cook pasta until al dente according to package directions; drain the pasta and add to skillet. Cook, stirring and tossing, for 1 minute, then sprinkle with cheese and serve.

Serves 6

Calories: 420.39
Fat: 6.20 grams
Saturated Fat: 1.94 grams
Cholesterol: 4.29 mg
Sodium: 630.14 mg

2 tablespoons olive oil
1 onion, chopped
4 cloves garlic, minced
2 jalapeño peppers, minced
2 cups sliced mushrooms
1 cup chopped plum tomatoes
2 teaspoons dried basil leaves
2 (14-ounce) cans diced tomatoes, undrained
¼ cup white wine
¼ cup tomato paste
¼ teaspoon salt
⅛ teaspoon cayenne pepper
1 (16-ounce) package ziti pasta
¼ cup grated Parmesan cheese

Garden Pasta

Lots of vegetables make this pasta dish colorful and healthy. You could add some cooked chicken or shrimp if you'd like.

Serves 6

Calories: 398.12
Fat: 5.39 grams
Saturated Fat: 1.93 grams
Cholesterol: 6.39 mg
Sodium: 583.52 mg

2 tablespoons olive oil
5 tomatoes, peeled and
    chopped
2 carrots, chopped
2 stalks celery, chopped
1 onion, chopped
3 cloves garlic, minced
8 green onions, chopped
1 teaspoon dried basil
    leaves
¼ teaspoon salt
⅛ teaspoon pepper
½ teaspoon dried
    oregano leaves
1 (16-ounce) package
    spaghetti pasta
3 tablespoons grated
    Parmesan cheese

1. Bring a large pot of water to a boil. Meanwhile, in large saucepan, combine olive oil, tomatoes, carrots, celery, onions, and green onions. Cook over medium heat, stirring occasionally, for 8 to 10 minutes until tender.

2. Add basil, salt, pepper, and oregano. Cook over medium-low heat for 5 minutes.

3. Meanwhile, cook spaghetti in boiling salted water until al dente. Drain and add to the sauce and toss well. Sprinkle with cheese and serve.

Peel Tomatoes

Peeling tomatoes doesn't have to be hard. Bring a large pot of water to a boil. Drop the tomatoes in and cook for 10 seconds. Remove the tomatoes and plunge them into ice water; let stand for 15 seconds. The peel should slip right off. The peel does contain fibers and nutrients, but in some sauces, the cooked peel can leave an unpleasant texture.

Macaroni and Cheese

There's nothing as comforting as macaroni and cheese on a cold night. This excellent recipe is very flavorful, despite the low-fat content. Be sure to use extra-sharp cheese.

1. Bring a large pot of water to a boil. Preheat oven to 350°F. Add macaroni and cook until almost al dente according to package directions; drain, rinse with cold water, and set aside.

2. In a large saucepan, heat olive oil over medium heat. Add onion; cook and stir until tender, about 6 minutes. Sprinkle with salt and pepper.

3. In a small bowl, combine cornstarch with ½ cup milk. Add remaining milk and stir with wire whisk. Add milk mixture to saucepan; cook and stir until thickened. Add ricotta and mustard and stir to blend.

4. Add cheddar and mozzarella cheeses and cook, stirring, until cheeses melt. Add cooked macaroni, and pour into 9" × 13" baking dish.

5. In a small bowl, stir together the bread crumbs, Parmesan cheese, and butter. Sprinkle over macaroni mixture. Bake until bread crumbs are browned and casserole is bubbly, about 25 to 35 minutes. Serve hot.

Serves 8

Calories: 304.24
Fat: 6.39 grams
Saturated Fat: 4.02 grams
Cholesterol: 19.42
Sodium: 410.24 mg

3 cups macaroni
1 tablespoon olive oil
1 onion, chopped
½ teaspoon salt
⅛ teaspoon pepper
2 tablespoons cornstarch
1½ cups skim milk
½ cup part-skim ricotta cheese
2 tablespoons Dijon mustard
1 cup shredded nonfat extra-sharp Cheddar cheese
1 cup shredded part-skim mozzarella cheese
⅓ cup seasoned dry bread crumbs
3 tablespoons grated Parmesan cheese
1 tablespoon butter, melted

Pasta with Summer Squash

Roasted garlic is one of the best ways to add flavor without fat. Use any vegetable you'd like; mushrooms or tomatoes work nicely.

Serves 4

Calories: 503.25
Fat: 8.39 grams
Saturated Fat: 1.94 grams
Cholesterol: 0.0 mg
Sodium: 380.24 mg

9 cloves garlic, peeled
½ teaspoon dried thyme leaves
½ teaspoon dried basil leaves
½ teaspoon salt
⅛ teaspoon pepper
2 tablespoons olive oil
1 (12-ounce) package fusilli pasta
2 yellow squash, chopped

1. Preheat oven to 450°F. Bring a large pot of water to a boil. Place whole garlic cloves in center of a piece of heavy-duty foil. Sprinkle with thyme, basil, salt, pepper, and olive oil. Crimp edges to close. Place on cookie sheet; bake for 20 to 30 minutes or until garlic is soft.

2. Meanwhile, about 5 minutes before garlic is done, cook pasta in boiling salted water until al dente. About 2 minutes before it is done, add squash to the pot. Scoop out ⅓ cup of the pasta cooking water and reserve.

3. Pour the contents of foil packet into large saucepan; mash garlic with fork. Add reserved pasta cooking water and cook over low heat until a sauce forms.

4. When the pasta is done, drain pasta and squash and add to saucepan. Toss thoroughly over low heat until pasta is coated with sauce; serve immediately.

Garlic

Garlic is a member of the lily family, which also includes onions. When fresh, it is quite strong and peppery and has a distinctive aroma. Cooking garlic softens the cloves and reduces the sulfur compounds, making it nutty and sweet. Garlic is a great source of vitamins C and B6, known to help prevent heart disease.

Chapter 13
Pasta and Bean Salads

California Black Bean Salad 184

Seafood Pasta Salad 185

Black and White Bean Salad 185

Chicken Pasta Salad 186

Sunshine Bean Salad 187

Orzo Salad 187

Salmon Tortellini Toss 188

Snow Pea Penne Salad 188

Mediterranean Lentil Bean Salad 189

Apple Gemelli Salad 189

Macaroni and Bean Salad 190

Herbed Pasta Salad 190

White Bean Pistachio Salad 191

Summer Peach Pasta Salad 192

Waldorf Pasta Salad 193

Tricolor Pepper Pasta Salad 194

California Black Bean Salad

This colorful salad can be served as a side dish for a grilled steak or as the main dish salad for a vegetarian lunch.

In a medium bowl, combine all ingredients and mix together until well blended. Cover and chill for 3 to 4 hours before serving.

Serves 8

Calories: 134.78
Fat: 3.25 grams
Saturated Fat: 0.49 grams
Cholesterol: 0.0 mg
Sodium: 318.49 mg

1 (15-ounce) can black beans, drained and rinsed
2 cups frozen corn, thawed
2 tomatoes, chopped
½ cup chopped red onion
1 green bell pepper, chopped
1 yellow bell pepper, chopped
2 cloves garlic, minced
¾ cup Low-Fat Italian Salad Dressing (page 273)
1 tablespoon chopped flat-leaf parsley
⅛ teaspoon hot pepper sauce
1 teaspoon chili powder

Seafood Pasta Salad

Just a small amount of seafood combined with lots of pasta and vegetables makes a refreshing low-fat main dish salad.

1. Bring a large pot of salted water to a boil. Add pasta; cook until al dente according to package directions. Drain and rinse with cold water, drain again.

2. While pasta is cooking, in medium bowl, combine mayonnaise, yogurt, mustard, and milk and mix well with wire whisk. Add drained pasta, shrimp, crabmeat, carrots, squash, and red pepper; toss to coat.

3. Cover and chill salad for 3 to 4 hours before serving. Store leftovers in refrigerator.

Serves 4 to 6

Calories: 253.57
Fat: 7.81 grams
Saturated Fat: 1.29 grams
Cholesterol: 68.53 mg
Sodium: 557.83 mg

1 (8-ounce) package shell pasta
⅓ cup low-fat mayonnaise
⅓ cup plain low-fat yogurt
2 tablespoons mustard
2 tablespoons skim milk
1 cup cooked medium shrimp
4 ounces cooked crabmeat
½ cup shredded carrots
1 cup sliced summer squash
1 red bell pepper, chopped

Black and White Bean Salad

Beans are a refreshing low-fat food, full of fiber and protein. And they taste wonderful too, with a mild nutty flavor.

1. Thoroughly drain the beans. In serving bowl, combine beans, corn, tomatoes, and red onion and toss to mix.

2. In a small bowl, combine remaining ingredients and whisk to blend. Pour over bean mixture and stir to coat. Cover and chill for 2 to 3 hours before serving.

Serves 6

Calories: 226.65
Fat: 5.24 grams
Saturated Fat: 0.78 grams
Cholesterol: 0.0 mg
Sodium: 377.27 mg

1 (15-ounce) can cannellini beans, rinsed
1 (15-ounce) can black beans, rinsed
1 cup frozen corn, thawed
2 cups grape tomatoes
½ cup diced red onion
2 tablespoons extra-virgin olive oil
3 tablespoons lime juice
¼ teaspoon salt
⅛ teaspoon cayenne pepper
1 tablespoon minced mint leaves
2 tablespoons minced cilantro

Chicken Pasta Salad

Buy small amounts of low-calorie or low-fat salad dressings until you are sure you like the taste. Then stock up!

Serves 6

Calories: 246.38
Fat: 3.07 grams
Saturated Fat: 0.79 grams
Cholesterol: 59.60 mg
Sodium: 155.53 mg

1 (12-ounce) package
    pasta shells
1 (10-ounce) package
    frozen broccoli
¾ cup Herbed Yogurt
    Dressing (page 271)
3 tablespoons Dijon
    mustard
2 tablespoons skim milk
3 cups cooked, cubed
    chicken
1 pint grape tomatoes
½ cup diced red onion
1 English cucumber,
    sliced

1. Bring a large pot of salted water to a boil. Cook pasta until al dente according to package directions.

2. While the pasta cooks, prepare broccoli in microwave according to package directions. When pasta and broccoli are done, drain well and place in serving bowl; top hot pasta and broccoli with salad dressing.

3. Add chicken, grape tomatoes, red onion, and cucumber and mix well. Cover and chill for 2 to 3 hours before serving.

English Cucumbers

English cucumbers are longer and thinner than regular cucumbers, and they usually come wrapped in plastic wrap. The skin is not waxed, which means you don't have to peel it before using. The seeds are also very small and not as bitter as regular cucumber seeds, so they don't have to be removed before eating.

Sunshine Bean Salad

This recipe tastes like it came from California; it's fresh, sweet, and tangy. Serve it alongside a grilled fish.

1. In serving bowl, combine all ingredients except salad dressing; toss to combine. Add about ¾ cup of the dressing and toss to coat. Cover and chill for 2 to 3 hours before serving.

2. Serve on mixed greens with additional dressing, if desired.

Serves 8

Calories: 153.95
Fat: 3.10 grams
Saturated Fat: 1.09 grams
Cholesterol: 31.92 mg
Sodium: 419.39 mg

1 (15-ounce) can garbanzo beans, rinsed and drained
2 cups frozen corn, thawed
1 cup sliced celery
½ cup chopped red onion
¼ cup chopped green onion
1 red bell pepper, chopped
1 green bell pepper, chopped
1 recipe Golden Cooked Salad Dressing (page 270)
8 cups mixed salad greens

Orzo Salad

You can add any fresh vegetable to this simple cold salad; chopped yellow squash or sliced mushrooms are delicious.

1. Bring a large pot of water to a boil. Meanwhile, combine pesto and yogurt in large bowl.

2. Cook pasta in boiling water according to package directions until al dente; drain well. Add to pesto mixture along with bell pepper and peas; stir gently to coat. Cover and chill for 2 to 3 hours before serving.

Serves 6

Calories: 350.93
Fat: 11.49 grams
Saturated Fat: 2.10 grams
Cholesterol: 10.39 mg
Sodium: 259.93 mg

1 cup Low-Fat Spinach Pesto (page 286)
½ cup plain nonfat yogurt
1 (16-ounce) package orzo pasta
1 red bell pepper, chopped
2 cups baby frozen peas, thawed

Salmon Tortellini Toss

Tortellini are small stuffed pastas that are usually sold frozen.
They come stuffed with everything from cheese to beef.

Serves 4

Calories: 395.93
Fat: 10.10 grams
Saturated Fat: 4.06 grams
Cholesterol: 61.92 mg
Sodium: 683.94 mg

1 (19-ounce) package
    frozen cheese tortellini
1 cup plain low-fat yogurt
2 tablespoons mustard
1 tablespoon skim milk
½ teaspoon dried
    oregano leaves
2 tablespoons grated
    Parmesan cheese
3 tablespoons chopped
    flat-leaf parsley
4 carrots, thinly sliced
1 zucchini, sliced
1 red bell pepper, chopped
2 (6-ounce) cans salmon,
    drained

1. Bring a large pot of water to a boil. Cook tortellini as directed on package. Meanwhile, in large bowl combine yogurt, mustard, milk, oregano, cheese, and parsley and mix well.

2. When tortellini are tender, toss with yogurt mixture. Add remaining ingredients and toss to coat. Cover and refrigerate for 2 to 3 hours before serving.

Snow Pea Penne Salad

Snow peas and penne are about the same size, so this salad
looks pretty and tastes great.

Serves 6

Calories: 293.59
Fat: 4.90 grams
Saturated Fat: 1.39 grams
Cholesterol: 0.0 mg
Sodium: 130.94 mg

1 pound snow peas
1 small red onion,
    chopped
¼ cup chopped mint
    leaves
2 cups uncooked penne
    pasta
2 tablespoons raspberry
    vinegar
1 tablespoon olive oil
¼ teaspoon salt
⅛ teaspoon pepper
1 tablespoon honey

1. Bring a large pot of water to a boil. Meanwhile, in a steamer, steam the snow peas for 3 to 5 minutes until crisp-tender. Rinse under cold water, drain, and combine with red onion and mint in serving bowl; set aside.

2. Cook pasta according to package direction until al dente. In a small bowl, combine vinegar, oil, salt, pepper, and honey and whisk to blend. Pour over snow pea mixture and toss to coat.

3. When pasta is cooked, drain and immediately add to snow pea mixture. Stir gently to coat. Cover and chill for 2 to 3 hours before serving.

Mediterranean Lentil Bean Salad

Beans, lentils, and celery make a delicious and flavorful side salad perfect to serve with a grilled steak.

1. Preheat broiler. Cut bell peppers in half and remove membranes and seeds. Place, skin-sideup, on a broiler pan. Broil peppers for 10 to 12 minutes, or until the skin is blackened and blistered.

2. Remove from the broiler and, when cool enough to handle, pull away the blackened skin; cut peppers into narrow strips. Combine the peppers, beans, lentils, celery, basil, and parsley in a medium bowl.

3. In a small bowl, combine vinegar, olive oil, mustard, salt, and pepper and blend well. Pour over salad and toss to coat. Cover and chill for at least 1 hour before serving.

Serves 6

Calories: 245.91
Fat: 4.29 grams
Saturated Fat: 1.39 grams
Cholesterol: 0.0 mg
Sodium: 319.92 mg

3 red bell peppers
1 (15-ounce) can white beans, drained
2 cups drained cooked lentils
1 cup diced celery
¼ cup chopped fresh basil
¼ cup chopped flat-leaf parsley
⅓ cup balsamic vinegar
2 tablespoons olive oil
2 tablespoons Dijon mustard
½ teaspoon salt
⅛ teaspoon white pepper

Apple Gemelli Salad

You can use golden raisins or dark colored raisins in this classic and easy salad. Substitute dried currants for a slightly sweeter taste.

1. Bring a large pot of salted water to a boil. Meanwhile, drain pineapple, reserving juice.

2. In a serving bowl, combine pineapple, apples, celery, and raisins and mix well. Cook pasta according to package directions until al dente; drain well.

3. Add pasta to apple mixture. In a small bowl, combine 3 tablespoons reserved pineapple liquid, yogurt, mayonnaise, cinnamon, and salt and mix well. Pour over salad and toss to coat. Cover and refrigerate for 3 to 4 hours before serving.

Serves 6

Calories: 179.94
Fat: 2.49 grams
Saturated Fat: 0.21 grams
Cholesterol: 5.20 mg
Sodium: 130.94 mg

2 Granny Smith apples, peeled and chopped
1 (8-ounce) can crushed pineapple
½ cup diced celery
⅓ cup raisins
½ (12-ounce) package gemelli pasta
½ cup plain low-fat yogurt
¼ cup plain nonfat mayonnaise
½ teaspoon cinnamon
⅛ teaspoon salt

Macaroni and Bean Salad

Beans and pasta together provide complete protein. This vegetarian main dish salad is a good choice for a light lunch.

Serves 4

Calories: 430.92
Fat: 4.39 grams
Saturated Fat: 1.19 grams
Cholesterol: 0.0 mg
Sodium: 329.39 mg

1 (15-ounce) can kidney beans, drained
1 red onion, chopped
2 cloves garlic, minced
3 celery stalks, chopped
½ cup raisins
2 cups elbow macaroni
2 tablespoons olive oil
2 teaspoons curry powder
2 tablespoons honey
⅓ cup apple cider vinegar
¼ teaspoon salt
⅛ teaspoon pepper

1. Bring a large pot of water to a boil. Meanwhile, combine kidney beans, red onion, garlic, celery, and raisins in a large bowl.

2. Cook macaroni as directed on package until al dente; drain well. Add to kidney bean mixture.

3. In a small bowl, combine olive oil, curry powder, honey, vinegar, salt, and pepper and blend well. Pour over salad and toss to coat. Cover and chill for 2 hours before serving.

Herbed Pasta Salad

You can add more herbs to this salad, especially if you have fresh on hand. Chopped fresh parsley, chives, and tarragon will repeat the flavors in the homemade dressing.

Serves 6

Calories: 385.94
Fat: 6.39 grams
Saturated Fat: 1.79 grams
Cholesterol: 14.39 mg
Sodium: 620.93 mg

1 cup cooked broccoli florets
1 cup cooked cauliflower florets
½ cup thinly sliced carrots
1 red bell pepper, chopped
1 (4-ounce) jar marinated artichoke hearts, drained
⅓ cup sliced black olives
2 tomatoes, chopped
4 green onions, sliced
1 (12-ounce) package rotelle pasta
¾ cup Buttermilk Dressing (page 272)

1. Bring a large pot of water to a boil. In serving bowl, combine broccoli, cauliflower, carrots, bell pepper, artichoke hearts, olives, tomatoes, and green onions; toss gently to mix.

2. Cook pasta according to package directions until al dente; drain well. Add to salad along with salad dressing and stir gently to coat. Cover and chill for 2 to 3 hours before serving.

White Bean Pistachio Salad

Pistachios actually lower cholesterol levels, so don't worry about including them in a low-fat diet.

1. In a large bowl, combine all ingredients except vinegar, olive oil, sugar, salt, pepper, and salad greens; toss to blend.

2. In a small bowl, combine vinegar, oil, sugar, salt, and pepper and mix well to blend. Pour over other ingredients in bowl and stir gently. Cover and chill for 2 to 3 hours.

3. To serve, arrange salad greens on plates and top with bean mixture. Serve immediately.

Serves 4

Calories: 184.92
Fat: 5.93 grams
Saturated Fat: 0.94 grams
Cholesterol: 0.0 mg
Sodium: 320.96 mg

1 (15-ounce) can small white beans, rinsed and drained
2 cups sliced celery
½ cup diced red onion
⅓ cup pistachios, chopped
2 tablespoons fresh thyme leaves
1 teaspoon dried tarragon leaves
¼ cup apple cider vinegar
2 tablespoons extra-virgin olive oil
2 tablespoons sugar
¼ teaspoon salt
½ teaspoon pepper
4 cups mixed salad greens

Summer Peach Pasta Salad

This refreshing salad can be made into a main-dish salad by adding some cubed cooked chicken or ham.

Serves 6

Calories: 385.93
Fat: 8.49 grams
Saturated Fat: 2.91 grams
Cholesterol: 10.35 mg
Sodium: 180.93 mg

2 tablespoons olive oil
1 cup torn spinach leaves
1 zucchini, thinly sliced
6 peaches
⅓ cup grated Parmesan
    cheese
¼ cup chopped basil
    leaves
2 tablespoons white wine
    vinegar
¼ teaspoon pepper
1 (12-ounce) package
    penne pasta
½ cup low-fat peach
    yogurt

1. In a skillet, heat oil over medium heat. Add spinach and zucchini and sauté until spinach is limp, about 5 minutes. Place in large bowl. Peel peaches and slice; add along with cheese, basil, vinegar, and pepper to spinach mixture and toss to coat.

2. Cook pasta according to package directions until al dente. Drain and add to salad along with yogurt; stir gently to coat. Cover and chill for 2 to 3 hours before serving.

Peeling Peaches

You can peel peaches using a swivel-bladed peeler, but it's easier to blanch them. Bring a large pot of water to a boil, and drop the peaches in. Boil for 10 seconds, then remove and place in cold water. The skins will slip off easily, then you can cut the fruit in half, remove the pit, and slice or dice according to the recipe.

Waldorf Pasta Salad

Waldorf salads are usually made with just apples, mayonnaise, and walnuts; this twist is delicious and easy to make.

1. In a serving bowl, combine apples, red grapes, green grapes, and oranges and toss to coat.

2. In a small bowl, combine yogurt, thyme, and honey and mix well. Pour over salad and add cooked pasta and walnuts; toss to coat. Serve on lettuce leaves.

Grapes

Grapes contain flavonoids, which is what gives them their beautiful color. The redder the grape, the higher the concentration of this compound. These chemicals, also found in red wine, help protect against LDL cholesterol and can help reduce blood clot formation. They also contain resveratrol, which helps maintain heart health.

Serves 6

Calories: 250.93
Fat: 4.29 grams
Saturated Fat: 1.29 grams
Cholesterol: 4.39 mg
Sodium: 53.29 mg

2 Granny Smith apples, chopped
1 cup red grapes
1 cup green grapes
2 oranges, peeled and sliced
1 (8-ounce) package rotini pasta, cooked and drained
1 cup plain low-fat yogurt
½ teaspoon dried thyme leaves
1 tablespoon honey
⅓ cup chopped walnuts, toasted
6 large lettuce leaves

Tricolor Pepper Pasta Salad

Serves 8

Calories: 159.35
Fat: 4.02 grams
Saturated Fat: 1.49 grams
Cholesterol: 0.0 mg
Sodium: 250.39 mg

2 red bell peppers,
  chopped
1 yellow bell pepper,
  chopped
1 green bell pepper,
  chopped
3 celery stalks, chopped
2 large cucumbers,
  peeled and chopped
1 red onion, chopped
2 cups grape tomatoes
1 (16-ounce) package
  penne pasta
¼ cup lime juice
⅓ cup olive oil
2 cloves garlic, minced
2 tablespoons mustard
½ teaspoon salt
⅛ teaspoon cayenne
  pepper
⅓ cup chopped flat-leaf
  parsley

*Use any combination of colored peppers in this easy salad. This
is a good one to take to a picnic or potluck.*

1. Bring a large pot of water to a boil. Meanwhile, combine all of the peppers with the celery, cucumbers, red onion, and tomatoes in serving bowl.

2. Cook pasta according to package directions. Meanwhile, in small bowl, combine lime juice, olive oil, garlic, mustard, salt, pepper, and parsley and mix well.

3. When pasta is cooked al dente, drain and add to pepper mixture. Pour dressing over all and stir to coat. Cover and chill for 3 to 4 hours before serving.

Peppers

Bell peppers come in many different colors. Red and green peppers are the same variety, just picked at different stages of maturity. The other colors, including yellow, orange, purple, and black, are different varieties. Their crisp texture and sweet taste make them a salad favorite, and they're packed with antioxidants for your health.

Chapter 14
Side Salads

Potato Green Bean Salad 196

Glorified Brown Rice 197

Summer Potato Salad 198

Caesar Salad 198

Chinese Coleslaw 199

Hearts of Palm Salad 200

Apricot Green Salad 201

Fruity Coleslaw 201

Avocado-Citrus Salad 202

Cold Sesame Noodles 203

Peach Spinach Salad 204

Four Bean Salad 205

Busy Day Salad 205

Manhattan Deli Salad 206

Chili Pepper Potato Salad 206

Gazpacho Salad 207

Pineapple Pear Mold 207

Dijon Coleslaw 208

Potato Green Bean Salad

Serves 8

Calories: 165.72
Fat: 3.83 grams
Saturated Fat: 0.53grams
Cholesterol: 0.0 mg
Sodium: 74.28 grams

*2 pounds red new
    potatoes
1 pound green beans
¼ cup apple cider vinegar
2 tablespoons Dijon
    mustard
2 tablespoons olive oil
1 tablespoon apple juice
2 cloves garlic, minced
⅛ teaspoon pepper
4 celery stalks, chopped
1 red bell pepper,
    chopped
1 red onion, chopped*

This simple salad is a wonderful 1-dish meal for summer, but you can vary the ingredients as the seasons change to enjoy all year round. Serve it with hot breadsticks and an ice cream salad for dessert.

1. Bring a large pot of water to a boil over high heat. Scrub potatoes and cut into quarters. Add potatoes to boiling water and bring back to a simmer. Cover, reduce heat to medium, and simmer until potatoes are nearly tender, about 10 minutes.

2. Add green beans to potatoes and cook for 3 to 4 minutes longer or until potatoes are tender and beans are crisp-tender. Drain well and place in bowl.

3. In a small bowl, combine vinegar, mustard, olive oil, apple juice, garlic, and pepper and mix well. Drizzle over potatoes and beans and toss to coat.

4. Add remaining ingredients and toss gently to coat. Serve immediately or cover and chill for 2 to 4 hours before serving.

Glorified Brown Rice

Glorified Rice is usually a very sweet salad, more like a dessert.
This healthier version is tangy and just slightly sweet.

Serves 6

Calories: 171.85
Fat: 3.67 grams
Saturated Fat: 0.71 grams
Cholesterol: 1.23 mg
Sodium: 91.82 mg

*1 (16-ounce) can fruit
    cocktail*
3 cups cooked brown rice
1 cup sliced celery
*½ cup sliced green
    onions*
*2 tablespoons red wine
    vinegar*
*1 tablespoon extra-virgin
    olive oil*
*2 tablespoons Dijon
    mustard*
½ cup plain low-fat yogurt
*½ teaspoon dried
    tarragon leaves*
⅛ teaspoon white pepper

1. Drain fruit cocktail, reserving ¼ cup of the liquid. In a large bowl, toss together fruit, brown rice, celery, and green onions.

2. In a small bowl, combine reserved liquid from fruit cocktail, vinegar, olive oil, mustard, yogurt, tarragon, and pepper and mix with wire whisk until blended. Pour over rice mixture and stir to coat.

3. Cover salad and chill for 1 to 2 hours before serving.

Fruit Cocktail

There are lots of varieties of fruit cocktail on the market. You can find it canned or bottled in the refrigerated section of the produce aisle in most supermarkets. The combination usually includes cherries, grapes, diced pears, pineapple, and diced peaches. It's packed in water or a light or heavy syrup.

Summer Potato Salad

Cumin and mustard are an unusual, flavorful combination in this easy potato salad recipe.

Serves 8

Calories: 109.94
Fat: 3.29 grams
Saturated Fat: 0.79 grams
Cholesterol: 1.93 mg
Sodium: 129.94 mg

1 cup plain low-fat yogurt
2 tablespoons mustard
1 teaspoon cumin
2 tablespoons chopped cilantro
½ teaspoon pepper
2 (16-ounce) packages frozen Southern-style hash brown potatoes
1 red onion, chopped
3 radishes, thinly sliced

1. Preheat oven to 400°F. Spread potatoes on large cookie sheet. Bake for 15 to 20 minutes, turning once with a spatula, until potatoes are tender and just beginning to brown.

2. While potatoes are baking, combine yogurt, mustard, cumin, cilantro, and pepper in large bowl; mix well. Add hot potatoes, red onion, and radishes and stir to coat.

3. Cover and refrigerate for 3 to 4 hours before serving. Refrigerate leftovers.

Caesar Salad

Caesar Salad usually has coddled egg yolk in the dressing, but this recipe uses yogurt for a safer recipe with less fat.

Serves 4

Calories: 150.94
Fat: 6.39 grams
Saturated Fat: 1.59 grams
Cholesterol: 5.39 mg
Sodium: 120.94 mg

1 head romaine lettuce
1 clove garlic, cut in half
2 tablespoons olive oil
2 cloves garlic, minced
½ teaspoon anchovy paste
1 teaspoon Worcestershire sauce
¼ cup nonfat plain yogurt
3 tablespoons lemon juice
2 tablespoons grated Parmesan cheese
⅛ teaspoon pepper

1. Rinse romaine lettuce, pat dry with paper towels, and tear leaves into large pieces. Place in bowl that has been rubbed with the halved garlic.

2. In a small bowl, combine remaining ingredients and whisk until blended. Pour over leaves and toss to coat; serve immediately.

Chinese Coleslaw

This crisp and fresh-tasting salad is perfect matched with grilled turkey burgers for a summer cookout.

1. Drain pineapple, reserving juice. In a large bowl, combine mayonnaise, pineapple juice, five-spice powder, and ground ginger and mix well.

2. Add all remaining ingredients, including drained pineapple, and stir to coat. Cover and refrigerate for 2 to 3 hours to blend flavors before serving. Store leftovers in refrigerator.

Five-Spice Powder

Chinese five-spice powder is a blend of spices distinctive to Asian cuisine. If you can't find it in the grocery store, you can make your own. Blend a teaspoon of ground Szechuan peppercorns, ½ teaspoon ground anise, ½ teaspoon ground cloves, 2 teaspoons ground fennel seed, and 2 teaspoons ground cinnamon; store in an airtight container.

Serves 6

Calories: 89.94
Fat: 1.49 grams
Saturated Fat: 0.49 grams
Cholesterol: 5.29 mg
Sodium: 194.93 mg

1 (8-ounce) can crushed pineapple
⅓ cup low-fat mayonnaise
¼ cup reserved pineapple juice
½ teaspoon five-spice powder
½ teaspoon ground ginger
4 cups shredded Chinese cabbage
1 (8-ounce) can sliced water chestnuts, drained
1 cup chopped flat-leaf parsley
½ cup sliced green onions

Hearts of Palm Salad

This exotic salad is a great choice for a cookout. It's tender, crisp, and sweet, with gorgeous color and texture.

Serves 4

Calories: 259.39
Fat: 4.93 grams
Saturated Fat: 1.08 grams
Cholesterol: 0.0 mg
Sodium: 420.95 mg

4 hearts of palm,
   quartered
4 Belgian endives, sliced
2 bunches watercress,
   chopped
4 tomatoes, sliced
2 tablespoons lemon juice
2 teaspoons curry powder
1 tablespoon red wine
   vinegar
1 tablespoon mustard
¼ teaspoon salt
⅛ teaspoon white pepper
1 tablespoon extra-virgin
   olive oil
½ cup mango chutney
1 tablespoon minced
   chives

1. On a large chilled serving platter, arrange hearts of palm, endive, watercress, and tomatoes in layers.

2. In a small bowl, combine remaining ingredients except chives and whisk to combine. Drizzle over the salad, sprinkle with chives, and serve immediately.

Hearts of Palm

Hearts of palm are literally the center of the palmetto tree, the state tree of both Florida and South Carolina. It's also known as swamp cabbage. It's almost always sold canned. The hearts are tender and juicy, with almost no fat and no cholesterol. You can use them in any salad to add crunch and flavor.

Apricot Green Salad

You can serve this salad dressing with any type of mixed salad greens or a combination of baby spinach and toasted walnuts.

1. Drain apricots, reserving 3 tablespoons syrup. In a small bowl, combine reserved syrup, vinegar, olive oil, soy sauce, ginger, and pepper and mix well.

2. Slice apricots. In serving bowl, toss apricots with salad greens, cilantro, green onions, and water chestnuts. Drizzle with salad dressing, toss well, and serve immediately.

Serves 6

Calories: 149.93
Fat: 1.59 grams
Saturated Fat: 0.39 grams
Cholesterol: 0.0 mg
Sodium: 320.95 mg

1 (17-ounce) can apricot
  halves in syrup
3 tablespoons white wine
  vinegar
1 tablespoon extra-virgin
  olive oil
1 tablespoon low-sodium
  soy sauce
½ teaspoon ground ginger
Dash white pepper
6 cups mixed salad greens
¼ cup minced cilantro
¼ cup sliced green onions
1 (8-ounce) can sliced
  water chestnuts,
  drained

Fruity Coleslaw

Coleslaw is usually made with cabbage and root vegetables like carrots and broccoli. This fruity version is fun and easy for the family to make.

1. Place cabbages in large bowl. Toss pears and apple with lemon juice and add to cabbage mixture along with currants.

2. In a small bowl, combine yogurt, lemon zest, honey, and salt and mix well. Pour over cabbage mixture, toss to coat, and cover. Refrigerate for 1 to 2 hours before serving to blend flavors.

Serves 6

Calories: 148.52
Fat: 1.30 grams
Saturated Fat: 0.52 grams
Cholesterol: 3.29 mg
Sodium: 183.25 mg

2 cups shredded green
  cabbage
2 cups shredded red
  cabbage
3 pears, diced
1 Granny Smith apple,
  diced
3 tablespoons lemon juice
½ cup dried currants
1 cup vanilla low-fat yogurt
1 teaspoon grated lemon
  zest
2 tablespoons honey
⅛ teaspoon salt

Avocado Citrus Salad

Serves 6

Calories: 209.39
Fat: 5.93 grams
Saturated Fat: 1.08 grams
Cholesterol: 0.0 mg
Sodium: 129.97 mg

3 (6-inch) corn tortillas
1 tablespoon chili powder
¼ teaspoon fine salt
4 oranges
4 grapefruits
3 tablespoons honey
2 tablespoons raspberry
* vinegar*
2 tablespoons extra-virgin
* olive oil*
1 avocado, peeled and
* diced*
6 mint sprigs

*This unusual salad features a tangy combination of textures,
colors, and flavors that will make it a family favorite.*

1. Preheat oven to 275°F. Slice tortillas into very thin strips, about ¼ inch wide and arrange in single layer on cookie sheet. Bake until golden brown, about 15 minutes, turning with spatula halfway through cooking time. Toss with chili powder and salt while still warm. Remove to cool on wire rack.

2. Grate 2 teaspoons orange zest and set aside. Remove peel from oranges and grapefruits, and cut fruit into wedges between the sections. Squeeze the membrane to retrieve 3 tablespoons juice; reserve. Place fruit in serving bowl.

3. In a small bowl, combine reserved juice, honey, raspberry vinegar, olive oil, and orange zest and whisk to blend. Drizzle over fruit.

4. Top with avocado, tortilla strips, and mint and serve immediately.

Making Salad Ahead of Time

Most fruit and vegetable salads can be made ahead of time. Omit any vegetables that may wilt and fruits that will turn brown. Add them just before serving time. Do not make salads using lettuce or spinach ahead of time because the dressing will wilt the greens.

Cold Sesame Noodles

The sauce is very highly seasoned because the noodles are so bland. You can make this dish ahead of time; add more soy sauce and tea if needed to moisten.

1. Bring a large pot of water to a boil. Meanwhile, combine garlic, ginger root, and water in a food processor. Add tahini, soy sauce, tea, sesame oil, vinegar, sugar, five-spice powder, and chili oil and process to blend.

2. Cook noodles in boiling water until al dente according to package directions. Drain and place in large bowl; immediately pour garlic mixture over and toss to coat. Sprinkle with green onions and serve immediately, or cover and chill to blend flavors.

Serves 6

Calories: 430.92
Fat: 12.59 grams
Saturated Fat: 1.84 grams
Cholesterol: 0.0 mg
Sodium: 539.92 mg

10 cloves garlic, minced
2-inch piece ginger root, minced
3 tablespoons water
⅓ cup tahini
3 tablespoons low-sodium soy sauce
⅓ cup strong brewed tea
1 tablespoon Asian sesame oil
1 tablespoon white wine vinegar
1 tablespoon sugar
½ teaspoon five-spice powder
½ teaspoon chili oil
1 pound thin buckwheat noodles
6 green onions, thinly sliced

3 cups baby spinach
1 cup peeled, sliced cucumber
1 peach, peeled and sliced
2 plums, pitted and sliced
¼ cup sliced green onion
⅔ cup low-fat lemon yogurt
2 tablespoons sugar
¼ teaspoon dried dill weed

Peach Spinach Salad

This fresh, colorful, and tender salad is full of sweet and tangy flavor. It's perfect for a side salad when you're grilling outside.

1. In serving bowl, combine spinach, cucumber, peaches, plums, and green onion and toss to coat.

2. In a small bowl, combine yogurt, sugar, and dill weed; stir to combine. Let stand for 10 minutes, then drizzle over salad; toss to coat and serve immediately.

Baby Spinach

If you think you don't like spinach, try fresh baby spinach. It's tender and nutty, with a sweet aftertaste. To prepare, rinse in cold water. You may want to pull off the stems, but they are usually tender enough to eat. Arrange spinach in a kitchen towel, roll up, and refrigerate for 1 to 2 hours. Then use in salads and recipes.

Four Bean Salad

Typically, Four Bean Salad is made with a sweet and sour dressing. This is a nice, spicy change.

Serves 8

Calories: 260.39
Fat: 2.19 grams
Saturated Fat: 0.15 grams
Cholesterol: 0.0 mg
Sodium: 730.96 mg

Place all the beans in a large colander or strainer; rinse under cold running water. Drain thoroughly and combine in large bowl with remaining ingredients; stir until coated. Cover and refrigerate for 2 to 3 hours before serving.

1 (15-ounce) can garbanzo beans
1 (15-ounce) can red kidney beans
1 (15-ounce) can black beans
1 (15-ounce) can Great Northern Beans
1 onion, diced
1 cup diced celery
⅔ cup Low-Fat Italian Salad Dressing (page 273)
2 tablespoons chopped flat-leaf parsley

Legumes

Legumes, including chickpeas, black beans, red beans, white beans, and kidney beans, are a great source of protein and fiber in a low-fat diet. They have a nice nutty taste and creamy texture. Use them in salads, sandwiches, and soups. Keep several canned varieties on hand to make salads and snacks.

Busy Day Salad

This easy salad is a vegetarian main dish delight. You can make it in minutes for a quick lunch for two.

Serves 2

Calories: 219.38
Fat: 1.82 grams
Saturated Fat: 0.20 grams
Cholesterol: 0.0 mg
Sodium: 439.82 mg

Combine all ingredients in medium bowl; divide among chilled salad plates and serve immediately.

2 cups mixed salad greens
⅓ cup shredded carrots
⅓ cup canned garbanzo beans, rinsed and drained
1 tomato, sliced
½ cup chopped red onion
⅓ cup low-fat ranch salad dressing

Manhattan Deli Salad

Deli salads are delicious but can be quite high in fat. Control what you eat with this easy salad, which can be served as a side dish or vegetarian main dish.

Serves 6

Calories: 367.49
Fat: 4.98 grams
Saturated Fat: 1.27 grams
Cholesterol: 4.29 mg
Sodium: 573.34 mg

1 cup sliced black olives
1 red bell pepper, chopped
1 green bell pepper,
    chopped
1 red onion, chopped
¼ cup grated Parmesan
    cheese
¼ cup chopped flat-leaf
    parsley
1 tablespoon capers
¾ cup Low-Fat Italian
    Salad Dressing (page
    273)
1 (12-ounce) package
    fusilli or rotini pasta

1. Bring a large pot of water to a boil. In a large bowl, combine olives, bell peppers, onion, cheese, parsley, capers, and salad dressing; mix well.

2. Cook pasta according to package directions. When al dente, drain and add to salad. Toss to coat, then cover and refrigerate for 2 to 3 hours to blend flavors before serving.

Chili Pepper Potato Salad

Depending on how spicy you like your food, you can add a jalapeño or habanero pepper to this easy and delicious salad.

Serves 8

Calories: 187.48
Fat: 4.39 grams
Saturated Fat: 0.64 grams
Cholesterol: 4.29 mg
Sodium: 345.21 mg

2 pounds russet potatoes
½ cup low-fat mayonnaise
½ cup plain low-fat yogurt
1 tablespoon lemon juice
2 tablespoons mustard
½ teaspoon salt
⅛ teaspoon white pepper
¼ cup 1% milk
3 stalks celery, chopped
1 red onion, chopped
1 (4-ounce) can chopped
    green chilies, drained
1 avocado, peeled and
    chopped
1 pint grape tomatoes

1. Peel potatoes and cut into cubes. Drop into a saucepan of cold water as you work. Place saucepan over high heat, bring to a boil, then reduce heat, cover pan, and simmer potatoes for 10 to 12 minutes or until tender.

2. While potatoes are cooking, combine mayonnaise, yogurt, lemon juice, mustard, salt, pepper, and milk in serving bowl and mix well. When potatoes are done, drain well and immediately add to mayonnaise mixture.

3. Add remaining ingredients and stir gently to coat. Cover and chill for at least 4 hours before serving.

Gazpacho Salad

Gazpacho is a Spanish soup. It's served cold and is made of tomato juice and fresh vegetables.

1. Place ¼ cup each of the cucumber, tomato, bell pepper, onion, and the tomato juice in a food processor; process until blended.

2. In a large bowl, combine blended mixture with remaining cucumber, tomato, bell pepper, and onion. Stir in remaining tomato juice along with the vinegar, oil, Tabasco, salt, pepper, and garlic. Cover and chill for at least 2 hours before serving.

Serves 4

Calories: 102.84
Fat: 3.92 grams
Saturated Fat: 0.58 grams
Cholesterol: 0.0 mg
Sodium: 196.79 mg

2 cucumbers, peeled and sliced
3 tomatoes, chopped
1 green bell pepper, chopped
1 red sweet onion, chopped
1 cup low-sodium tomato juice, divided
¼ cup red wine vinegar
1 tablespoon olive oil
½ teaspoon Tabasco sauce
¼ teaspoon salt
¼ teaspoon white pepper
2 cloves of garlic, minced

Pineapple Pear Mold

A molded salad is a refreshing old-fashioned recipe. This one is full of vitamin C and would be delicious for breakfast on a hot day.

1. In a small saucepan, soften the gelatin in ½ cup orange juice for 5 minutes. Add sugar, then place over low heat and stir until the gelatin and sugar dissolve. Drain, pineapple, reserving juice.

2. In a 4-cup glass measuring cup, combine remaining orange juice, pineapple-orange juice, and enough reserved pineapple liquid to equal 2½ cups. Stir into gelatin mixture with drained crushed pineapple. Cover and chill until partially set, about 30 minutes.

3. Fold the pears into the pineapple mixture and transfer to a 6-cup mold. Cover and chill until firm, about 2 to 3 hours. To unmold, dip the bottom of the mold in hot water for 10 seconds, then invert onto a plate.

Serves 6

Calories: 174.55
Fat: 0.33 grams
Saturated Fat: 0.01 grams
Cholesterol: 0.0 mg
Sodium: 7.49 mg

2 (0.25-ounce) envelopes unflavored gelatin
⅓ cup sugar
1 cup orange juice, divided
1 (20-ounce) can crushed pineapple
2 (6-ounce) cans pineapple-orange juice
2 pears, peeled and diced

Dijon Coleslaw

Serves 6

Calories: 128.94
Fat: 1.38 grams
Saturated Fat: 0.03 grams
Cholesterol: 2.39 mg
Sodium: 240.99 mg

*1 small head cabbage,
    shredded*
4 green onions, chopped
1 red onion, diced
*1 green bell pepper,
    chopped*
½ cup shredded carrots
⅓ cup golden raisins
½ cup low-fat mayonnaise
½ teaspoon celery seeds
¼ cup nonfat sour cream
½ cup buttermilk
*2 tablespoons Dijon
    mustard*
*1 tablespoon apple cider
    vinegar*
2 teaspoons sugar
¼ teaspoon salt
⅛ teaspoon pepper

*Coleslaw can be served as a salad, or you can also try it as a
sandwich topping on a corned beef sandwich.*

1. In a large bowl, combine the cabbage, green onions, red onion, bell
    pepper, carrots, and raisins

2. In a small bowl, whisk together all the remaining ingredients. Add
    the mayonnaise mixture to the cabbage mixture and stir to combine.
    Refrigerate for 2 to 3 hours to blend flavors.

Cabbage

*Cabbage is a member of the cruciferous Brassica family, and it can be
a potent partner in the fight against disease. It's an excellent source of
vitamins A and C. It also contains chemicals called indoles, which have
been found to inhibit breast cancer cell growth. Serving it raw in coleslaws and in other salads also prevents the sulfur smell you get from
cooking it!*

Chapter 15
Soups

Cioppino 210

Onion Soup 211

Broccoli-Leek Soup 212

Chilled Cucumber Mint Soup 212

Curried Chicken Mushroom Soup 213

Light Corn Chowder 214

Black Bean Stew 215

Bacon Corn Chowder 216

Chilled Potato Soup 216

Spicy Pink Bean Stew 217

Pumpkin Cheese Chowder 218

Autumn Soup 219

Potato Garbanzo Stew 220

Creamy Borscht 220

Savory Tomato Soup 221

Tuna Chowder 221

Creamy Vegetable Soup 222

Chicken and Dumpling Stew 223

Chicken Lime Soup 224

Cioppino

Serves 6

Calories: 330.47
Fat: 7.46 grams
Saturated Fat: 1.06 grams
Cholesterol: 92.58 mg
Sodium: 705.44 mg

2 tablespoons olive oil
1 onion, chopped
3 cloves garlic, minced
1 green bell pepper,
    chopped
1 red bell pepper,
    chopped
4 cups clam juice
2 (14.5-ounce) cans no-
    salt diced tomatoes,
    undrained
½ cup dry white wine
1 bay leaf
½ teaspoon dried basil
    leaves
½ teaspoon salt
⅛ teaspoon white pepper
12 mussels, scrubbed
    and debearded
12 clams, scrubbed
18 medium shrimp,
    deveined
1 pound cod fillet, cubed
½ pound sea scallops
3 tablespoons chopped
    flat-leaf parsley

Cioppino is a rich, hearty Italian soup that is full of seafood. Serve it with some toasted bread to soak up all the fabulous broth.

1. In a large soup or stock pot, heat olive oil over medium heat. Add onion and garlic; cook and stir for 3 minutes. Add green and red bell peppers; cook and stir for 3 minutes longer.

2. Add clam juice, tomatoes, wine, bay leaf, basil, salt, and pepper and bring to a boil. Reduce heat to low, cover, and simmer for 30 minutes.

3. Uncover and remove bay leaf. Add all of the seafood and bring back to a simmer over medium heat. Cover and reduce heat to low; simmer for 5 to 8 minutes or until shrimp are pink and curled, cod is opaque, and clams and mussels open. Discard clams or mussels that do not open. Sprinkle with parsley and serve immediately.

Onion Soup

Using chicken broth and beef broth lightens up traditional Onion Soup. This soup is a whole meal—don't serve it as a starter because it's too filling.

1. In a large stock pot, heat 1 tablespoon olive oil and butter over medium heat. Add onions and garlic and reduce heat to low. Cook and stir until onions begin to turn brown, about 25 to 35 minutes.

2. Add the wines, thyme, and pepper and simmer for 15 minutes. Add the broths and bring back to a simmer; simmer for 1 hour.

3. Preheat the broiler. Brush the French bread with remaining 2 tablespoons olive oil. In a small bowl, combine the cheeses. Sprinkle cheeses over the bread.

4. Ladle the soup into ovenproof bowls. Top each serving with a slice of the bread. Place on a heavy duty cookie sheet and slide under the broiler. Broil for 2 to 3 minutes or until cheese bubbles and starts to brown. Serve immediately.

Sliced or Chopped?

You can slice or chop onions when making onion soup. Chopped onions make the soup easier to eat because they fit neatly onto a soup spoon, while the thin slices can slip off the spoon. The flavor will be the same with either type of prepared onion, so it's your choice.

Serves 8

Calories: 299.15
Fat: 10.67 grams
Saturated Fat: 3.46 grams
Cholesterol: 11.20 mg
Sodium: 345.42 mg

3 tablespoons olive oil, divided
1 tablespoon butter
6 large onions, chopped
3 cloves garlic, minced
1 cup dry red wine
½ cup Marsala wine
1 tablespoon dried thyme leaves
½ teaspoon pepper
4 cups fat-free, low-sodium chicken broth
4 cups fat-free, low-sodium beef broth
8 slices French bread, toasted
⅓ cup grated Parmesan cheese
⅓ cup grated Gruyere cheese

Broccoli-Leek Soup

Serves 6

An immersion blender is an invaluable tool for making soup recipes neat and simple. If you don't have one, you can use a blender or food processor.

Calories: 174.02
Fat: 4.95 grams
Saturated Fat: 1.55 grams
Cholesterol: 6.11 mg
Sodium: 336.32 mg

1 tablespoon olive oil
2 leeks, rinsed and
    chopped
3 cloves garlic, minced
1 pound red potatoes,
    peeled and chopped
1½ pounds broccoli,
    chopped
5 cups low-sodium, fat-
    free chicken broth
⅛ teaspoon white pepper
½ cup plain low-fat yogurt
⅓ cup grated Parmesan
    cheese
Pinch white pepper
2 tablespoons chopped
    fresh chives

1. In a large soup pot, heat olive oil over medium heat. Add leeks and garlic; cook and stir until tender, about 5 to 7 minutes. Add potatoes and broccoli and cook, stirring frequently, for 2 minutes.

2. Add broth and ⅛ teaspoon white pepper and bring to a simmer. Reduce heat to low, cover pot, and simmer until vegetables are tender, about 15 to 20 minutes. Purée soup using an immersion blender.

3. In a small bowl, combine yogurt, cheese, pinch white pepper, and chives and mix well. Serve soup immediately and spoon the yogurt mixture on top.

Chilled Cucumber Mint Soup

Serves 4

For a hot summer day, nothing beats a cold soup; you don't even have to cook this one! The two kinds of mint add a wonderful fresh flavor. Garnish the soup with whole mint leaves.

Calories: 109.19
Fat: 2.37 grams
Saturated Fat: 1.41 grams
Cholesterol: 9.77 mg
Sodium: 245.27 mg

2 cucumbers, peeled and
    seeded
⅓ cup chopped green
    onion
2 tablespoons chopped
    fresh mint leaves
2 cups 1% milk
1 cup plain low-fat yogurt
2 drops mint extract
¼ teaspoon salt
⅛ teaspoon white pepper

1. Chop cucumbers and combine with all ingredients in blender or food processor. Cover and blend or process until smooth.

2. Cover soup and chill for 2 to 3 hours before serving.

Curried Chicken Mushroom Soup

Chopped turkey breast can be substituted for the chicken if you'd prefer. Top this easy soup with some chopped fresh parsley for more color.

1. In a small bowl, combine the mushrooms with the boiling water; set aside for 20 minutes to rehydrate.

2. In a large saucepan, heat olive oil over medium heat. Add chicken breasts; cook and stir until almost cooked, about 4 to 5 minutes. Remove chicken from saucepan and set aside. Add leeks and mushrooms to saucepan; cook and stir for 4 to 5 minutes or until crisp-tender.

3. Add curry powder, flour, pepper, and chervil to saucepan; cook and stir until bubbly. Add milk and chicken broth; stir well and bring to a simmer.

4. Meanwhile, drain mushrooms, reserving liquid. Squeeze out excess liquid and coarsely chop mushrooms. Strain liquid through a coffee filter. Add to soup along with the mushrooms and chicken. Bring to a simmer; simmer for 10 to 15 minutes to blend flavor. Serve immediately.

Curry Powder

India, where curry consumption is high, has a very low incidence of Alzheimer's disease. Studies indicate this may be because curry powder contains turmeric, which contains an antioxidant that also has an anti-inflammatory function. So eat lots of curry; if you blend your own, include lots of turmeric!

Serves 4

Calories: 204.74
Fat: 6.07 grams
Saturated Fat: 1.18 grams
Cholesterol: 40.35 mg
Sodium: 199.66 mg

1 ounce mixed dried
    mushrooms
2 cups boiling water
1 tablespoon olive oil
2 boneless, skinless
    chicken breasts,
    chopped
1½ cups chopped leek
2 cups chopped cremini
    mushrooms
1 tablespoon curry
    powder
2 tablespoons flour
⅛ teaspoon white pepper
½ teaspoon dried chervil
    leaves
1 cup skim milk
1 cup low-fat chicken
    broth

Light Corn Chowder

*Corn chowder, filled with vegetables, is a creamy, rich delight.
Evaporated milk is the secret ingredient. It provides creaminess
with very little fat.*

Serves 6

Calories: 178.87
Fat: 4.90 grams
Saturated Fat: 1.56 grams
Cholesterol: 7.65 mg
Sodium: 239.29 mg

2 (14-ounce) cans fat-free
   chicken broth
1 cup broccoli florets
1 tablespoon olive oil
1 cup sliced mushrooms
1 onion, chopped
1 red bell pepper, chopped
2 cloves garlic, minced
2 tablespoons flour
⅛ teaspoon salt
⅛ teaspoon white pepper
2 (13-ounce) cans
   evaporated skim milk
1½ cups frozen corn
   kernels, thawed and
   drained
⅓ cup grated Parmesan
   cheese

1. In a small saucepan, combine chicken broth and the broccoli and bring to a boil. Reduce heat to low and simmer for 3 minutes; remove from heat and let stand.

2. In a large saucepan, heat olive oil over medium heat. Add mushrooms, onion, red bell pepper, and garlic; cook and stir for 5 minutes. Add flour, salt, and pepper; cook and stir until bubbly.

3. Add evaporated milk all at once; cook and stir until thickened. Add broccoli and broth along with corn; cook and stir for 3 minutes. Add cheese, stir until melted, and serve immediately.

Black Bean Stew

Black beans, also known as turtle beans, are full of fiber and protein. Their color coat contains at least eight types of flavonoids, which are antioxidants.

Serves 8

Calories: 276.41
Fat: 5.75 grams
Saturated Fat: 1.41 grams
Cholesterol: 3.67 mg
Sodium: 287.68 mg

2 cups black beans
2 tablespoons olive oil
1 onion, chopped
1 large bunch cilantro, chopped
8 cloves garlic, minced
2 teaspoons ground cumin
2 tablespoons chili powder
½ teaspoon dried oregano leaves
1 teaspoon crushed red pepper flakes
1 (28-ounce) can tomato purée
½ teaspoon pepper
3 cups fat-free, low-sodium chicken broth
¼ cup brandy, if desired
⅓ cup grated Parmesan cheese

1. Cover beans with cold water and let soak overnight. Drain beans and place in large soup pot. Add water to cover, bring to a boil over high heat, then reduce heat to low, cover pot, and simmer for 2½ to 3 hours or until beans are tender.

2. In a large skillet, heat olive oil over medium heat. Add onion, cilantro, garlic, cumin, chili powder, oregano, and pepper flakes; sauté until onions are tender. Add tomatoes, pepper, and chicken broth; cook for 5 to 8 minutes until blended.

3. Drain beans and purée half of them in a blender or food processor; return to pot along with contents of the skillet and stir to blend. Add brandy and cook until heated through. Garnish with Parmesan cheese.

Antioxidants

Antioxidants are important because they help your body resist the effects of aging at the cellular level. Antioxidant intake is usually inversely proportional to death from diseases like heart disease. In other words, the more antioxidants you eat, the better your chance for a long, healthy life. Eat lots of legumes and brightly colored fruits and vegetables.

Bacon Corn Chowder

Just a bit of bacon adds a smoky flavor to this simple soup. The marjoram adds a delicious depth of flavor.

Serves 6
___

Calories: 210.43
Fat: 3.04 grams
Saturated Fat: 1.20 grams
Cholesterol: 10.49 mg
Sodium: 222.90 mg

3 slices bacon
1 onion, minced
3 cloves garlic, minced
1 green bell pepper,
 chopped
½ teaspoon dried
 marjoram leaves
2 cups frozen corn kernels
2 cups water
2 cups 1% milk
1 (13-ounce) can
 evaporated skim milk
1 potato, peeled and diced
2 tablespoons cornstarch
⅛ teaspoon pepper
3 dashes Tabasco sauce

1. In a large saucepan, fry bacon until crisp. Transfer bacon to paper towels, crumble, and set aside. Pour off all but 1 tablespoon bacon drippings.

2. Cook onion, garlic, and bell pepper in the drippings, stirring until crisp-tender, about 5 minutes. Add corn, water, milk, evaporated milk, and marjoram potato and stir. Bring to a boil, reduce heat to low, cover pan, and simmer for 15 to 20 minutes or until potato is tender.

3. Ladle 1 cup of the liquid into a small bowl and stir in cornstarch, pepper, and Tabasco. Return this mixture to the saucepan and cook over medium heat, stirring frequently, until soup thickens and just comes to a boil. Garnish with bacon and serve.

Chilled Potato Soup

Chilled potato soup is also known as vichyssoise. It's elegant and delicious, and gorgeous served in chilled glass bowls.

Serves 4
___

Calories: 82.09
Fat: 2.34 grams
Saturated Fat: 1.27 grams
Cholesterol: 7.22 mg
Sodium: 458.81 mg

1 (10-ounce) can cream
 of potato soup
1¼ cups fat-free, low-
 sodium chicken broth
¾ cup buttermilk
1 small onion, chopped
2 green onions, minced
⅛ teaspoon white pepper
3 tablespoons minced
 chives

Combine all ingredients except chives in blender or food processor. Cover and blend or process until smooth. Pour into a serving bowl, cover, and chill for 4 to 6 hours before serving. Garnish with chives.

Spicy Pink Bean Stew

Any type of dried beans will work in this hearty recipe. Serve it with some crackers for a hearty winter meal.

1. Pick over the beans and sort, then rinse and drain. Cover with cold water and let soak overnight.

2. The next day, drain the beans and add water. Bring to a boil over medium heat, then reduce heat and simmer.

3. Heat olive oil in a skillet and cook onion and garlic until tender, about 5 to 6 minutes. Add to bean mixture along with chicken broth, chili powder, cumin, pepper, and oregano leaves. Cover and simmer for 2 to 3 hours until beans are tender.

4. Using a potato masher, mash half of the beans. Stir in tomatoes and bring to a simmer. In a small bowl combine tomato sauce and cornstarch; mix well. Stir into bean mixture and simmer for 8 to 10 minutes until thickened.

Preparing Beans

Dried beans sometimes have sticks, twigs, or small rocks packed in with them, so they must be carefully sorted, rinsed, and drained before using. Do not add salt or acidic ingredients while the beans cook for the first 1 to 2 hours, as those ingredients slow down the softening of the beans.

Serves 6

Calories: 153.34
Fat: 4.95 grams
Saturated Fat: 0.70 grams
Cholesterol: 0.0 mg
Sodium: 340.83 mg

1 pound dried pink beans
4 cups water
2 tablespoons olive oil
1 onion, chopped
4 cloves garlic, minced
2 cups fat-free chicken broth
1 tablespoon chili powder
½ teaspoon cumin
⅛ teaspoon pepper
½ teaspoon dried oregano leaves
1 (14-ounce) can diced tomatoes
1 (8-ounce) can tomato sauce
2 tablespoons cornstarch

Pumpkin Cheese Chowder

This pumpkin chowder is served in a pumpkin! Place it on a very large platter with sides to prevent leaks.

Serves 8

Calories: 154.67
Fat: 5.70 grams
Saturated Fat: 2.41 grams
Cholesterol: 8.62 mg
Sodium: 314.49 mg

*1 large pumpkin, about 5
     pounds, scrubbed*
*1 tablespoon butter,
     melted*
1 tablespoon olive oil
2 onions, chopped
3 stalks celery, chopped
4 cloves garlic, minced
*5 cups low-sodium
     vegetable broth*
*1 (15-ounce) can solid-
     packed pumpkin*
½ teaspoon pepper
½ teaspoon nutmeg
1½ cups 1% milk
2 tablespoons cornstarch
*1 cup grated extra-sharp
     low-fat Cheddar
     cheese*
⅓ cup dry white wine
*⅓ cup minced flat-leaf
     parsley*

1. Preheat oven to 350°F. Cut top off pumpkin and remove seeds. Brush inside with melted butter. Replace top and put pumpkin on a baking sheet. Bake for 40 to 50 minutes or until pumpkin is tender when pierced with a fork, but still holds it shape.

2. Meanwhile, heat olive oil in a large soup pot over medium heat. Add onion, celery, and garlic and sauté until tender, about 5 to 7 minutes. Add broth, pumpkin, pepper, and nutmeg. Cover and simmer for 20 minutes.

3. Using an immersion blender, purée the soup. Combine ½ cup milk with cornstarch and blend well; add remaining milk and stir. Add milk mixture, cheese, and wine to soup and heat until the cheese melts and soup is hot, stirring frequently.

4. Place the baked pumpkin on a large serving platter with sides and pour in the soup. Sprinkle with parsley.

5. To serve, ladle soup at the table, scooping a bit of the pumpkin into each serving, being careful not to pierce the shell.

Autumn Soup

The squash gives this one-pot meal a beautiful golden color. It's also delicious served cold; you may need to thin it with some additional buttermilk.

1. In a large soup pot, combine broth, onion, garlic, bread, apples, and the squash quarters. Bring to a boil, reduce heat to low, cover, and simmer for 40 minutes.

2. Remove squash quarters and let stand for 10 minutes. Scoop flesh from the rind and return to pot; discard rind. Add rosemary, marjoram, and pepper.

3. Using an immersion blender, purée the soup. In a small bowl, combine eggs and buttermilk and beat well. Stir some of the hot soup into the egg mixture, beating with a wire whisk. Add all of the warmed egg mixture to the soup.

4. Cook soup, stirring frequently, until steam rises, but do not let the soup boil. Serve immediately.

Preparing Squash

Winter squashes can take some skill to prepare. Using a sharp chef's knife, cut the squash in half. Once it is cut in half, turn the squash cut side down and cut each half in half. Scoop out the seeds with a large spoon and proceed with the recipe.

Serves 6

Calories: 220.25
Fat: 3.25 grams
Saturated Fat: 1.16 grams
Cholesterol: 73.77 mg
Sodium: 420.26 mg

4 cups fat-free chicken broth
1 onion, chopped
3 cloves garlic, minced
2 slices firm white bread, cut into cubes
2 Granny Smith apples, cored and chopped
1 butternut squash, quartered and seeded
1 tablespoon fresh rosemary leaves, minced
½ teaspoon dried marjoram leaves
½ teaspoon pepper
2 eggs
1 cup buttermilk

Serves 4

Calories: 346.23
Fat: 5.15 grams
Saturated Fat: 0.70 grams
Cholesterol: 0.0 mg
Sodium: 360.93 mg

1 tablespoon olive oil
1 onion, chopped
3 cloves garlic, minced
1 teaspoon paprika
3 tomatoes, chopped
1 teaspoon dried oregano
    leaves
2 potatoes, peeled and
    diced
4 cups fat-free, low-
    sodium chicken broth
1 (15-ounce) can
    garbanzo beans,
    rinsed and drained
½ cup chopped fresh
    basil leaves
¼ teaspoon salt
⅛ teaspoon pepper
½ cup chopped fresh
    parsley

Potato Garbanzo Stew

Potatoes and beans may sound like a strange combination, but it is heart-warming and delicious.

1. In a large saucepan, heat olive oil over medium heat. Add onion and garlic; cook and stir until crisp-tender, about 5 minutes. Add paprika, tomatoes, and oregano. Reduce heat to low and cook, stirring frequently, for 5 minutes.

2. Add potatoes and broth, cover, and bring to a boil. Reduce heat to low and simmer for 5 minutes, stirring occasionally. Add garbanzo beans and cook until potatoes are tender, 5 to 8 minutes longer.

3. Add basil, salt, and pepper and simmer for 3 to 5 minutes longer to heat through. Sprinkle with parsley and serve.

Serves 4

Calories: 213.10
Fat: 6.18 grams
Saturated Fat: 3.80 grams
Cholesterol: 21.60 mg
Sodium: 417.40 mg

1 (16-ounce) jar pickled
    beets, drained
2 cups buttermilk
1 tablespoon honey
1 tablespoon sugar
2 tablespoons lemon juice
⅛ teaspoon pepper
½ cup low-fat sour cream
¼ cup snipped chives

Creamy Borscht

Serve this gorgeous pink soup in tiny cups or mugs as an unusual appetizer before a German or Polish meal.

1. In a blender or food processor, combine beets, buttermilk, honey, sugar, lemon juice, and pepper and blend or process until smooth. Cover and chill for 1 to 2 hours before serving.

2. To serve, ladle into cups or mugs and top with sour cream and chives.

Savory Tomato Soup

Tomato soup made from fresh tomatoes tastes nothing like the condensed variety. This fresh soup is excellent served with grilled cheese sandwiches.

1. In a large skillet, heat olive oil over medium heat. Add shallots; cook and stir until tender, about 5 to 6 minutes. Add tomatoes and chicken broth; bring to a simmer. Simmer, stirring occasionally, for 15 minutes.

2. Add sugar, evaporated milk, and seasonings. Using an immersion blender, purée the soup. Heat until soup steams, but do not boil. Serve immediately.

Serves 4

Calories: 164.11
Fat: 4.10 grams
Saturated Fat: 0.70 grams
Cholesterol: 4.15 mg
Sodium: 254.57 mg

1 tablespoon olive oil
2 shallots, minced
5 large tomatoes, diced
1 cup fat-free chicken broth
1 teaspoon sugar
1 (13-ounce) can nonfat evaporated milk
1 teaspoon dried basil leaves
½ teaspoon dried oregano leaves
⅛ teaspoon pepper

Tuna Chowder

You can use canned salmon or shrimp in this rich chowder if you prefer.

1. In a large soup pot, heat olive oil over medium heat. Add onion, celery, and garlic; cook and stir for 3 minutes. Add potato; cook and stir until potato is almost tender, about 4 to 5 minutes longer.

2. Add flour, salt, and pepper to pot; cook and stir until bubbly. Add milk, cook and stir until soup thickens, about 5 to 6 minutes.

3. Add tuna, cheese, and herbs. Cook over medium-low heat for 5 to 8 minutes or until soup is hot and cheese melts. Serve immediately.

Serves 6

Calories: 234.13
Fat: 7.51 grams
Saturated Fat: 2.35 grams
Cholesterol: 24.22 mg
Sodium: 444.44 mg

2 tablespoons olive oil
1 onion, chopped
3 stalks celery, chopped
3 cloves garlic, minced
1 large potato, peeled and chopped
3 tablespoons flour
¼ teaspoon salt
⅛ teaspoon pepper
3 cups 1% milk
2 (6-ounce) cans water-packed tuna, drained
1 cup grated low-fat extra-sharp Cheddar cheese
1 teaspoon dried thyme leaves
½ teaspoon dried dill weed

Creamy Vegetable Soup

Cruciferous vegetables like broccoli and cauliflower are so good for you because they can help prevent cancer. These veggies are high in fiber, vitamins, and antioxidants.

Serves 4

Calories: 164.75
Fat: 3.15 grams
Saturated Fat: 1.70 grams
Cholesterol: 8.98 mg
Sodium: 458.86 mg

1½ cups water
3 cups broccoli florets
2 carrots, chopped
1 onion, chopped
2 cloves garlic, minced
1 cup chopped cauliflower
¼ teaspoon salt
⅛ teaspoon pepper
1 tablespoon mustard
2 cups 1% milk
1 cup shredded low-fat
    sharp Cheddar cheese
2 tablespoons cornstarch
1 cup diced yellow
    summer squash

1. In a large saucepan, bring water to a boil. Add the broccoli, carrot, onion, garlic, and cauliflower and bring back to a boil. Simmer for 5 to 6 minutes until vegetables are almost tender.

2. Let cool slightly, then transfer to food processor. Add salt, pepper, mustard, and milk and process until smooth. Return to saucepan.

3. Bring soup to a boil, then reduce heat and simmer until vegetables are cooked, about 5 to 6 minutes longer.

4. Coat cheese with cornstarch and add to saucepan along with squash. Cook over medium heat, stirring frequently, until soup thickens slightly and cheese melts. Serve immediately.

Chicken and Dumpling Stew

Ancient Greeks and Egyptians praised chicken soup's healing properties, and twenty-first century scientists have backed them up. One bowl gives your body much-needed liquids, electrolytes, protein, and nutrients. This homemade version is a better option than the sodium-filled canned soups.

1. Cut chicken into cubes and combine in large soup pot with potatoes, carrots, onions, celery, and sweet potatoes. Pour chicken broth over, and add thyme, sage, and salt. Place over high heat, bring to a boil, then reduce heat to low and cook for 15 minutes.

2. Meanwhile, in food processor, combine flour, parsley, baking powder, and salt. Cut in butter with short pulses until particles are fine. Add milk and process for just a few seconds. The dough will be stiff.

3. Add peas to the soup and bring back to a simmer. Drop flour mixture by tablespoons into the soup pot, cover, and simmer for 10 to 15 minutes or until dumplings are cooked through. Serve immediately.

Dumplings

There are some rules to follow for making the best dumplings. First, mix the batter only until blended. Then, be sure the soup is simmering but not boiling when you add the dumplings. Finally, do not lift the lid while the dumplings are cooking. Break one open to test it; the dough should be cooked through.

Serves 8

Calories: 367.00
Fat: 4.40 grams
Saturated Fat: 2.23 grams
Cholesterol: 42.31 mg
Sodium: 745.05 mg

4 boneless, skinless chicken breasts
4 russet potatoes, peeled and cubed
2 carrots, sliced
2 onions, sliced
2 celery stalks, chopped
2 sweet potatoes, peeled and cubed
8 cups fat-free, low-sodium chicken broth
1 teaspoon dried thyme leaves
1 teaspoon dried sage leaves
¼ teaspoon salt
1 cup flour
3 tablespoons chopped flat-leaf parsley
¼ teaspoon salt
1 teaspoon baking powder
2 tablespoons butter
½ cup 1% milk
2 cups frozen baby peas

Chicken Lime Soup

This savory, tangy soup is one version of a Yucatan classic.
Serve with a fruit salad and some guacamole with chips.

Serves 6
_____

Calories: 288.67
Fat: 8.99 grams
Saturated Fat: 3.92
grams
Cholesterol: 63.17 mg
Sodium: 765.02 mg

1 pound boneless,
*   skinless chicken*
*   breasts*
6 cups fat-free chicken
*   broth*
¼ cup lime juice
1 teaspoon dried oregano
*   leaves*
½ teaspoon dried basil
*   leaves*
1 jalapeño pepper,
*   minced*
1 bay leaf
½ teaspoon salt
⅛ teaspoon white pepper
2 tomatoes, peeled and
*   chopped*
1 red onion, chopped
2 tablespoons minced
*   cilantro*
¼ pound low-fat Monterey
*   Jack cheese,*
*   shredded*
2 cups baked corn
*   tortillas, slightly*
*   crushed*
½ cup nonfat sour cream

1. Place chicken breasts in a saucepan, add water to cover, and bring to a simmer over medium heat. Reduce heat to low and poach for about 10 minutes, or until cooked through. Drain and let cool, then shred the meat. Set aside.

2. Combine the broth, lime juice, oregano, basil, jalapeño, bay leaf, salt, and pepper in a saucepan. Bring to a boil, reduce the heat to low, and simmer for 15 minutes.

3. Add chicken, tomato, red onion, and minced cilantro. Return to a simmer and cook for 5 minutes. Remove bay leaf, then ladle the soup into a large bowl. Add the cheese. Garnish with tortillas and sour cream.

Chapter 16
Side Dishes

Pesto Potatoes 226

Cauliflower Purée 226

Tomato Potatoes 227

Stuffed Baked Potatoes 228

Scallion Tabbouleh 229

Curried Cauliflower 230

Sweet Potato Apple Bake 230

Green Beans with Garlic 231

Baked Acorn Squash 232

Dilled Green Beans 232

Orange Sweet Potatoes 233

Sweet Potato Apple Purée 233

Lemon Asparagus and Carrots 234

Coriander Carrots 235

Glazed Baby Carrots 235

Buttermilk Mashed Potatoes 236

Roasted Potatoes with Rosemary 236

Pesto Potatoes

Serves 4

Calories: 393.26
Fat: 2.74 grams
Saturated Fat: 0.62 grams
Cholesterol: 0.69 mg
Sodium: 130.65 mg

12 red new potatoes
¼ cup Low-Fat Spinach Pesto (page 286)
⅛ teaspoon pepper

Potatoes—with their nutty and earthy flavor—and pesto—with its spicy and fresh flavor—blend perfectly in this simple side dish recipe.

Steam the potatoes until tender, about 15 minutes. Remove from the steamer, place in a bowl, and add the pesto. Toss well, season with salt and pepper, and serve.

Cauliflower Purée

Serves 8

Calories: 99.16
Fat: 4.16 grams
Saturated Fat: 0.71 grams
Cholesterol: 0.92 mg
Sodium: 91.88 mg

2 tablespoons olive oil
1 onion, finely chopped
2 leeks, white parts only, chopped
3 cloves garlic, minced
½ cup fat-free vegetable broth
2 cauliflowers, cut into florets
½ cup plain low-fat yogurt
⅛ teaspoon white pepper

Instead of potatoes, serve this creamy and flavorful purée with meat loaf or roast chicken.

1. In a large saucepan, heat olive oil over medium heat. Add onion, leeks, and garlic; cook and stir until tender, about 7 to 8 minutes.

2. Add vegetable broth and cauliflower florets; bring to a boil. Cover pan, reduce heat, and simmer for 25 to 35 minutes or until vegetables are very tender.

3. Remove from heat and, using an immersion blender, purée the mixture. Add yogurt and pepper; heat through until steaming, then serve.

Cauliflower's Health Benefits

Phenethyl isothiocyanate is the compound in cauliflower that helps lower your risk of cancer. However, it stops forming when cauliflower is cooked. To get the most of this health benefit, let cauliflower stand at room temperature for 15 minutes when you cut it, before cooking it. The compound will develop in this time frame, and cooking doesn't destroy it.

Tomato Potatoes

This casserole can be a vegetarian main dish or a hearty side dish to serve with meat loaf.

1. Preheat oven to 325°F. Spray 3-quart baking dish with nonstick cooking spray and set aside.

2. In a large skillet, heat oil and the butter over medium heat. Add onions and garlic and sauté for 1 minute. Cover skillet, reduce heat to low, and cook until onions are translucent, about 5 minutes. Remove from heat and add tomatoes, salt, pepper, parsley, basil, and oregano. Mix well.

3. Spread one-third of the onion mixture in a prepared dish. Arrange half of the sliced potatoes on top, then sprinkle with half of the cheese. Repeat layers, then top with remaining onion mixture. Cover tightly

4. Bake for 70 to 80 minutes. Uncover dish and continue baking until potatoes are tender and cheese browns, about 20 to 30 minutes. Serve immediately.

Serves 8

Calories: 230.94
Fat: 5.20 grams
Saturated Fat: 1.85 grams
Cholesterol: 12.93 mg
Sodium: 304.12 mg

1 tablespoon olive oil
1 tablespoon butter
2 onions, chopped
6 cloves garlic, minced
2 (14-ounce) cans diced tomatoes, drained
½ teaspoon salt
⅛ teaspoon pepper
2 tablespoons minced flat-leaf parsley
1 teaspoon dried basil leaves
1 teaspoon dried oregano leaves
2½ pounds russet potatoes, thinly sliced
⅓ cup grated Parmesan cheese

Stuffed Baked Potatoes

Stuffed potatoes are usually stuffed with fat and calories! This version is just as rich-tasting but much lower in fat.

Serves 8

Calories: 329.53
Fat: 11.48 grams
Saturated Fat: 6.49 grams
Cholesterol: 46.93 mg
Sodium: 298.36 mg

4 large russet potatoes
2 tablespoons butter
4 cloves garlic, minced
½ cup 1% milk
*1 cup part-skim ricotta
    cheese*
½ teaspoon salt
⅛ teaspoon pepper
*¼ cup grated Parmesan
    cheese*

1. Preheat oven to 400°F. Scrub potatoes and pierce skins with a fork. Place directly on wire racks in oven and bake 1 hour. Remove from oven and reduce oven temperature to 375°F. Meanwhile, in microwave-safe bowl, combine butter and garlic; cook on high for 30 seconds.

2. Cut potatoes in half. Scoop out the potato flesh into a bowl, being careful not to tear the skins. Set skins aside on baking sheet.

3. Add butter mixture to the potatoes and mash. Then add the milk, ricotta cheese, salt, pepper, and Parmesan cheese to the potatoes and stir until combined.

4. Spoon the potato mixture into the potato skins, mounding the top. Bake until heated through, about 30 to 35 minutes.

Mashing Potatoes

When you mash potatoes, it's important that you add the oil or butter first. The fat coats the starch granules in the potatoes so they don't over combine and become gluey. And don't overmix mashed potatoes; stir just until all ingredients are combined.

Scallion Tabbouleh

Bulgur, or cracked wheat, is a nutritious and tasty side dish that's chewy and nutty. It is high in fiber, which fills you up and keeps you satisfied hours after lunch.

1. In a medium bowl, combine bulgur and boiling water. Cover and let stand for 20 minutes, or according to package directions, until tender.

2. Drain to remove excess moisture, if necessary, then transfer to a serving bowl. Add parsley, raisins, currants, and green onion; toss to mix well. In a small bowl, stir together lime juice, oil, salt, and pepper. Add to the bulgur mixture, toss well, and serve.

3. Mixture can be heated in the microwave, if desired. Microwave on 50 percent power for 2 to 3 minutes, remove, and stir. Continue microwaving on 50 percent power for 1 minute intervals until mixture is steaming. Let stand for 5 minutes, then serve.

Serves 8

Calories: 129.98
Fat: 2.10 grams
Saturated Fat: 0.40 grams
Cholesterol: 0.0 mg
Sodium: 162.03 mg

1 cup bulgur
2 cups boiling water
½ cup chopped flat-leaf parsley
⅓ cup raisins
⅓ cup dried currants
½ cup chopped green onion
¼ cup lime juice
1 tablespoon olive oil
½ teaspoon salt
⅛ teaspoon pepper

Curried Cauliflower

*Cauliflower is mild and nutty and adapts well to almost any spice
or herb. Roasted with curry, it becomes tender and spicy.*

1. Preheat oven to 400°F. Place cauliflower, onion, and garlic in roasting pan and toss to mix. In a small saucepan, combine remaining ingredients; heat over low heat until butter melts.

2. Drizzle butter mixture over vegetables and toss to coat. Roast for 25 to 35 minutes or until cauliflower is tender when pierced with a knife. Serve immediately.

Sweet Potato Apple Bake

*This is an excellent side dish to serve at Thanksgiving. You can
easily double it and bake it in two casseroles.*

1. Preheat oven to 350°F. In a large bowl, toss the apple slices with the lemon juice. In a 1½-quart baking dish, alternate layers of the sweet potatoes and apples.

2. In a small bowl, combine apple juice, salt, pepper, thyme, and butter and mix well. Pour over the layers in the baking dish. Cover and bake until apples and potatoes are tender and juice is bubbling, about 70 to 80 minutes.

Green Beans with Garlic

Green beans, garlic, and tomatoes combine in a delicious side dish that's perfect with grilled chicken.

Serves 6

Calories: 64.05
Fat: 1.49 grams
Saturated Fat: 0.21 grams
Cholesterol: 0.0 mg
Sodium: 225.93 mg

1 pound green beans
1 tablespoon olive oil
1 onion, chopped
3 cloves garlic, minced
1 tablespoon flour
¼ teaspoon salt
⅛ teaspoon pepper
*1 (14-ounce) can diced
     tomatoes*

1. Assemble a steamer and place water in bottom section. Bring to a simmer over high heat. Trim beans and add to top of steamer. Cook until beans are tender, about 5 to 7 minutes. Remove from steamer and set aside.

2. In a medium saucepan, heat oil over medium heat. Add onion and garlic; cook and stir until tender, about 6 minutes. Sprinkle flour, salt, and pepper over onions; cook and stir until bubbly.

3. Drain tomatoes, reserving liquid. Add liquid to saucepan; cook and stir until thickened. Add green beans and drained tomatoes; cook and stir over medium heat for 2 to 3 minutes until blended. Serve immediately.

Green Beans

Green beans are a wonderful source of vitamins A and C, both antioxidants. They stop cholesterol from oxidizing, which can slow plaque formation in your arteries. They're also a good source of fiber, potassium, and magnesium. Don't overcook the beans; they're best cooked until crisp-tender. They'll also retain more color cooked that way.

Baked Acorn Squash

This simple way of treating squash adds wonderful flavor to this healthy vegetable. Serve with a roasted chicken.

Serves 4

Calories: 103.94
Fat: 0.79 grams
Saturated Fat: 0.78 grams
Cholesterol: 7.40 mg
Sodium: 231.94 mg

1 acorn squash
1 tablespoon butter
2 tablespoons brown
    sugar
¼ teaspoon salt
⅛ teaspoon white pepper
½ teaspoon dried tarragon
    leaves

1. Preheat oven to 400°F. Cut squash in half and scoop out seeds. Place squash in a glass baking dish, cut-side up. Spread with butter and sprinkle with brown sugar, salt, pepper, and tarragon.

2. Pour 1 inch of water into the baking dish around the squash. Bake the squash for 40 to 50 minutes, or until tender. Cut each half into half again, and serve immediately.

Dilled Green Beans

Serve these fresh, low calorie green beans as a side dish to grilled fish, along with a fruit salad and some angel food cake for dessert. The red pepper flakes add a little bit of zing to an already flavorful dish.

Serves 6

Calories: 53.05
Fat: 0.20 grams
Saturated Fat: 0.01 grams
Cholesterol: 0.0 mg
Sodium: 189.84 mg

1 pound green beans,
    trimmed
3 cloves garlic, minced
2 tablespoons chopped
    fresh dill weed
½ teaspoon crushed red
    pepper flakes
½ teaspoon dry mustard
1 cup apple cider vinegar
1 cup water
2 tablespoons sugar
½ teaspoon salt

1. Steam the beans until tender, about 5 minutes, then immediately plunge in cold water to cool. Drain.

2. Place beans in large bowl. Add garlic, dill, red pepper flakes, and mustard and stir to coat.

3. In a small saucepan, combine vinegar, water, sugar, and salt and bring to a boil. Pour the hot marinade over the beans and let cool. Cover and chill overnight before serving.

Orange Sweet Potatoes

Stuffed sweet potatoes are quite a treat. They're delicious and have the most wonderful color.

1. Preheat oven to 400°F. Pierce potatoes with a fork and place directly on oven rack. Bake for 50 to 60 minutes or until tender.

2. Cut potatoes in half lengthwise and scoop out the flesh, keeping the skin intact. Mash pulp with the butter, then beat in orange juice, salt, pepper, and ginger.

3. Cut oranges into small pieces and stir into potato mixture. Spoon back into the potato skins and place on baking sheet. Top with almonds.

4. Bake until potatoes are hot and almonds are toasted, about 25 to 35 minutes. Serve immediately.

Serves 6

Calories: 195.34
Fat: 4.05 grams
Saturated Fat: 0.89 grams
Cholesterol: 5.01 mg
Sodium: 95.35 mg

3 sweet potatoes
1 tablespoon butter
¼ cup orange juice
¼ teaspoon salt
⅛ teaspoon pepper
½ teaspoon ground ginger
3 oranges, peeled
¼ cup sliced almonds

Sweet Potato Apple Purée

Now this is a dish for the holidays! You can keep it warm in a slow cooker if you'd like; stir occasionally.

1. In a large saucepan, place potatoes and cover with water. Cover saucepan, bring to a boil, reduce the heat to medium-low, and cook until tender, about 15 minutes. Drain.

2. Meanwhile, in a small saucepan, combine the apples with apple juice. Bring to a simmer over medium heat and cook until tender, about 5 minutes.

3. Transfer potatoes and undrained apples to a food processor. Add butter, nutmeg, salt, and pepper and purée until smooth. Sprinkle with sunflower seeds and serve.

Serves 12

Calories: 149.93
Fat: 3.29 grams
Saturated Fat: 1.83 grams
Cholesterol: 10.32 mg
Sodium: 140.92 mg

3 pounds sweet potatoes, peeled and cubed
2 Granny Smith apples, peeled and cubed
½ cup apple juice
2 tablespoons butter
½ teaspoon ground nutmeg
1 teaspoon salt
¼ teaspoon white pepper
¼ cup toasted sunflower seeds

Lemon Asparagus and Carrots

Steaming is one of the best ways to cook vegetables. It retains nutrients and keeps the bright color you want.

Serves 6

Calories: 83.95
Fat: 2.94 grams
Saturated Fat: 0.98 grams
Cholesterol: 0.0 mg
Sodium: 93.29 mg

1 pound baby carrots
1 pound fresh asparagus
2 tablespoons lemon juice
1 tablespoon olive oil
1 tablespoon mustard
½ teaspoon lemon pepper
½ teaspoon salt

1. Steam the carrots until crisp tender, about 15 minutes, then plunge them into cold water to cool. Drain and place in a bowl. Steam asparagus until tender.

2. In a small bowl, combine lemon juice, oil, mustard, lemon pepper, and salt and mix well. Arrange carrots and asparagus on a platter and drizzle with lemon mixture; serve.

3. To serve, arrange the carrots and asparagus on a platter. Sprinkle with a little lemon juice and lemon pepper.

Steaming Vegetables

To steam vegetables, place water in a large saucepan and bring to a simmer. Cover with a steamer insert or a metal colander, making sure that the insert or colander sits above the water. Add the vegetables to the insert, cover, and simmer for 10 to 15 minutes or until tender. Stir the vegetables occasionally for even steaming.

Coriander Carrots

Coriander and bay leaf add a nice spicy touch to tender carrots. Serve this with grilled chicken or rice dishes.

1. Heat oil in large saucepan over medium heat. Add onion; cook and stir until crisp-tender, about 4 minutes. Add water, bay leaf, salt, carrots, and currants and bring to a simmer.

2. Cover pan, reduce heat to low, and simmer for 10 to 15 minutes or until carrots are tender when tested with a fork. Drain carrots, removing bay leaf, and return saucepan to heat. Add butter, coriander, lemon juice, and parsley; cook and stir over low heat for 2 to 3 minutes or until carrots are glazed. Serve immediately.

Serves 6

Calories: 95.34
Fat: 2.69 grams
Saturated Fat: 0.33 grams
Cholesterol: 5.39 mg
Sodium: 253.94 mg

1 tablespoon olive oil
1 onion, chopped
1 cup water
1 bay leaf
½ teaspoon salt
1½ pounds carrots, thickly sliced
¼ cup dried currants
1 tablespoon butter
2 teaspoons ground coriander
2 tablespoons lemon juice
3 tablespoons minced flat-leaf parsley

Glazed Baby Carrots

Baby carrots are sweet and tender and fun to eat. When glazed with butter and herbs, they are one of the best side dish recipes.

1. Place carrots in large saucepan and add water to cover. Cover pan and bring to a boil. Reduce heat to low and simmer until tender, about 8 to 10 minutes.

2. Drain all but 3 tablespoons water from the pan and add the butter. Bring to a boil over medium high heat. Boil, shaking the pan frequently, until water evaporates and carrots are coated with butter, about 5 to 8 minutes. Add salt, pepper, and herbs, toss to coat, and serve immediately.

Serves 8

Calories: 75.20
Fat: 2.16 grams
Saturated Fat: 1.80 grams
Cholesterol: 7.39 mg
Sodium: 95.25 mg

2 pounds baby carrots
2 tablespoons butter
½ teaspoon salt
⅛ teaspoon pepper
2 tablespoons chopped flat-leaf parsley
1 tablespoon chopped fresh dill weed
¼ cup chopped fresh mint

Buttermilk Mashed Potatoes

Mashed potatoes don't have to be full of fat. Buttermilk adds a creamy richness to this classic dish.

Calories: 106.39
Fat: 2.39 grams
Saturated Fat: 1.53 grams
Cholesterol: 6.93 mg
Sodium: 49.23 mg

3 pounds potatoes,
    peeled and quartered
2 tablespoons butter
1 onion, chopped
1½ cups buttermilk
⅛ teaspoon nutmeg
½ teaspoon salt
⅛ teaspoon white pepper

1. Place potatoes in a large pot with water to cover. Bring to a boil, cover, reduce the heat to medium, and cook until tender, about 20 minutes.

2. Meanwhile, in small saucepan melt butter over medium heat. Cook onion, stirring occasionally, until tender, about 7 minutes.

3. When potatoes are done, drain, return to the hot pot, add onion mixture, and mash until smooth. Gradually add the buttermilk, stirring constantly. Stir in nutmeg, salt, and pepper. Serve immediately.

Roasted Potatoes with Rosemary

You can also roast russet potatoes with this method. Just cut into large chunks and roast for 55 to 65 minutes.

Serves 8

Calories: 126.34
Fat: 3.66 grams
Saturated Fat: 0.44 grams
Cholesterol: 0.0 mg
Sodium: 159.32 mg

2 pounds red new
    potatoes, sliced
2 tablespoons olive oil
4 cloves garlic, minced
2 tablespoons fresh
    rosemary, minced
½ teaspoon salt
⅛ teaspoon white pepper

Preheat oven to 375°F. In a large baking dish, toss the potatoes with the oil, garlic, rosemary, salt, and pepper. Bake until the potatoes are tender when pierced with a fork, about 40 to 50 minutes, stirring potatoes once during cooking time. Serve immediately.

Roasting Potatoes

When potatoes are roasted, their flavor concentrates and the insides become creamy as the skin and exterior becomes crisp. For best results, stir or turn the potatoes using a spatula about halfway through cooking time. The potatoes are done when they are tender and the outside edges begin to brown.

Chapter 17

Chilled Desserts, Puddings, and Sorbets

Strawberry Soup 238

Buttermilk Fruit Sherbet 238

Pineapple Sherbet 239

Orange Sherbet 239

Cranberry Sherbet 240

Tangy Lime Pie 241

Coffee Almond Float 242

Pumpkin Pudding 242

Peach Sorbet 243

Strawberry Sorbet 244

Spicy Cold Pears 245

Light Lemon Pudding 246

Buttermilk Pops 246

Sweet Vanilla Sauce 247

Chocolate "Ice Cream" 247

Sweet Cocoa Sauce 248

Blueberry "Ice Cream" 249

Pears in Orange Sauce 250

Frozen Yogurt with Berry Sauce 251

Spiced Cherry Sauce 252

Strawberry Soup

This beautifully colored and flavorful soup is an unusual end to a summer dinner. Serve with more sliced strawberries or float some raspberries on top.

Serves 6

Calories: 279.43
Fat: 3.85 grams
Saturated Fat: 2.05 grams
Cholesterol: 12.74 mg
Sodium: 147.93 mg

3 cups strawberries, chopped
½ teaspoon cinnamon
½ cup frozen orange juice concentrate
½ cup water
¼ cup dry red wine, if desired
Pinch ground cloves
2 tablespoons cornstarch
2 tablespoons water
1 pint vanilla low-fat frozen yogurt
1 pint low-fat strawberry yogurt

1. In a large saucepan, combine strawberries, cinnamon, orange juice concentrate, ½ cup water, wine, and cloves. Bring to a boil over high heat, then reduce heat to low and simmer for 10 minutes.

2. In a small bowl, combine cornstarch with 2 tablespoons water and mix well. Add to the strawberry mixture; cook until thickened, about 5 minutes. Puree using an immersion blender.

3. Remove from heat, let cool for 1½ hours at room temperature, then add the frozen yogurt and strawberry yogurt. Stir until yogurt melts, then cover and refrigerate for 2 to 3 hours before serving.

Buttermilk Fruit Sherbet

This almost-instant dessert can be served as is or topped with a dessert sauce.

Serves 4

Calories: 65.92
Fat: 0.44 grams
Saturated Fat: 0.01 grams
Cholesterol: 0.69 mg
Sodium: 33.02 mg

2 cups frozen blueberries
1 cup frozen raspberries
¾ cup low-fat buttermilk, divided
2 tablespoons honey
Pinch salt
1 teaspoon vanilla

1. In a food processor, combine frozen berries with ½ cup buttermilk; process until berries are chopped.

2. Continue processing, adding remaining ¼ cup buttermilk, honey, salt, and vanilla. Uncover and stir, then process again until mixture is smooth and has the texture of frozen custard. Don't overprocess. Serve immediately.

Pineapple Sherbet

This flavorful sherbet is delicious placed between two graham crackers and frozen for an ice cream sandwich.

1. In a medium bowl, combine milk and sugar; stir well and let stand for 15 minutes, until sugar dissolves.

2. Add remaining ingredients and mix well. Pour into a 9" × 5" loaf pan and freeze until firm, about 4 to 5 hours. Stir the mixture twice during freezing time for a lighter consistency.

Serves 4

Calories: 206.56
Fat: 3.79 grams
Saturated Fat: 2.01 grams
Cholesterol: 15.89 mg
Sodium: 55.89 mg

1¾ cups 1% milk
½ cup sugar
*1 (8-ounce) can crushed
    pineapple, undrained*
2 tablespoons lemon juice
¼ cup orange juice
Pinch salt

Orange Sherbet

This can be lemon sherbet if you use lemonade concentrate.

1 In a blender, combine all ingredients and blend until smooth.

2. Pour into an 8" × 4" loaf pan and freeze until almost firm, about 2 hours. Turn out of pan into a bowl and beat with a fork. Return to pan and freeze until firm.

Freezing Without an Ice Cream Maker

It's possible to freeze ice creams, sherbets, and sorbets without an ice cream maker. Commercial ice cream makers work by chilling the mixture while adding air at the same time. You can replicate this process by occasionally beating the sherbet while it is freezing. This takes time but results in a creamier product.

Serves 2

Calories: 178.49
Fat: 0.30 grams
Saturated Fat: 0.14 grams
Cholesterol: 6.03 mg
Sodium: 189.34 mg

*1 cup nonfat dry milk
    powder*
½ cup water
*¼ cup frozen orange juice
    concentrate*

Cranberry Sherbet

This sherbet can be a gorgeous deep pink or a light pink depending on whether you use regular or white cranberry juice.

Serves 4

Calories: 292.58
Fat: 0.15 grams
Saturated Fat: 0.01 grams
Cholesterol: 2.78 mg
Sodium: 105.34 mg

1½ teaspoons unflavored
    gelatin
2 cups cranberry juice,
    divided
½ cup sugar
Pinch salt
2 tablespoons nonfat dry
    milk powder
½ cup corn syrup
3 tablespoons lemon juice

1. In a small saucepan, combine gelatin and 1 cup of the cranberry juice; let stand for 5 minutes. Place over low heat and heat until gelatin dissolves completely.

2. Add sugar and salt; stir over low heat until dissolved. Remove from heat and add remaining cranberry juice.

3. Sprinkle milk powder over the cranberry mixture; beat in with a wire whisk or egg beater. Add corn syrup and lemon juice and mix well until combined.

4. Pour mixture into a 9" × 5" loaf pan and freeze until almost firm, about 2 hours. Spoon back into the bowl and beat until fluffy. Pour back into loaf pan, cover, and freeze until firm, about 2 to 3 hours longer.

Corn Syrup

There are two types of corn syrup: light and dark. Dark corn syrup has more flavor because it has added caramel flavoring and coloring, along with a molasses derivative. In some recipes, they can be used interchangeably. But when you're making a delicately flavored dessert, like this sherbet, use the light corn syrup for best results.

Tangy Lime Pie

This signature dessert is equally tangy and sweet, with a smooth fluffy texture. Serve it on chilled plates, garnished with more lime peel.

1. For crust, combine crushed graham crackers and melted butter in a small bowl. Press into bottom and up sides of a 9" pie plate; place in freezer.

2. For filling, in medium saucepan combine juice concentrate with gelatin; let stand for 5 minutes. Stir in the sugar; place over low heat, and cook, stirring frequently, until gelatin and sugar dissolve.

3. Pour into medium bowl and add lime zest, lime juice, and vanilla; stir well. Cover and chill until mixture is consistency of unbeaten egg whites, about 30 minutes.

4. Whip chilled mixture until fluffy. Add yogurt and beat again until smooth. Pour into prepared pie crust, cover, and chill until firm, about 4 to 5 hours.

Unflavored Gelatin

Don't confuse unflavored gelatin, which comes in small packets of about 1 tablespoon, with the preflavored kind containing sugar. Using unflavored gelatin lets you avoid artificial colors and flavors and lets you add the amount of sugar you want to your desserts. Follow the recipe instructions exactly for best results.

Serves 8

Calories: 220.04
Fat: 7.09 grams
Saturated Fat: 4.53 grams
Cholesterol: 42.08 mg
Sodium: 244.89 mg

12 low-fat graham crackers, crushed
3 tablespoons butter, melted
⅓ cup frozen apple juice concentrate, thawed
1 (0.25-ounce) envelope unflavored gelatin
½ cup sugar
1 teaspoon grated lime zest
⅓ cup lime juice
1 teaspoon vanilla
1 cup plain low-fat yogurt
½ cup lime or lemon flavored low-fat yogurt

Coffee Almond Float

Floats are fun desserts. You could use this cold coffee mixture over any flavor of frozen yogurt or sorbet.

Serves 2

Calories: 173.85
Fat: 2.81 grams
Saturated Fat: 1.76 grams
Cholesterol: 10.98 mg
Sodium: 128.09 mg

1 tablespoon brown sugar
½ cup cold brewed coffee
1 teaspoon orgeat (almond)
    syrup or vanilla
¼ cup ice cubes
1 cup 1% milk
½ cup chocolate low-fat
    frozen yogurt

1. In a small bowl, combine sugar and coffee; stir until dissolved. Add orgeat, stirring to mix well. Add ice cubes and milk and stir well; let stand for 5 minutes. Remove ice cubes.

2. Divide milk mixture between two parfait glasses and top with the frozen yogurt. Serve immediately.

Pumpkin Pudding

Serve this elegant pudding instead of pumpkin pie for Thanksgiving dessert. Dollop with some candied ginger and nonfat whipped topping.

Serves 4

Calories: 285.69
Fat: 6.01 grams
Saturated Fat: 2.07 grams
Cholesterol: 169.95 mg
Sodium: 390.87 mg

2 cups low-fat cottage
    cheese
⅛ teaspoon salt
1 (15-ounce) can solid-
    packed canned
    pumpkin
3 eggs
2 egg whites
⅓ cup brown sugar
¼ cup honey
½ teaspoon nutmeg
⅛ teaspoon ginger

1. Preheat oven to 350°F. Spray four individual custard cups with nonstick cooking spray and set aside.

2. In a blender or food processor, combine all ingredients. Blend or process until smooth. Pour into the prepared custard cups. Place cups in a baking pan.

3. Pour hot water into the pan to reach halfway up the sides of the custard cups. Bake until a knife inserted near center comes out clean, about 35 to 40 minutes.

4. Remove custard cups from water bath and cool on wire rack for 1 hour. Cover and chill for 4 to 5 hours before serving.

Peach Sorbet

With some canned peaches on hand, you can have your own homemade sorbet any time you like.

1. Drain peaches; add liquid to measuring cup. Add water, if necessary, to measure 1½ cups. Pour into a small saucepan and sprinkle with gelatin. Let stand for about 5 minutes to allow the gelatin to soften. Place the pan over medium heat and heat, stirring constantly, until the gelatin dissolves, just a few minutes.

2. Add the lemon juice, sugar, honey, salt, and extract. Stir over low heat until sugar and honey dissolve, about 5 minutes. Set aside for 30 minutes.

3. In a food processor, purée the peaches until smooth. Add the gelatin mixture and process until thoroughly combined. Pour into a 9" × 13" baking pan, and place in the freezer for 2 hours.

4. Transfer the peach mixture to a chilled bowl, and beat with a rotary beater or an electric mixer until the mixture is fluffy. Return to the metal pan, and freeze for 2 hours more. Scoop into individual dishes to serve.

Serves 6

Calories: 73.05
Fat: 0.06 grams
Saturated Fat: 0.01 grams
Cholesterol: 0.0 mg
Sodium: 19.55 mg

1 (16-ounce) can sliced peaches, drained
1 (0.25-ounce) package unflavored gelatin
1 tablespoon lemon juice
2 tablespoons sugar
2 tablespoons honey
Pinch salt
½ teaspoon almond extract

Strawberry Sorbet

Serves 8

Calories: 74.53
Fat: 0.32 grams
Saturated Fat: 0.10 grams
Cholesterol: 0.58 mg
Sodium: 23.59 mg

2 cups strawberries
¾ cup orange juice
½ cup skim milk
¼ cup sugar, divided
1 tablespoon honey
2 pasteurized egg whites
⅛ teaspoon cream of
*   tartar*

An ice cream maker will make a smoother sorbet, but you can also freeze it according to these directions.

1. Hull strawberries and place in food processor; sprinkle with 2 tablespoons sugar and let stand for 20 minutes, until sugar dissolves.

2. Add orange juice, milk, and honey to strawberries and process until smooth. Pour into a 9" baking pan, cover, and freeze until firm, about 3 hours.

3. In a medium bowl, beat egg whites with cream of tartar until foamy. Gradually add remaining 2 tablespoons sugar, beating until stiff peaks form.

4. Break the frozen strawberry mixture into chunks and transfer to a large mixer bowl. Beat until smooth, then fold in egg whites. Return to the pan and freeze until firm, about 6 hours, stirring every 2 hours.

Pasteurized Egg Whites

Pasteurized egg whites have been heated to a temperature that destroys bacteria, so they are safe to use uncooked. They can take longer to beat to stiff peaks; just keep working until the mixture thickens. Be careful to follow the expiration dates on these eggs. They expire much more quickly than regular eggs do.

Spicy Cold Pears

Fruit, especially when flavored with spices and citrus, makes a wonderful fat-free dessert.

Serves 4

Calories: 199.50
Fat: 0.89 grams
Saturated Fat: 0.04 grams
Cholesterol: 0.0 mg
Sodium: 15.39 mg

4 pears, peeled and cored
2 cups cranberry juice
3 tablespoons sugar
½ teaspoon cinnamon
¼ teaspoon cloves
1 teaspoon grated orange zest
1 teaspoon grated lemon zest

1. Cut pears in half. In a large saucepan, combine remaining ingredients and mix well. Add pears and bring to a simmer over medium heat.

2. Reduce heat, cover pan, and simmer until pears are tender, about 12 to 17 minutes. Remove from heat and let cool for 30 minutes. Chill pears in liquid until very cold, about 3 to 4 hours. Serve pears with the liquid and low-fat sour cream or frozen yogurt.

Light Lemon Pudding

For the ice water, let ice cubes and water sit for 20 minutes, then measure the amount of water you need.

Serves 6

Calories: 92.40
Fat: 0.08 grams
Saturated Fat: 0.02 grams
Cholesterol: 1.05 mg
Sodium: 38.89 mg

1 (0.25-ounce) envelope
    unflavored gelatin
½ cup cold water
1 cup boiling water
½ cup sugar
⅓ cup lemon juice
1 teaspoon grated lemon
    zest
Pinch salt
½ cup nonfat dry milk
    powder
½ cup ice water
¼ teaspoon vinegar

1. In a small bowl, combine gelatin and cold water; let stand for 4 minutes. Add boiling water and stir to dissolve the gelatin. Add the sugar, lemon juice, lemon zest, and salt and mix well. Chill until very thick, about 1½ hours.

2. Chill a deep mixing bowl and beaters. When cold, add milk powder, ice water, and vinegar. Beat at high speed until very fluffy, then cover and chill.

3. When both mixtures are cold, add the lemon mixture to the dry milk mixture and beat until fluffy. Spoon into serving dishes, cover, and chill until firm, about 4 to 5 hours.

Buttermilk Pops

Buttermilk adds a creamy texture to these simple popsicles. Use any type of frozen juice concentrate you'd like.

Yields 10

Calories: 73.64
Fat: 0.31 grams
Saturated Fat: 0.15 grams
Cholesterol: 2.30 mg
Sodium: 52.64 mg

1 (6-ounce) can frozen
    orange juice
    concentrate
1 cup low-fat buttermilk
1 cup evaporated skim
    milk
¼ cup sugar
⅛ teaspoon salt

1. Thaw the orange juice concentrate. Combine in medium bowl with remaining ingredients. Stir until mixture blends and sugar dissolves.

2. Pour into 10 4-ounce paper drink cups or popsicle molds and freeze until thickened, about 20 to 25 minutes.

3. Insert popsicle sticks and return to freezer. Freeze until firm, about 3 to 4 hours. To serve, peel off the paper cup.

Sweet Vanilla Sauce

Sweet sauces add flavor and texture to desserts without adding much fat. This sauce is beautiful served over a mixed bowl of cherries, strawberries, and raspberries.

In a small bowl, combine all ingredients and mix well. Cover and refrigerate for 2 to 3 hours to blend flavors. Serve over fresh fruit or angel food cake.

Yields 1¼ cups; serving size 2 tablespoons

Calories: 14.93
Fat: 0.13 grams
Saturated Fat: 0.08 grams
Cholesterol: 0.52 mg
Sodium: 23.05 mg

¼ cup nonfat buttermilk
2 tablespoons sugar
1 cup vanilla low-fat yogurt
½ teaspoon vanilla
Pinch salt

Chocolate "Ice Cream"

It's hard to believe that something that tastes this rich is actually low in fat; but it is. Serve this with marshmallow topping for a great dessert.

1. In a medium bowl, combine pudding mix, sugar, cocoa powder, and salt. Add evaporated milk, 1% milk, melted butter, and vanilla and beat until blended.

2. Pour into ice cream maker and freeze according to manufacturer's instructions. Freeze for 2 to 3 hours before serving.

Serves 4

Calories: 262.63
Fat: 3.23 grams
Saturated Fat: 2.00 grams
Cholesterol: 11.12 mg
Sodium: 280.50 mg

1 (3-ounce) package instant chocolate pudding mix
¼ cup sugar
1 tablespoon cocoa powder
Pinch salt
1 (13-ounce) can evaporated skim milk
⅔ cup 1% milk
2 teaspoons butter, melted
½ teaspoon vanilla

Sweet Cocoa Sauce

*This cocoa sauce can be served over everything from fresh fruit
to cake or sherbet.*

**Yields 1 cup; serving
size 2 tablespoons**

Calories: 32.04
Fat: 0.35 grams
Saturated Fat: 0.14 grams
Cholesterol: 0.0 mg
Sodium: 56.94 mg

*½ cup cocoa powder
¼ cup sugar
¼ cup brown sugar
¼ cup water
Pinch salt
1 teaspoon vanilla*

1. In a small saucepan, combine cocoa powder, sugar, and brown sugar and mix well. Add water and salt. Bring to a boil over high heat, stirring constantly with a wire whisk. Boil for 1 minute.

2. Remove from heat and stir in vanilla. Cover and refrigerate for 3 to 4 hours before serving. You may add some skim milk or heat in the microwave or in a saucepan over low heat to thin before serving.

Blueberry "Ice Cream"

Make this delicious creamy dessert with raspberries or strawberries too.

Serves 6

Calories: 239.05
Fat: 0.51 grams
Saturated Fat: 0.10 grams
Cholesterol: 4.97 mg
Sodium: 149.93 mg

2 cups blueberries
½ cup sugar, divided
Pinch salt
1 tablespoon cornstarch
1 (13-ounce) can
*   evaporated skim milk*
2 pasteurized egg whites
1 teaspoon grated lemon
*   zest*
2 tablespoons lemon juice
1 teaspoon vanilla

1. In a saucepan, combine the blueberries with ¼ cup of the sugar. Place over medium heat and heat, stirring constantly, until the sugar dissolves, about 5 minutes. Remove from the heat.

2. Place a strainer over a bowl and pour the blueberry mixture into the stainer. Press the berries with the back of a spoon. Scrape the mashed berries from the outside of the strainer into the bowl with the blueberry juice. Place the bowl in the refrigerator. Do not rinse the saucepan.

3. Add the remaining ¼ cup sugar, salt, and cornstarch to the saucepan. Stir in two-thirds of the evaporated milk. Place over medium heat and bring to a boil, stirring constantly. Cook the mixture until it is as thick as pudding.

4. Remove from heat and add egg whites and the remaining evaporated milk, mixing well. Stir the milk mixture into the blueberry purée in bowl. Add the lemon zest, lemon juice, and vanilla. Stir until blended. Chill for 20 minutes.

5. Pour into an ice cream maker and freeze according to the manufacturer's instructions.

Ice Cream Makers

It used to be that to make ice cream you'd have to pack a large container with ice and rock salt, and turn a crank for a long time. Now there are automatic ice cream makers that are super easy to use. You just freeze the inner container, add the ice cream mixture, put the machine together, and turn it on.

Pears in Orange Sauce

Fruit in a sweet sauce makes a satisfying
dessert with almost no fat. You can serve the pears on
top of angel food cake or frozen yogurt.

Serves 4

Calories: 124.93
Fat: 0.37 grams
Saturated Fat: 0.01 grams
Cholesterol: 0.0 mg
Sodium: 150.94 mg

1 cup water
2 pears
⅔ cup orange juice
2 tablespoons lemon juice
1 tablespoons cornstarch
3 tablespoons honey
Pinch salt
¼ teaspoon grated
   orange zest
Fresh mint

1. In a large skillet, bring water to a boil. Meanwhile, cut the pears in half lengthwise and remove the core. Add pears to the water, reduce heat, and cook over low heat until pears are tender when pierced with a knife, about 8 to 10 minutes. Set aside.

2. In a small saucepan, combine remaining ingredients except mint; mix well. Cook and stir over medium heat until mixture boils and thickens, about 10 minutes.

3. Remove pears from water and add to orange sauce. Chill until cold, about 2 to 3 hours, then serve garnished with mint.

Smooth Sauces

For the smoothest dessert sauces, be sure you combine the cornstarch with the liquid ingredients very well. A wire whisk works best to beat the sauce before it starts cooking and while it's on the heat. Make sure that you reach into the corners of the pan with the whisk, and stir constantly while the sauce is cooking.

Frozen Yogurt with Berry Sauce

This beautiful dessert can be made any time of year. It's nice to serve in the winter, when fresh fruits are more expensive and of lesser quality.

Serves 4

Calories: 186.94
Fat: 1.57 grams
Saturated Fat: 0.89 grams
Cholesterol: 5.93 mg
Sodium: 69.34 mg

1 (10-ounce) package frozen strawberries, thawed
1 teaspoon vanilla
½ cup raspberries
1 tablespoon lemon juice
1 pint low-fat frozen vanilla yogurt

1. In a blender or food processor, combine strawberries, vanilla, raspberries, and lemon juice; blend or process until smooth.

2. Spoon yogurt into four dessert dishes and top with strawberry sauce. Sauce can be stored, covered, in refrigerator up to 4 days. Use for other things, like topping cake or other fruits.

Berry Combinations

Use your imagination when making sauces with fresh or frozen berries. Blackberries and raspberries are delicious together, as are boysenberries and blueberries. Use this basic formula to make the sauce. The sauce can be frozen after it is made; freeze in pint containers for up to 3 months. To thaw, let stand in refrigerator overnight.

Spiced Cherry Sauce

This sauce is delicious over everything from Sherry Custard with Spiced Cherries (page 268) to Angel Food Cake (page 254) and sorbets.

Yields 2 cups; serving size 2 tablespoons

Calories: 53.06
Fat: 1.09 grams
Saturated Fat: 0.40 grams
Cholesterol: 0.0 mg
Sodium: 79.94 mg

1 (14.5-ounce) can tart cherries, undrained
2 tablespoons sugar
2 teaspoons cornstarch
1 tablespoon lemon juice
¼ teaspoon cinnamon
⅛ teaspoon cloves
Pinch ground ginger
Pinch salt

1. Make sure cherries do not have pits. In a small saucepan, combine cherries and their juice with sugar. Bring to a simmer over medium heat.

2. In a small bowl, combine cornstarch with lemon juice. Add to pan with cherries and cook, stirring, until sauce is clear, about 5 minutes. Stir in the spices.

3. Remove sauce from heat and serve warm. Or cover and refrigerate for 2 to 3 hours before serving. Drizzle over frozen yogurt or angel food cake. Store sauce, covered, in refrigerator up to 5 days.

Freezing Sauces

You can freeze most cornstarch-based sauces. Cool completely, then pack into hard-sided freezer container, leaving about 1 inch of headspace to allow for expansion. Label and seal the container, then freeze for up to 3 months. To thaw, let stand in refrigerator overnight. You may need to stir the sauce to recombine it before serving.

Chapter 18
Baked Desserts

Angel Food Cake 254

Strawberry Angel Cake 255

Sweet Potato Tart. 256

Peachy Angel Cake 257

Sweet Potato Pudding. 258

Graham Cracker Crust 258

Margarita Pie 259

Low-Fat Pumpkin Pie 259

Lemon Cheesecake. 260

Lemon Meringue Pie 261

Fresh Peach Pie. 262

Strawberry Pie 263

Peanut Butter Chocolate Bars. 264

Baked Pears 265

Spice Cake 266

Applesauce Pound Cake 267

Sherry Custard with Spiced Cherries 268

Angel Food Cake

Angel food cake is delicious served with sliced strawberries mixed with some sugar and lemon juice.

Serves 10 to 12

Calories: 228.84
Fat: 0.12 grams
Saturated Fat: 0.01 grams
Cholesterol: 0.0 mg
Sodium: 150.57 mg

12 egg whites
1 teaspoon cream of tartar
¼ teaspoon salt
1 cup sugar
2 teaspoons vanilla
½ teaspoon almond extract
1 cup sifted cake flour
1 cup powdered sugar

1. Preheat oven to 350°F. In a large bowl, with electric mixer, beat egg whites with cream of tartar and salt until foamy. Add sugar, 1 tablespoon at a time, beating constantly until sugar is dissolved and egg whites are glossy. They should stand in stiff peaks.

2. Beat in vanilla and almond extract. In sifter, combine cake flour and powdered sugar. Sift over the egg white mixture in 4 portions, gently folding the 2 mixtures together.

3. Spoon mixture into an ungreased 10-inch tube pan. Bake for 35 to 45 minutes or until the cake is deep golden brown and the top springs back when lightly touched. Invert pan onto a funnel to cool. Remove from pan when cooled completely.

Angel Food Cake

Angel food cake is the premiere nonfat cake; it's fluffy and sweet with a light and tender texture. It must be baked in an ungreased pan so the delicate structure has something to hold onto as it rises. Inverting the cake as it cools helps maintain the height, because the egg protein structure will stretch as it sets.

Strawberry Angel Cake

You can use any flavor or fruit in this simple recipe. Try peach frozen yogurt and sliced canned peaches, or raspberry yogurt and raspberries.

1. Cut cake in half horizontally. Spread the frozen yogurt on bottom half of cake, then cover with half of the strawberries. Repeat layers.

2. Place cake on serving plate and freeze for 3 to 4 hours until firm. Sprinkle with powdered sugar and slice to serve.

Serves 8 to 10

Calories: 284.66
Fat: 1.09 grams
Saturated Fat: 0.49 grams
Cholesterol: 2.38 mg
Sodium: 185.44 mg

1 Angel Food Cake (page 254)
2 cups strawberry frozen yogurt
1 pint strawberries, sliced
2 tablespoons powdered sugar

Sweet Potato Tart

This pie is a great way to use up sweet potatoes after Thanksgiving. You can use sweet potatoes that are glazed and seasoned; just cut down on the spices in the pie.

Serves 10

Calories: 204.20
Fat: 4.96 grams
Saturated Fat: 2.75 grams
Cholesterol: 12.58 mg
Sodium: 222.69 mg

*1 cup crushed graham
    cracker crumbs
1 teaspoon cinnamon
1 tablespoon butter, melted
1 egg white
4 baked sweet potatoes
6 egg whites
⅓ cup brown sugar
¼ teaspoon salt
¼ teaspoon cinnamon
¼ teaspoon nutmeg
½ teaspoon ginger
¼ teaspoon cloves
2 teaspoons vanilla
¼ cup maple syrup
2 (3-ounce) packages
    light cream cheese,
    softened
¼ cup orange juice*

1. Preheat oven to 350°F. Spray a 12-inch tart pan thoroughly with non-stick baking spray containing flour. For the crust, combine cracker crumbs, 1 teaspoon cinnamon, 1 tablespoon melted butter, and 1 egg white in small bowl; mix until combined. Pat onto the bottom of a prepared tart pan.

2. For filling, peel the sweet potatoes if necessary and cut into cubes. Place in large bowl and mash with a fork. Add the egg whites, brown sugar, salt, ¼ teaspoon cinnamon, nutmeg, ginger, and cloves; beat until smooth.

3. Add vanilla, maple syrup, cream cheese, and orange juice and continue to beat until smooth. Pour into crust.

4. Bake until center of the tart is firm and not sticky to the touch, about 30 to 45 minutes. Transfer to wire rack and let cool for 30 minutes, then refrigerate for at least 1 hour before serving.

Peachy Angel Cake

This dessert can be made with other fruits as well. Try canned pears with lemon gelatin or canned cherries with cherry gelatin.

Serves 8

Calories: 330.54
Fat: 0.18 grams
Saturated Fat: 0.01 grams
Cholesterol: 0.75 mg
Sodium: 214.99 mg

1 Angel Food Cake (page 254)
1 (8-ounce) can sliced peaches
1 (3-ounce) package orange-flavored gelatin
⅓ cup ice water
½ cup nonfat milk powder
1 tablespoon powdered sugar
2 tablespoons lemon juice

1. Cut ½-inch-thick slice off the top of the cake and set aside. With the point of a knife, cut a ring ½-inch in from the edge of the base and ½-inch in from the center hole. Pull out soft cake to form a trough 1½ inches deep.

2. Drain peaches, reserving juice in a microwave-safe glass measuring cup. Chop peaches and set aside. Add water to juice if necessary to measure ½ cup. Heat in microwave on full power for 2 to 3 minutes until boiling.

3. Place gelatin in small bowl and pour in boiling liquid, stirring until gelatin mixture is completely dissolved. Chill until slightly thickened, about 30 minutes.

4. For filling, mix ice water, dry milk, and powdered sugar in small mixing bowl and beat until thick. Add the lemon juice and beat until stiff. Using the same beaters, beat thickened gelatin until smooth, then fold in the whipped milk mixture. Divide the filling in half.

5. Add the peaches to half of the filling and transfer to the cake shell, spreading evenly. Replace the top of the cake. Chill the remaining gelatin mixture until desired spreading consistency, about 1 hour. Frost the top and sides of the cake. Store in refrigerator.

Dissolving Gelatin

Gelatin must be completely dissolved in order for the recipe to work. Take a bit of the mixture of gelatin and liquid in a steel spoon and look at it under the light. If you don't see any grains of gelatin and sugar, it's dissolved.

Serves 8

Calories: 345.43
Fat: 8.43 grams
Saturated Fat: 3.99 grams
Cholesterol: 43.00 mg
Sodium: 270.43 mg

1⅔ cups flour
1 cup sugar
⅓ cup brown sugar
1 teaspoon baking soda
¼ teaspoon baking powder
¼ teaspoon salt
1 teaspoon cinnamon
½ teaspoon allspice
¼ teaspoon cardamom
1 cup mashed cooked
*   sweet potatoes*
¼ cup butter
⅓ cup skim milk
1 egg

Sweet Potato Pudding

You can serve this pudding for Thanksgiving dinner; just top it with some crumbled sugar cookies to duplicate the crust of a sweet potato pie.

1. Preheat oven to 350°F. Spray an 8" square cake pan with nonstick baking spray containing flour and set aside.

2. In a large bowl, combine flour, sugar, brown sugar, baking soda, baking powder, salt, cinnamon, allspice, and cardamom. Add sweet potato, butter, and milk to flour mixture.

3. Using electric mixer, beat for 2 minutes. Add egg and beat for another minute. Pour batter into the prepared cake pan. Bake about 35 to 40 minutes until set. Let cool for 30 minutes, then serve warm.

Serves 8

Calories: 119.30
Fat: 4.23 grams
Saturated Fat: 2.13 grams
Cholesterol: 7.63 mg
Sodium: 123.97 mg

9 double low-fat graham
*   crackers*
2 tablespoons finely
*   chopped walnuts*
2 tablespoons brown
*   sugar*
2 tablespoons butter,
*   melted*
1 egg white, slightly
*   beaten*

Graham Cracker Crust

Egg white helps hold together the crumbs and reduces the fat in this crisp and crunchy pie crust.

1. Preheat oven to 375°F. Crush graham crackers until very fine crumbs form. In a medium bowl, combine with walnuts and brown sugar; toss to mix well.

2. Add melted butter and egg white; mix well with a fork until well blended. Press mixture onto bottom and up sides of 9" pie plate.

3. Bake pie crust for 8 to 10 minutes or until set. Cool completely on wire rack before filling.

Margarita Pie

Lots of lime, in the forms of juice and zest, make this pie tart and refreshing. Serve strawberries as a sweet-tasting complement.

1. In a small saucepan, combine gelatin, sugar, and salt and mix well. Add egg substitute, lime juice, and lime zest and mix well with wire whisk. Let stand for 5 minutes.

2. Cook mixture over medium heat, stirring frequently, until gelatin and sugar dissolve, about 5 to 6 minutes. Remove from heat and let cool for 30 minutes.

3. Stir in tequila and chill in refrigerator until mixture thickens. Fold whipped topping into tequila mixture, then spoon into crust. Chill until firm, about 4 to 6 hours. Garnish with lime slices just before serving.

Serves 8

Calories: 225.93
Fat: 5.90 grams
Saturated Fat: 1.03 grams
Cholesterol: 0.0 mg
Sodium: 201.55 mg

1 package unflavored gelatin
⅔ cup sugar
¼ teaspoon salt
½ cup egg substitute
½ cup fresh lime juice
1 teaspoon grated lime zest
¼ cup tequila or apple cider
1½ cups nonfat whipped topping
1 (9-inch) Graham Cracker Crust (page 258)
8 very thin lime slices

Low-Fat Pumpkin Pie

Pumpkin pie is a must for Thanksgiving. This low-fat version is creamy and delicious, just like the original.

1. Preheat oven to 450°F. In a large bowl, stir together sugar, brown sugar, salt, cinnamon, ginger, and nutmeg. Beat in the pumpkin, vanilla, evaporated milk, orange zest, and egg whites until smooth.

2. Pour into pie crust. Bake for 10 minutes, then reduce heat to 325°F and continue to bake until a knife inserted in the filling comes out clean, about 35 to 45 minutes. Cool on wire rack for 1 hour, then cover and chill in refrigerator for 3 to 4 hours before serving.

Serves 8

Calories: 230.34
Fat: 6.93 grams
Saturated Fat: 1.93 grams
Cholesterol: 1.86 mg
Sodium: 204.11 mg

⅓ cup sugar
⅓ cup brown sugar
⅛ teaspoon salt
1 teaspoon cinnamon
½ teaspoon ginger
¼ teaspoon nutmeg
1½ cups canned solid-packed pumpkin
1½ teaspoons vanilla
1½ cups evaporated skim milk
1 teaspoon orange zest
3 egg whites
1 Graham Cracker Crust (page 258), baked and cooled

Lemon Cheesecake

Serves 8

Calories: 220.88
Fat: 6.05 grams
Saturated Fat: 2.20 grams
Cholesterol: 62.98 mg
Sodium: 370.90 mg

12 graham crackers, crushed
2 tablespoons butter, melted
2 tablespoons lemon juice
1 pound 1% small-curd cottage cheese
2 eggs
2 egg whites
½ cup evaporated skim milk
½ cup sugar
1 tablespoon grated lemon zest
⅓ cup lemon juice
¼ cup flour

The lemon adds zing to this light, creamy cheesecake. To enhance the presentation, use a zester to peel off long curls of lemon zest and arrange them on top of the cake.

1. For crust, mix together the crumbs, butter, and 2 tablespoons lemon juice in a bowl. Transfer crumb mixture to 9" springform pan and press onto the bottom. Place in the freezer.

2. Preheat oven to 300°F. For filling, in a food processor, combine the cottage cheese, eggs, egg whites, evaporated milk, sugar, lemon zest, and ⅓ cup lemon juice. Process until smooth. Add flour and process a few seconds longer.

3. Remove crust from freezer and pour cottage cheese mixture into it. Bake until the filling has set, about 55 to 65 minutes. Cool on a rack, then chill in refrigerator for 4 to 5 hours before serving. Release the pan sides and slide onto a serving plate. Decorate with the lemon slices, if desired.

Cheesecake Cracking

Cheesecakes sometimes crack as they cool. You can prevent this by baking them in a water bath. Wrap the springform pan in foil and place in a larger pan. Add hot water to come 1 inch up the side of the springform pan. Bake as directed. If the top still cracks, just top it with a thin layer of low-fat sour cream mixed with some powdered sugar and lemon juice.

Lemon Meringue Pie

Putting lemon filling in a graham cracker pie crust not only adds flavor and texture to this classic recipe, but it reduces the fat content.

Serves 6

Calories: 430.32
Fat: 12.80 grams
Saturated Fat: 4.03 grams
Cholesterol: 88.79 mg
Sodium: 203.54 mg

1½ cups sugar
3 tablespoons cornstarch
3 tablespoons flour
⅛ teaspoon salt
⅓ cup water
2 egg yolks
2 tablespoons butter
½ cup lemon juice
1 Graham Cracker Crust
   (page 258)
3 egg whites
⅛ teaspoon cream of
   tartar
6 tablespoons sugar

1. In a saucepan, combine 1½ cups sugar, cornstarch, flour, and salt. Using a wire whisk, stir in water until smooth. Bring to a boil over high heat, stirring constantly. Reduce heat to medium. Cook, stirring, until slightly thickened, about 8 minutes.

2. Remove from heat. In a bowl, lightly beat egg yolks. Stir a small amount of the hot mixture into egg yolks, beating well. Then add egg yolk mixture to saucepan. Bring to a boil over high heat, stirring constantly.

3. Reduce the heat to low and cook, stirring, 4 minutes longer. Remove from heat. Add butter and lemon juice, mixing well. Cool for 20 minutes, stirring occasionally. Pour into the pie crust and cool for 30 minutes. Place in refrigerator and cool completely.

4. Preheat oven to 350°F. In a large bowl, on high speed, beat egg whites with cream of tartar until soft peaks form. Gradually add 6 tablespoons sugar, beating until stiff peaks form and the sugar is dissolved. Spread over the cooled filling, sealing to the edges of the pastry.

5. Bake until meringue browns, about 12 to 15 minutes. Cool on wire rack for 30 minutes, then chill for at least 4 hours in the refrigerator before serving.

Fresh Peach Pie

Serves 8

Calories: 391.33
Fat: 12.43 grams
Saturated Fat: 2.77 grams
Cholesterol: 12.33 mg
Sodium: 203.54 mg

1 Graham Cracker Crust
    (page 258), baked and
    cooled
1 cup brown sugar,
    divided
2½ cups flour, divided
1 teaspoon cinnamon,
    divided
¼ teaspoon ginger
⅛ teaspoon salt
8 peaches, peeled and
    sliced
2 tablespoons lemon juice
3 tablespoons butter,
    melted
2 tablespoons peach
    nectar

When peaches are in season, there's nothing better than this pie. The crunchy cinnamon topping complements the sweet and juicy peaches. Serve it warm with some vanilla ice milk.

1. Preheat oven to 400°F. In a medium bowl, combine ⅔ cup brown sugar, 1¾ cups flour, ½ teaspoon cinnamon, ginger, and salt, mixing well. Add peaches and lemon juice to the sugar-flour mixture, tossing gently.

2. Pour the peach mixture into pie crust. In a small bowl, combine ⅓ cup brown sugar, ¾ cup flour, and ½ teaspoon cinnamon; mix well. Add melted butter and peach nectar; work with fork until crumbs form. Sprinkle over peach mixture.

3. Bake for 10 minutes, then reduce the heat to 375°F and continue to bake until streusel topping is golden brown and peaches are tender when pierced with a fork, about 50 to 55 minutes. Cool on wire rack. Serve warm or at room temperature.

Fruit Pies

You can reduce the fat on many fruit pies, even those that use a full-fat rolled pie crust. Just omit the top crust, and use a streusel topping or sprinkle the top with coconut or nuts. You can also omit the crust altogether, and make a crumble or crisp instead, which is made with a fruit bottom and a streusel topping.

Strawberry Pie

This light and airy dessert is delicious when strawberries are in season. Garnish with a few whole berries.

1. Bake and cool the pie crust; set aside. In a large bowl, combine egg white with cream of tartar and lemon juice. Beat until foamy, then add the sugar and strawberries. Continue to beat until the mixture holds soft peaks, about 10 to 12 minutes.

2. Spoon into pie crust and chill thoroughly before serving. Pie can also be frozen; let stand at room temperature for 15 minutes before slicing.

Serves 8

Calories: 249.84
Fat: 4.98 grams
Saturated Fat: 2.34 grams
Cholesterol: 7.65 mg
Sodium: 156.43 mg

1 Graham Cracker Crust (page 258)
2 pasteurized egg whites
⅛ teaspoon cream of tartar
¼ teaspoon lemon juice
⅓ cup sugar
1½ cups sliced strawberries

Egg White Foams

Egg white foams are created when air is beaten into egg whites. You'll have a higher foam if you let the egg white stand at room temperature for about 20 minutes before you start beating. Cream of tartar and lemon juice help stabilize the foam by adding acid to the protein web of the foam.

Peanut Butter Chocolate Bars

This crunchy and creamy bar cookie is really delicious, and only ⅓ calories come from fat!

Yields 36 squares

Calories: 189.98
Fat: 6.03 grams
Saturated Fat: 3.02 grams
Cholesterol: 15.65 mg
Sodium: 61.51 mg

5 tablespoons butter, softened
⅓ cup reduced-fat peanut butter
1 egg
1 egg white
1 cup brown sugar
1 cup flour
¾ cup crisp peanut butter-flavored cereal squares, finely crushed
1 cup quick-cooking oatmeal
¼ teaspoon salt
½ teaspoon baking soda
1 (13-ounce) can nonfat sweetened condensed milk
2 cups semisweet chocolate chips

1. Preheat oven to 350°F. Spray a 9" × 13" baking pan with nonstick cooking spray containing flour; set aside.

2. In a large bowl combine butter, peanut butter, egg, and egg white; beat until combined. Add brown sugar and beat until smooth. Stir in flour, finely crushed cereal, oatmeal, salt, and baking soda and mix until crumbly. Press half into prepared pan.

3. In a medium microwave-safe bowl, combine sweetened condensed milk and 1½ cups chocolate chips; microwave on 50 percent power for 2 minutes, then remove and stir until smooth. Spoon evenly over the crumbs in pan.

4. Top with remaining ½ cup chocolate chips, then remaining crumbs; press down lightly. Bake for 20 to 25 minutes or until bars are set. Cool completely, then cut into squares to serve.

Baked Pears

Make this dessert special by serving it in a stemmed goblet,
topped with some mint sprigs.

Serves 6

Calories: 143.54
Fat: 0.33 grams
Saturated Fat: 0.02 grams
Cholesterol: 0.0 mg
Sodium: 1.08 mg

2 tablespoons lemon juice
6 pears, peeled
4 tablespoons sugar
3 cups nonfat frozen
  yogurt

1. Preheat oven to 375°F. Place lemon juice in a 2-quart baking dish and add just enough water to cover the bottom. Cut pears in half, remove cores, and place pears in baking dish, cut-side down. Cover and bake until pears are tender when pierced with a knife, 20 to 25 minutes.

2. Remove from oven and sprinkle each pear with 2 teaspoons sugar. Bake, uncovered, for 10 minutes longer to glaze. Serve warm or chilled with frozen yogurt.

Baked Fruits

Baked fruit is a simple and nutritious low-fat dessert. You can make this dessert using other fruits like peaches or apples. The peaches would bake for about 15 minutes, and apples for about 40 to 50 minutes. Also think about adding some spices to the sugar glaze; cinnamon, cardamom, and nutmeg are delicious.

Spice Cake

Nothing smells as good as a spice cake cooling on a rack. Top this with nonfat whipped topping or some frozen vanilla yogurt.

Serves 6

Calories: 286.54
Fat: 1.02 grams
Saturated Fat: 0.49 grams
Cholesterol: 2.39 mg
Sodium: 175.44 mg

1 tablespoon butter
½ cup brown sugar
½ cup sugar
2 eggs
1 teaspoon baking soda
1 cup nonfat buttermilk
2 cups flour
⅛ teaspoon salt
1 teaspoon nutmeg
1 teaspoon cinnamon
½ teaspoon allspice
¼ teaspoon cardamom
¼ teaspoon cloves
1 cup raisins

1. Preheat oven to 350°F. Spray an 8" square pan with nonstick baking spray containing flour and set aside.

2. In a large bowl, cream together butter, brown sugar, and sugar. Add eggs and mix thoroughly. Dissolve the baking soda in buttermilk, and stir into sugar-egg mixture. In a medium bowl, sift together flour, salt, and spices. Beat into the sugar mixture and fold in raisins.

3. Pour batter into the prepared pan. Bake until a toothpick inserted in the center comes out clean, about 50 to 55 minutes. Cool on wire rack.

Applesauce Pound Cake

Yes, you can have pound cake, even on a low-fat diet. Applesauce is the secret ingredient that adds moisture and flavor.

1. Preheat oven to 325°F. Spray a 9" × 5" loaf pan with nonstick baking spray containing flour and set aside.

2. In a large bowl, combine milk, raisins, applesauce, brown sugar, sugar, and oil and mix well until combined. In sifter, combine cinnamon, salt, nutmeg, cake flour, baking powder, and baking soda. Sift over milk mixture and blend.

3. Fold in apples and walnuts. Spoon batter into prepared loaf pan. Bake for 65 to 75 minutes or until cake is deep golden brown and a cake tester inserted in center comes out clean. Let cool in pan for 5 minutes, then remove to wire rack to cool.

4. In a small bowl, combine powdered sugar with lemon juice and mix until smooth. Drizzle over the cake and let stand until firm.

Pound Cakes

Traditionally, pound cakes are made with a pound each of butter, eggs, sugar, and flour. The structure of the cake depended on the eggs and used little or no leavening. This cake is much healthier and just as delicious, using applesauce and finely chopped apples for moistness and flavor.

Serves 8

Calories: 329.98
Fat: 7.30 grams
Saturated Fat: 0.55 grams
Cholesterol: 0.66 mg
Sodium: 59.93 mg

1 cup skim milk
1 cup raisins
1 cup applesauce
½ cup brown sugar
¼ cup sugar
¼ cup vegetable oil
1 teaspoon cinnamon
¼ teaspoon salt
⅛ teaspoon nutmeg
2 cups cake flour
1 teaspoon baking powder
1 teaspoon baking soda
1 cup finely chopped peeled apples
½ cup chopped walnuts
1 cup powdered sugar
2 tablespoons lemon juice

Sherry Custard with Spiced Cherries

Serves 4

Calories: 128.04
Fat: 2.34 grams
Saturated Fat: 1.08 grams
Cholesterol: 12.45 mg
Sodium: 120.99 mg

2 tablespoons sugar
Pinch salt
1⅓ cups 1% milk
1 teaspoon vanilla
2 to 3 teaspoons sherry
3 egg whites
1 tablespoon sugar
½ recipe Spiced Cherry
*   Sauce (page 252)*

This custard is much more fragile than regular custards made with egg yolks, but it still has a creamy texture. The Spiced Cherry Sauce makes it just perfect!

1. Preheat oven to 325°F. Spray a 2-cup baking dish with nonstick cooking spray and place in a baking pan; set aside.

2. In a small saucepan, combine 2 tablespoons sugar, salt, and milk. Cook over low heat until sugar dissolves, about 5 minutes. Remove from heat and add vanilla and sherry.

3. In a medium bowl, combine egg whites with 1 tablespoon sugar; beat until very soft peaks form. Stir into milk mixture.

4. Strain mixture through a sieve into prepared baking dish. Pour hot water into the baking pan to reach halfway up the sides of the dish. Bake until a knife inserted near center comes out clean, about 50 to 60 minutes. Let cool for 30 minutes; serve warm with the Spiced Cherry Sauce.

Chapter 19
Sauces and Dressings

Golden Cooked Salad Dressing 270

Honey Orange Salad Dressing. 270

Herbed Yogurt Dressing. 271

Buttermilk Dressing. 272

Horseradish Salad Dressing. 272

Hoisin Dressing 273

Low-Fat Italian Salad Dressing 273

Green Salsa. 274

Southwestern Apricot Salsa. 275

Stone Fruit Salsa 276

Tangy Peach Salsa 276

California Salsa 277

Tomato Citrus Salsa. 278

Basic Low-Fat White Sauce. 278

Low-Fat Country Gravy 279

Low-Fat Cheese Sauce 280

Creamy Mustard Sauce 280

Light Alfredo Sauce 281

Pear and Apple Sauce. 282

Golden Cooked Salad Dressing

This gorgeous salad dressing can be substituted for Caesar dressing or used in a salad with fruit and greens.

Yields 1½ cups; serving size 2 tablespoons

Calories: 42.63
Fat: 1.39 grams
Saturated Fat: 0.74 grams
Cholesterol: 20.17 mg
Sodium: 109.76 mg

⅓ cup sugar
½ teaspoon dry mustard
½ teaspoon salt
⅛ teaspoon white pepper
2 tablespoons flour
1 egg
½ cup white wine vinegar
½ cup water
1 tablespoon butter

1. In a small bowl, combine sugar, mustard, salt, pepper, and flour; mix well. Add egg; beat until well blended.

2. In a small saucepan, combine vinegar, water, and butter; heat over medium heat until mixture simmers. Remove from heat and gradually beat in the egg mixture.

3. Return saucepan to the heat; cook over medium heat, stirring constantly with wire whisk, until dressing is smooth and thick, about 3 to 4 minutes. Cover and chill. Store covered, in refrigerator, up to 1 week.

Honey Orange Salad Dressing

This simple salad dressing is perfect to serve drizzled on spinach leaves or mixed salad greens.

Yields 1¼ cups; serving size 2 tablespoons

Calories: 66.33
Fat: 2.74 grams
Saturated Fat: 0.38 grams
Cholesterol: 0.0 mg
Sodium: 58.90 mg

¼ cup water
¼ cup honey
3 tablespoons white vinegar
⅔ cup orange juice
¼ teaspoon salt
Dash white pepper
2 tablespoons extra-virgin olive oil

1. In a small saucepan, combine water, honey, and vinegar; bring to a simmer. Simmer for 2 minutes, then remove from heat and cool.

2. Stir in orange juice, salt, and pepper along with olive oil; mix well. Cover and store in refrigerator for up to 4 days.

Herbed Yogurt Dressing

*This delicious dressing can be served over baby spinach leaves,
or try it as an appetizer dip.*

**Yields 2½ cups; serving
size 2 tablespoons**

Calories: 16.41
Fat: 0.11 grams
Saturated Fat: 0.03 grams
Cholesterol: 0.49 mg
Sodium: 66.48 mg

2 cups plain low-fat yogurt
*½ cup chopped flat-leaf
    parsley*
*½ cup chopped fresh dill
    weed*
2 cloves garlic, minced
3 tablespoons lemon juice
*2 tablespoons Dijon
    mustard*
¼ teaspoon salt
⅛ teaspoon white pepper

In a medium bowl, combine all ingredients and mix well. Cover and
chill for 2 to 3 hours before serving. Store, covered, in the refrigerator
for up to 5 days.

Fresh Herbs

*Fresh herbs do not have a long shelf life, so buy them just before you
want to use them. Parsley can be the exception if it is stored properly.
Cut off the tips of the stems and stand it upright in a glass. Add cold
water and store it in the refrigerator. It can stay fresh and crisp for a
week; just snip off what you need.*

**Yields 1 cup; serving
size 2 tablespoons**

Calories: 23.73
Fat: 1.43 grams
Saturated Fat: 0.30 grams
Cholesterol: 0.92 mg
Sodium: 124.92 mg

¾ cup buttermilk
2 tablespoons nonfat
    mayonnaise
3 tablespoons minced
    flat-leaf parsley
3 tablespoons minced
    chives
1 clove garlic, minced
1 tablespoon minced
    tarragon leaves
1 tablespoon lemon juice
Dash Worcestershire sauce
¼ teaspoon salt
⅛ teaspoon white pepper

**Yields ¾ cup; serving
size 2 tablespoons**

Calories: 29.72 mg
Fat: 0.43 grams
Saturated Fat: 0.21 grams
Cholesterol: 1.23 mg
Sodium: 58.28 mg

2 tablespoons lemon juice
2 tablespoons rice wine
    vinegar
2 tablespoons freshly
    grated horseradish
1 tablespoon honey
½ cup plain low-fat yogurt
1 tablespoon mustard

Buttermilk Dressing

*Buttermilk and fresh herbs combine to make a delicious salad
dressing that is good on everything from watercress to baby spinach.*

In a small bowl, combine all ingredients and mix well. Cover and refrigerate for 2 hours before serving. Store, covered, in refrigerator up to 4 days.

Buttermilk

Despite its name, buttermilk is naturally low in fat. It's the liquid left over when most of the fat is removed from heavy cream in the butter-making process. Despite its low fat content, it has a rich and thick texture. It blends well with other ingredients and makes a smooth and creamy salad dressing.

Horseradish Salad Dressing

*Horseradish is an extremely pungent root vegetable that is used
in small quantities. If you like hot food, increase the amount in
this easy salad dressing.*

Combine all ingredients in a small bowl and stir well. Cover and chill for 3 hours before serving. To store, cover and keep refrigerated for up to 4 days.

Hoisin Dressing

This Asian-inspired salad dressing can be used on cabbage or spinach for a salad, or as a marinade for grilled chicken or pork.

Combine all ingredients in small jar with a screw-top lid. Close lid and shake well. Cover and chill for at least 2 hours before serving. Store in refrigerator for up to 4 days.

Hoisin Sauce

Hoisin means seafood in Chinese, but it doesn't contain any seafood. It's a sweet, thick, and spicy sauce used as a marinade and addition to stir-fries. It is made of vinegar, garlic, fermented soybeans, and chili peppers. It keeps for a long time in the refrigerator.

Low-Fat Italian Salad Dressing

You can increase the herbs and spices in this dressing if you'd like; just add them to taste.

1. In a small microwave-safe bowl, combine cornstarch, water, and sugar. Microwave on high for 1 minute, remove, and stir. Microwave for 30 second intervals, stirring in between each interval, until mixture is thick and smooth, about 1 to 2 minutes.

2. Beat in vinegar and remaining ingredients except olive oil, stirring well with wire whisk or eggbeater. Then slowly beat in the olive oil until blended.

3. Cover and chill for 2 to 3 hours before serving. Store covered in refrigerator up to 5 days.

Yields ¾ cup; serving size 1 tablespoon

Calories: 32.48
Fat: 2.76 grams
Saturated Fat: 0.46 grams
Cholesterol: 0.08 mg
Sodium: 67.94 mg

6 tablespoons rice vinegar
2 tablespoons peanut oil
2 tablespoons hoisin sauce
1 tablespoon sesame seeds
2 tablespoons minced ginger root
⅛ teaspoon salt
⅛ teaspoon white pepper

Yields 1 cup; serving size 2 tablespoons

Calories: 43.76
Fat: 3.39 grams
Saturated Fat: 0.47 grams
Cholesterol: 0.00 mg
Sodium: 146.02 mg

1 tablespoon cornstarch
½ cup water
2 tablespoons sugar
⅓ cup apple cider vinegar
½ teaspoon dry mustard powder
1 teaspoon dried basil leaves
½ teaspoon dried oregano leaves
½ teaspoon dried thyme leaves
½ teaspoon paprika
½ teaspoon salt
⅛ teaspoon pepper
2 tablespoons olive oil

Green Salsa

Green salsa served with blue corn tortilla chips makes a colorful and delicious appetizer for a Tex-Mex meal.

Yields 1½ cups; serving size 2 tablespoons

Calories: 32.50
Fat: 2.38 grams
Saturated Fat: 0.33 grams
Cholesterol: 0.0 mg
Sodium: 67.69 mg

2 jalapeño peppers, minced
6 small green tomatoes, chopped
2 tablespoons chopped cilantro
1 teaspoon ground cumin
2 tablespoons red wine vinegar
¼ cup diced red onion
2 tablespoons extra-virgin olive oil
2 tablespoons water

1. In a blender or food processor, combine all ingredients except olive oil and water. Blend or process until smooth.

2. With the motor running, add olive oil and water; blend until mixed. Chill for at least 1 hour before serving.

Southwestern Apricot Salsa

This sweet and spicy salsa is delicious served with crisp crackers and Melba toast. You could also use it for a sandwich topping.

1. Drain apricots, reserving 2 tablespoons juice. Chop apricots and combine in medium bowl with remaining ingredients, including reserved juice. Stir to blend.

2. Cover and refrigerate for 2 hours before serving. Store in refrigerator for up to 4 days.

Canned Fruit

You can find canned fruit packed in water, in light syrup, and in heavy syrup. The difference is in the amount of sugar added to the liquid used to pack the fruit. Use the type called for in the recipe, even though they are interchangeable. To use, drain the fruit thoroughly in a colander or strainer; do not rinse.

Yields 2 cups; serves 8

Calories: 36.44
Fat: 1.81 grams
Saturated Fat: 0.24 grams
Cholesterol: 0.0 mg
Sodium: 74.82 mg

1 (16-ounce) can apricots in light syrup
½ cup chopped red onion
1 tablespoon olive oil
2 tablespoons chopped fresh cilantro
2 tablespoons lime juice
2 jalapeño peppers, minced
1 teaspoon grated lime zest
½ teaspoon cumin
½ teaspoon salt
⅛ teaspoon white pepper

Stone Fruit Salsa

Stone fruits have a pit instead of seeds. These sweet and juicy fruits are delicious combined with lemon, mint, and the spice of cayenne pepper.

Yields 2 cups; serves 8

Calories: 58.72
Fat: 0.21 grams
Saturated Fat: 0.03 grams
Cholesterol: 0.0 mg
Sodium: 76.02 mg

2 peaches, peeled
3 plums
½ cup dried cherries, chopped
½ cup chopped red onion
2 cloves garlic, minced
2 tablespoons lemon juice
1 tablespoon chopped fresh mint
¼ teaspoon salt
⅛ teaspoon cayenne pepper

1. Remove pit from peaches and dice. Dice plums and combine with peaches and dried cherries in medium bowl.

2. Stir in red onion and remaining ingredients and stir to mix. Cover and chill for 2 to 4 hours before serving.

Tangy Peach Salsa

Serve as an appetizer with crackers and pita chips, or top grilled fish or chicken with a spoonful or two.

Yields 2 cups; serves 8

Calories: 81.68
Fat: 0.20 grams
Saturated Fat: 0.02 grams
Cholesterol: 0.0 mg
Sodium: 84.41 mg

4 peaches, peeled
½ cup orange marmalade
½ cup thinly sliced green onions
¼ teaspoon salt
⅛ teaspoon red pepper flakes
2 tablespoons lime juice
1 tablespoon minced fresh ginger root

Cut peaches in half and remove pit. Chop peaches and combine in medium bowl with remaining ingredients. Mix to combine, then cover and refrigerate for 1 to 2 hours before serving.

Marmalade

Marmalade is made from orange peel, juice, sugar, and a thickening agent. The British version is bitter and sweet, while the American version is almost always sweet. Marmalade originated in Britain in the seventeenth century, when citrus fruits became more readily available.

California Salsa

Salsa is easy to make and is a great low-fat treat. Serve it with baked potato chips, tortilla chips, bell pepper wedges, and celery sticks for a healthy appetizer.

Combine all ingredients in medium bowl and mix well. Cover tightly and chill for 2 to 3 hours before serving.

Yields 2 cups; 8 servings

Calories: 30.37
Fat: 0.16 grams
Saturated Fat: 0.04 grams
Cholesterol: 0.0 mg
Sodium: 263.97 mg

2 cups chopped tomatoes
2 stalks celery, chopped
1 red onion, chopped
1 yellow bell pepper,
    chopped
½ teaspoon salt
2 tablespoons apple cider
    vinegar
1 tablespoon sugar
1 green chili pepper,
    minced
¼ teaspoon white pepper
⅛ teaspoon cayenne
    pepper

*3 tomatoes, chopped
2 cloves garlic, minced
1 tablespoon minced
    chives
1 red onion, finely
    chopped
1 jalapeño pepper,
    minced
2 tablespoons lime juice
1 tablespoon orange juice
½ teaspoon salt
⅛ teaspoon white pepper*

Tomato Citrus Salsa

*Orange juice adds a bit of sweetness to this fresh and spicy salsa.
Serve it with blue corn tortilla chips for a great color contrast.*

1. Combine all ingredients in medium bowl. Mix well, cover, and chill before serving.

2. Can be served as an appetizer or a topping on grilled fish, steak, or chicken.

Limes

Limes are usually quite hard to juice and each one doesn't yield very much. To get the most juice out of your limes, roll them on the counter using the palm of your hand. Then prick the limes with a fork and micro-wave for 10 to 20 seconds on high to help break up the cells.

Basic Low-Fat White Sauce

*Toasting the flour and cornstarch before adding the milk
enhances the flavor and keeps the sauce from tasting floury.*

*2 tablespoons flour
1 tablespoon cornstarch
½ teaspoon lemon pepper
⅛ teaspoon salt
1 cup 1% milk*

1. Combine flour and cornstarch in small saucepan. Place over medium-low heat; cook and stir until toasted but not browned, stirring constantly. Add lemon pepper, salt, and milk, stirring constantly.

2. Continue to cook and stir over medium-low heat until sauce is thickened, about 10 minutes. Use immediately as base for cheese sauce or gravy, or cover and store in refrigerator up to 3 days.

Low-Fat Country Gravy

This gravy can be served with sautéed pork chops or chicken breasts. It's also excellent served with biscuits.

1. In a small saucepan, combine Worcestershire sauce, onion soup mix, coffee, thyme leaves, and garlic; bring to a simmer over high heat.

2. Reduce heat to low and stir in white sauce and 1 tablespoon skim milk. Cook and stir until sauce is thick and onions and garlic are tender, adding more milk if necessary, until desired consistency is reached. Serve immediately.

Coffee as Flavoring

Coffee is the traditional flavoring in red-eye gravy, usually made with the drippings from a cooked ham. It adds flavor and color to this low-fat gravy recipe. For this recipe or any other cooking or baking recipe, you can brew it fresh, use leftover coffee, or make instant coffee according to the package directions.

Yields 1½ cups sauce; serving size 3 tablespoons

Calories: 27.34
Fat: 0.45 grams
Saturated Fat: 0.14 grams
Cholesterol: 0.69 mg
Sodium: 270.94 mg

1 tablespoon Worcestershire sauce
1 tablespoon low-sodium dried onion soup mix
2 tablespoons strong brewed coffee
¼ teaspoon dried thyme leaves
2 cloves garlic, minced
1 cup Basic Low-Fat White Sauce (page 278)
1 to 2 tablespoons skim milk

Yields 1½ cups
sauce; serving size
3 tablespoons

Calories: 37.39
Fat: 0.83 grams
Saturated Fat: 0.50 grams
Cholesterol: 2.75 mg
Sodium: 103.61 mg

1 cup Basic Low-Fat
   White Sauce (page
   278)
½ cup grated low-fat
   extra sharp Cheddar
   cheese
1 teaspoon mustard
1 to 2 tablespoons skim
   milk, as needed

Yields 1½ cups;
12 servings

Calories: 18.83
Fat: 0.23 grams
Saturated Fat: 0.05
grams
Cholesterol: 0.50 mg
Sodium: 83.91 mg

1 cup plain nonfat yogurt
¼ cup Dijon mustard
⅛ teaspoon white pepper
2 tablespoons low-fat
   cottage cheese
¼ teaspoon Tabasco
   sauce
2 tablespoons minced
   shallot
2 cloves garlic, minced
1 tablespoon lemon juice

Low-Fat Cheese Sauce

*You can use any low-fat or nonfat cheese in this super simple
sauce. Serve it over cooked vegetables or as a pasta sauce.*

Pour white sauce into a small saucepan and heat until it begins to
steam. Add the cheese and mustard; stir with wire whisk over low heat
until cheese is melted and sauce is smooth. Add milk if necessary for
desired consistency. Serve immediately.

Creamy Mustard Sauce

*Serve this sauce with grilled fish or chicken,
or use it as an appetizer dip with crudités.*

Combine all ingredients in small bowl and stir well to mix. Cover and
refrigerate up to 4 days.

Light Alfredo Sauce

Store this sauce, covered, in the refrigerator up to 3 days. Just reheat in the microwave before serving.

Heat the evaporated milk in a deep saucepan over medium heat. Bring to a simmer but do not boil. Add the Parmesan cheese and parsley. As soon as the cheese has melted and the sauce is thick and creamy, remove from the heat. Season with white pepper and red pepper flakes, if desired. Serve immediately.

Alfredo Sauce

This versatile Italian sauce can be used in so many ways. Toss it with cooked fettuccine or spaghetti and top with parsley. Use it in lasagna recipes as the base for the white sauce. Or try using it as a pizza sauce, topped with chicken and some white cheeses for a white pizza.

Yields 2½ cups; serving size 4 tablespoons

Calories: 50.67
Fat: 1.25 grams
Saturated Fat: 0.75 grams
Cholesterol: 5.18 mg
Sodium: 110.53 mg

1 (13-ounce) can evaporated nonfat milk
½ cup grated Parmesan cheese
½ cup chopped flat-leaf parsley
⅛ teaspoon white pepper
Pinch red pepper flakes, if desired

Pear and Apple Sauce

You own homemade applesauce is so delicious. Serve it with a baked ham or with turkey at Thanksgiving.

Yields about 5 cups; serving size ½ cup

Calories: 126.68
Fat: 0.11 grams
Saturated Fat: 0.01 grams
Cholesterol: 0.0 mg
Sodium: 41.08 mg

1 cup sugar
2 cups water
⅛ teaspoon salt
1 cinnamon stick
2 quinces
2 pears
3 Granny Smith apples

1. In a large saucepan over medium heat, combine the sugar, water, salt, and cinnamon stick. Cook, stirring occasionally, until sugar is dissolved.

2. Meanwhile, peel the quinces and cut into pieces. Add the quinces to the saucepan. Cover and cook, stirring occasionally, until fruit is tender, about 40 minutes.

3. Meanwhile, peel the pears and apples and cut into chunks. Add to the saucepan and cook for 20 to 25 minutes longer or until all the fruit is very tender. Remove cinnamon stick.

4. Using an immersion blender or potato masher, blend or mash the fruit mixture until desired consistency. Serve warm or cold. Store covered in refrigerator for up to 5 days.

Quinces

Quinces are not used very often in the United States. They are not eaten out of hand because the flesh is very tart, sour, and hard, but they make great puddings, jams, and sauces. The fruit itself is oblong in shape and bumpy, with a yellow or green skin. It adds a wonderful taste to applesauce because it has a very strong perfume.

Chapter 20
Condiments and Extras

Fruit Smoothie 284

Nectarine Chutney 284

Candy Corn 285

Mock Sour Cream. 286

Low-Fat Spinach Pesto 286

BBQ Sauce 287

Cranberry Chutney 288

Freezer Jam 289

Peach Leather 290

Daikon Salsa 291

Watermelon Salsa. 291

Smoky Salsa 292

Mid-East Buttermilk Shake 293

Cooked Applesauce. 293

Uncooked Applesauce 294

Fruit Smoothie

The trick to rich-tasting low-fat smoothies is not to use crushed ice. Use frozen fruit instead; it will thicken without diluting the flavor.

Serves 4

Calories: 82.94
Fat: 0.23 grams
Saturated Fat: 0.15 grams
Cholesterol: 2.73 mg
Sodium: 66.35 mg

1 (8-ounce) can fruit
   cocktail, chilled
1 cup skim milk
¼ cup nonfat dry milk
   powder
1 teaspoon vanilla
⅛ teaspoon cinnamon
1 frozen banana, cubed

In a blender container or food processor, combine all ingredients. Blend or process until smooth, then serve immediately.

Nectarine Chutney

Chutney makes a perfect low-fat—almost nonfat—sandwich spread. It pairs well with ham, chicken, and roast beef.

Yields 2 cups; serving size 2 tablespoons

Calories: 42.43
Fat: 1.08 grams
Saturated Fat: 0.09 grams
Cholesterol: 0.0 mg
Sodium: 24.03 mg

3 nectarines
1 onion, chopped
½ cup brown sugar
½ cup golden raisins
¼ cup apple cider vinegar
1 teaspoon chili powder
¼ teaspoon allspice
½ cup slivered almonds,
   toasted

1. Peel nectarines, remove pit, and chop. In 2-quart microwave-safe bowl, combine all ingredients except almonds.

2. Microwave on high for 20 to 25 minutes, stirring every 5 minutes, until mixture is very thick. Fruit should be tender.

3. Let mixture cool; cover, and refrigerate until cold. Stir in the almonds before serving. Chutney can be stored, covered, in refrigerator up to 2 weeks.

Candy Corn

Baking soda makes the sweet sugar syrup foam up so it more evenly coats the popcorn. You could add other candies to this delicious mix, like crushed hard candy.

Yields 4½ cups; serving size ¾ cup

Calories: 118.77
Fat: 4.12 grams
Saturated Fat: 2.47 grams
Cholesterol: 10.17 mg
Sodium: 84.34 mg

⅓ cup brown sugar
2 tablespoons butter
3 tablespoons corn syrup
⅛ teaspoon salt
¼ teaspoon baking soda
4½ cups popped corn

1. Preheat oven to 275°F. In a small saucepan, combine brown sugar, butter, corn syrup, and salt and bring to a boil. Remove from heat and add baking soda; mixture will foam up.

2. Place popcorn in large bowl; drizzle sugar mixture over the popcorn and toss with two spoons to coat.

3. Spread on a baking sheet and bake for 20 to 25 minutes until crisp and glazed, stirring every 8 minutes. Cool completely, then store at room temperature.

Making Popcorn

Air-popped popcorn is the most fat-free version, but you don't need an air popper. You can pop regular popcorn on the stovetop in a heavy saucepan over low heat without any oil. Cover the pan; when the corn starts to pop, start shaking it to prevent burning. When popping slows, remove pan from heat and pour the popcorn into a bowl.

Mock Sour Cream

This simple recipe is perfect for topping baked potatoes and gelatin salads. Don't use it in cooking or baking, however, or it may break down.

Yields 1½ cups; serving size 2 tablespoons

Calories: 17.54
Fat: 0.18 grams
Saturated Fat: 0.12 grams
Cholesterol: 0.97 mg
Sodium: 67.99

1 cup skim milk
¾ cup low-fat cottage cheese
2 to 4 teaspoons vinegar

1. Combine all ingredients in blender or food processor. Blend or process until smooth.

2. You may need to add more milk, cottage cheese, or vinegar to make the proper consistency and taste. Cover and refrigerate up to 4 days.

Low-Fat Spinach Pesto

Pesto is a flavorful sauce usually made with a lot of oil, nuts, and cheese. This slimmed-down version is just as delicious as the regular kind.

Yields 2 cups; serving size ¼ cup

Calories: 52.13
Fat: 3.08 grams
Saturated Fat: 0.66 grams
Cholesterol: 1.38 mg
Sodium: 200.16 mg

1 (10-ounce) package spinach
4 cloves garlic, chopped
1 cup fresh basil leaves
½ cup chopped flat-leaf parsley
½ teaspoon salt
⅛ teaspoon pepper
2 tablespoons olive oil
2 tablespoons lemon juice
2 to 4 tablespoons water
2 tablespoons grated Parmesan cheese

1. In a food processor, combine spinach, garlic, basil, parsley, salt, and pepper and process until finely chopped.

2. With motor running, slowly add olive oil and lemon juice, then add enough water to make a thick sauce. Add cheese and mix well. To store, cover and refrigerate for up to 3 days, or freeze for longer storage.

Freezing Pesto

Pesto is easily frozen for later use. Make it in the summer when fresh basil is readily available. Divide the pesto into ice cube trays and freeze until solid. Then pop out of the trays and place in a freezer bag; label, seal, and freeze up to 4 months. To use, thaw in the microwave oven or refrigerator.

BBQ Sauce

Your own homemade barbecue sauce is delicious slathered on everything from grilled chicken to ribs.

1. In a medium saucepan, combine all ingredients except ketchup. Bring to a boil over high heat, then reduce heat to low and simmer for 20 minutes.

2. Remove pan from heat and stir in ketchup. Use immediately, or cover and chill in refrigerator for up to 3 days.

Using BBQ Sauce

Since barbecue sauce is so high in sugar (from the sugar, onions, and ketchup) it can burn quite easily. When cooking with barbecue sauce on a grill or under the broiler, add it during the last 20 to 30 minutes of cooking, just long enough to heat the sauce through and form a glaze. If it cooks at high heat any longer, it will burn.

Yields 1 cup; serving size 2 tablespoons

Calories: 38.61
Fat: 0.11 grams
Saturated Fat: 0.01 grams
Cholesterol: 0.0 mg
Sodium: 176.53 mg

⅓ cup apple cider vinegar
½ cup water
1 tablespoon Dijon mustard
2 tablespoons brown sugar
½ teaspoon pepper
¼ cup lemon juice
1 onion, minced
2 tablespoons Worcestershire sauce
⅓ cup ketchup

Cranberry Chutney

This chutney is perfect to give as a gift at Christmas or Hanukkah. Ladle into 1-cup jars and tie with a beautiful bow.

Yields 4 cups; serving size 2 tablespoons

Calories: 29.54
Fat: 0.97 grams
Saturated Fat: 0.07 grams
Cholesterol: 0.0 mg
Sodium: 25.94 mg

¾ cup chopped walnuts, toasted
½ pound cranberries
½ cup golden raisins
1 small red onion, minced
¼ cup orange marmalade
¼ cup orange juice
1 tablespoon grated orange zest
3 tablespoons white wine vinegar
½ cup sugar
¼ cup brown sugar
½ teaspoon salt
¼ teaspoon cayenne pepper
½ teaspoon ground ginger
1 cinnamon stick
1 bay leaf

1. In a large saucepan, combine all ingredients and bring to a simmer over low heat, stirring frequently.

2. Cook until mixture thickens, about 30 minutes. Remove cinnamon stick and bay leaf. Stir chutney well, then ladle into sterilized jars. Cover tightly and store in refrigerator for up to 4 weeks.

Toasting Nuts

Toasting nuts helps bring out their flavors and keeps them crunchy even when cooked in moist mixtures. To toast nuts, spread on a cookie sheet and bake at 350°F for 8 to 10 minutes, shaking the pan occasionally, until fragrant. If you're running short on time, you can microwave the nuts on high for 1 to 2 minutes, stirring once, until fragrant. Let cool before chopping.

Freezer Jam

Making your own homemade jam is one way to preserve more exotic fruits like persimmons.

Yields 4 cups; serving size 2 tablespoons

Calories: 98.93
Fat: 0.01 grams
Saturated Fat: 0.0 grams
Cholesterol: 0.0 mg
Sodium: 5.03 mg

10 ripe persimmons
¼ cup lemon juice
1 (1.75-ounce) package powdered pectin
6 cups sugar
⅛ teaspoon salt

1. Cut off stem ends from persimmons, then force through a food mill or sieve. Measure 4 cups pulp and place in a deep saucepan. Add lemon juice and pectin and mix well with wire whisk.

2. Set pan over high heat and bring to a boil, stirring constantly. Add sugar and salt and mix well. Bring to a boil, stirring constantly. Boil without stirring for 4 minutes. Remove from the heat and stir, skimming off foam from the surface, for 5 minutes.

3. Spoon into sterilized 1-cup freezer containers and seal with sterilized lids. Let cool and freeze for up to 6 months. If the seal did not take, store in refrigerator for up to 1 month.

Freezer Jam

Freezer jam usually uses a bit less sugar than regular jam. It's easier to make because you don't have to process the jam in a boiling water bath, but make sure that you do freeze the jam. If the lids do not compress to indicate a good seal, store in the refrigerator and use promptly.

Peach Leather

Instead of buying fruit roll-ups, make your own!
This is a fun project for kids.

Calories: 192.04
Fat: 0.14 grams
Saturated Fat: 0.01 grams
Cholesterol: 0.0 mg
Sodium: 43.02 mg

3 pound peaches or apricots
1 cup sugar
⅛ teaspoon salt

1. Bring a saucepan of water to a boil. Add peaches or apricots to water for 30 seconds. Using a slotted spoon, transfer to a bowl of ice water, then slip off the skins. Slice the fruit, discarding the pits. You should have 10 cups.

2. Transfer to a large saucepan. Add salt and sugar and bring to a boil, stirring until the sugar is dissolved. Boil for 3 minutes. Pour into a blender and process until smooth. Cool to lukewarm.

3. Spray 4 baking sheets with nonstick cooking spray. Spread the purée ¼" thick on the prepared sheets, about 12" × 15" each.

4. Preheat oven to 150°F. Place the baking sheets in the oven and leave the door ajar. Let the fruit mixture dry for 12 to 16 hours, until no indentation remains when the surface is touched. Rotate and turn the baking sheets from time to time. Let leather cool completely.

5. To store, roll up the "leather" in plastic wrap. Wrap in more plastic wrap and seal tightly. The leather will keep at room temperature for a few days, in the refrigerator for 1 month, or in the freezer for 6 months.

Daikon Salsa

Daikon means "large root" in Japanese. It's another term for radish, also known as lo bok, winter radish, or Chinese radish.

In a medium bowl, combine vinegar, broth, soy sauce, sugar, and oil and beat to blend. Stir in radishes and carrots and toss to coat. Cover and chill for 3 to 4 hours before serving.

Yields 2 cups; serving size ½ cup

Calories: 29.84
Fat: 0.36 grams
Saturated Fat: 0.0 grams
Cholesterol: 0.0 mg
Sodium: 250.95 mg

2 tablespoons rice wine vinegar
1 tablespoon sake or chicken broth
1 tablespoon low-sodium soy sauce
1 teaspoon sugar
2 teaspoons sesame oil
10 daikon radishes, thinly sliced
1 carrot, shredded

Watermelon Salsa

Watermelon is an unusual ingredient in a salsa; it adds a fresh, clean sweet taste, which contrasts nicely with the peppers and lemon juice.

1. In a medium bowl, combine watermelon, orange, and strawberries and toss well to coat.

2. In a small bowl, combine remaining ingredients and stir with wire whisk to combine. Add to watermelon mixture and stir gently. Cover and refrigerate for 2 to 3 hours to blend flavors before serving. Store, covered, in refrigerator up to 1 week.

Yields 5 cups; serving size ⅓ cup

Calories: 20.70
Fat: 0.10 grams
Saturated Fat: 0.01 grams
Cholesterol: 0.0 mg
Sodium: 44.33 mg

2 cups chopped watermelon
1 orange, peeled and diced
1 cup chopped strawberries
2 tablespoons lemon juice
1 tablespoon honey
⅛ teaspoon salt
1 jalapeño pepper, minced
⅛ teaspoon cayenne pepper

Smoky Salsa

Yields 2 cups; serves 8

Calories: 23.63
Fat: 0.17 grams
Saturated Fat: 0.04 grams
Cholesterol: 0.0 mg
Sodium: 120.52 mg

8 plum tomatoes, halved
1 red onion, thickly sliced
½ bunch fresh cilantro
3 cloves garlic, minced
1 tablespoon chopped
    canned chipotle
    peppers in adobo
2 tablespoons adobo
    sauce
¼ teaspoon salt
2 tablespoons lemon juice
2 tablespoons chopped
    flat-leaf parsley

*The grill adds a fabulous smoky flavor to the tomatoes, onions,
and even the fresh cilantro used in this excellent salsa.*

1. Prepare and preheat grill. Place the tomatoes and red onion in a grill basket. Grill over medium-hot coals until partially charred, turning basket occasionally. Remove vegetables from basket as they cook. The onions will take the longest.

2. Place cilantro in grill basket and grill for 30 seconds, until it has a slightly smoky scent.

3. Chop tomatoes, red onion, and cilantro and combine with remaining ingredients in medium bowl. Cover and refrigerate for 2 to 3 hours before serving.

Chipotle Peppers in Adobo

Chipotle peppers are smoked jalapeño peppers. Unless they are dried, they are usually found packed in adobo sauce, a thick spicy red sauce. You can use the peppers, the sauce, or both in any recipe. Remove the peppers from the sauce and remove excess sauce with your fingers. Cut the peppers into small pieces and use in the recipe.

Mid-East Buttermilk Shake

This fresh, minty shake tastes rich, despite being almost fat-free. Buttermilk tastes rich, but it doesn't contain much fat.

Combine all ingredients in a blender. Blend until thick. Pour into a tall mug and garnish with more mint leaves; serve immediately.

Serves 1

Calories: 120.94
Fat: 2.09 grams
Saturated Fat: 1.07 grams
Cholesterol: 9.48 mg
Sodium: 379.96 mg

1 cup low-fat buttermilk
Pinch salt
2 tablespoons honey
¼ cup fresh mint leaves
½ cup ice cubes

Mint

Mint is an excellent herb to use when making low-fat foods. It adds a fresh and crisp aroma and taste that compensates for reduced fat. You can grow your own mint in a pot on the windowsill or in the garden. You can choose from several varieties of mint, including lemon mint and pineapple mint.

Cooked Applesauce

Applesauce is easy to make, especially when you use a slow cooker. It also freezes well.

1. Core and thinly slice apples. Combine all ingredients except lemon juice in a 4-quart slow cooker. Cover and cook on low for 8 to 10 hours or until apples are very soft.

2. Using an immersion blender or potato masher, blend or mash the apples until desired consistency. Stir in lemon juice, cool, and store, covered, in the refrigerator up to 5 days.

Yields 1 quart; serving size ½ cup

Calories: 168.27
Fat: 0.46 grams
Saturated Fat: 0.08 grams
Cholesterol: 0.0 mg
Sodium: 39.35 mg

10 large apples
1 teaspoon cinnamon
⅓ cup apple juice
¼ cup sugar
⅛ teaspoon salt
3 tablespoons lemon juice

Uncooked Applesauce

In just a few minutes, you can have a fresh applesauce that tastes like it took hours to make.

Yields 1½ cups;
serving size ¼ cup

Calories: 80.60
Fat: 0.26 grams
Saturated Fat: 0.04 grams
Cholesterol: 0.0 grams
Sodium: 10.85 mg

4 apples
⅓ cup apple juice
Pinch salt
½ teaspoon cinnamon
1 tablespoon lemon juice

1. Peel apples, core, and dice. Combine in food processor or blender with remaining ingredients. Blend or process until desired consistency. Cover and chill for 2 to 3 hours before serving.

2. Store covered in refrigerator for up to 4 days.

Apple Choices

Because this sauce is uncooked, you can use any apple that is good for eating out of hand. Choose a tart or sweet variety depending on whether you want your applesauce to be tart or sweet. Good snacking varieties include Red Delicious, Honeycrisp, Ambrosia, Braeburn, Empire, Gala, and Fuji.

Appendix A

Glossary

Al dente
An Italian phrase meaning "to the tooth" that describes pasta when it is properly cooked.

Angel food cake
A cake made of mostly egg whites, sugar, and flour. It is usually fat-free.

Applesauce
A sauce made of cooked or uncooked apples, usually flavored with sugar and spices. Used as a fat substitute in low-fat baking.

Arborio rice
A short-grain Italian rice used to make risotto. It has more starch that makes the sauce in the finished product creamy.

Aroma
A volatile, or airborne, compound which reacts with the body's olfactory system to produce a sense of smell.

Bake
To cook in an oven using dry heat. Baked goods include bread, casseroles, pastries, cookies, and cakes.

Barley
A cereal grain that is fat-free and contains a large amount of fiber and B vitamins. Barley is sold as whole grains, flakes, and flour.

Baste
To cover a food with liquid as it cooks. Basting helps preserve moisture and adds flavor.

Braise
To cook with wet heat. Braised food is usually browned, then cooked in a closed environment with water or other liquid.

Brown

In food, a reaction to heat that causes sugar and protein molecules to combine, creating a brown color on the surface.

Butter

A by-product of milk, butter is concentrated milk fat produced by agitating heavy cream. It is used in cooking and baking.

Cake flour

Flour made of low-protein wheat. The flour has a higher percentage of starch and less gluten, which results in a finer crumb and more tender texture.

Carbohydrate

One of the three main compounds which make up food, carbohydrates are chains of simple sugars. One gram of carbohydrates provides 4 calories.

Cheese

A dairy food made by coagulating milk using acids and enzymes. Cheese can be made from the milk of cows, sheep, and goats.

Chutney

A thick, low-fat sauce, usually sweet, made from fruits or vegetables and spices. Chutney is an accompaniment to Indian foods.

Cocoa

Cocoa is a powder made from the dried seed of the cacao tree. It is unsweetened and low in fat; used in cooking and baking.

Condensed milk

Milk which has been cooked to reduce the water content. Usually sweetened with sugar and sold as sweetened condensed milk.

Condiment

A sauce or highly flavored substance used to add flavor, usually after food is cooked. Condiments include pickles, mustard, and ketchup.

Cooking spray

A spray made of oils that is used to grease pans and sauté food with very little fat. Also can be combined with flour for baking purposes.

Cream of tartar

Potassium hydrogen tartrate is an acid salt used to stabilize egg white foams and, when paired with baking soda, creates baking powder.

Dijon mustard

A spicy mustard made from a French recipe. Instead of the typical vinegar, a substance called verjuice, made from unripe grapes, is used.

Dredge

To coat in flour, cornmeal, or another dry substance. Meats are usually dredged in flour before being sautéed.

Emulsify

To combine a fat and a liquid, two substances which repel each other. Emulsification can be produced by adding energy to the mixture, or ingredients, called emulsifiers, can be used.

En papillote

To cook wrapped in paper or foil. Foods cooked en papillote are more moist. Used in cooking delicate foods.

Evaporated milk

Milk that has had approximately 60 percent of its water removed. Usually found canned, can be whole, low-fat, or nonfat.

Fat

Compounds made of fatty acids and glycerol which are insoluble in water. Fats are necessary for life, and are found in many foods. One gram of fat provides 9 calories.

Fruit

The part of a plant which produces seeds. Fruits are usually edible, and usually sweet.

Gelatin

A substance used to thicken juices and other liquids, made from animals' connective tissue.

Glaze
A thin coating used to add flavor and improve appearance of foods. Glazes can be savory or sweet.

Grill
A dry-heat method of cooking, over charcoal or a strong heat source. Grilling cooks food quickly and adds flavor by caramelization.

Herbs
Deciduous plants, whether annual or perennial, that have edible leaves and provide flavor. Herbs include cilantro, basil, oregano, chives, and parsley.

Honey
A sweet, thick fluid produced by honeybees. Bees make the honey by using nectar from flowers they collect with their tongue.

Infuse
To permeate one substance with another. Extracts are made by infusing alcohol with aromatic substances from beans and berries.

Jalapeño
A medium-sized chili pepper that has moderate heat. Used to add spicy heat to foods.

Julienne
To cut food into small, thin strips, usually about ⅛-inch thick or less.

Knead
To manipulate a dough or other substance by pressing and pulling it with your hands.

Leavening
Substances, including baking powder and yeast, that add carbon dioxide to products, making them rise and giving them a fine texture.

Legumes
The dried fruit of plants, legumes develop in a pod. They are usually cooked before serving, and include black-eyed peas, chickpeas, kidney beans, and black beans.

Low-fat

A food which is low in fat, defined as 30 percent total calories from fat.

Margarine

A spread similar to butter, made from vegetable oils. Used in baking and cooking. Used to be full of trans fat, but new formulations have less.

Mayonnaise

An emulsification of egg yolks and vegetable oil. Lower-fat varieties, with gums and stabilizers added, are available.

Meat thermometer

A thermometer that registers the internal temperature of meat when it's cooked.

Monounsaturated fat

A fatty acid that contains one double bond between two carbons. Considered the healthiest of fats. This fat is liquid at room temperature, but usually becomes solid at refrigerator temperatures.

Mustard

A condiment made by combining ground mustard seeds with vinegar, wine, or verjuice. Mustards can be smooth or coarse, depending on the grind of the seeds.

Neufchatel cheese

Technically, a soft cheese from France with an edible rind. Sometimes, low-fat cream cheese is marketed as Neufchatel in the United States.

Nonfat

Free of fat. Either naturally nonfat, like fruits or water, or made nonfat by the removal of fat.

Olive oil

Oil high in monounsaturated fat, made by pressing olives. Olive oil comes in several types, the finest being cold-pressed extra-virgin.

Pan fry

To fry in a small amount of fat in a hot pan or skillet.

Pepper

The fruit of a flowering vine, dried and used to add spice to foods. Pepper can be black, red, white, green, and pink. Or the firm-fleshed fruits of the pepper plant. Peppers including habanero, jalapeño, bell pepper, and Scotch bonnet.

Pita bread

A low-fat bread made by baking at a very high oven temperature so the carbon dioxide explodes, creating a thin-shelled hollow. Pita breads are usually cut in half and filled with sandwich fillings.

Polyunsaturated fat

A fat that has two or more double bonds between four or more carbon molecules. The fat is liquid at room temperature.

Protein

One of the three compounds that make up life, proteins are made from chains of amino acids. One gram of protein provides 4 calories.

Reduced fat

Used as a descriptor on food labels; refers to a product which has 25 percent less fat than the original version.

Risotto

A dish made by cooking medium or short-grain rice with liquid or broths, stirring to release the starch from the rice.

Roast

A dry-heat cooking method; food is roasted in the oven at fairly high temperatures. Also refers to a cut of meat which has been roasted.

Roux

A combination of flour and fat, cooked until the starch granules in the flour swell. Used as the base for thickening sauces and soups.

Salt

Sodium chloride, a mineral compound added to foods to help enhance flavors. Also one category of taste bud.

Saturated fat

A fat with no double bonds between carbon molecules. All the carbon molecules are attached to each other and to hydrogen molecules. This fat is solid at room temperature.

Sauté

To cook food for a short amount of time over fairly high heat, stirring so the food cooks evenly.

Spices

Dried fruits, seeds, bark, or roots of plants that are used to season food. Spices include cinnamon, ginger, nutmeg, cardamom, and anise.

Taste

The ability to respond to chemicals in food, through the tongue and nose. There are five tastes the tongue can detect, including sweet, salty, bitter, sour, and umami. Taste is sensed in the brain.

Taste bud

Small papillae, or raised bumps, found on the tongue which contain receptors for the five tastes: sour, salty, sweet, bitter, and umami.

Umami

Salts of glutamic acid, umami is one of the five tastes on the tongue. Described as a meaty taste, this compound is found in MSG, mushrooms, and soy.

Unsaturated fat

A fat which has one or more double bonds between the carbon molecules of the fatty acid. Unsaturated fats can be monounsaturated or polyunsaturated.

Vegetable

A usually savory edible part of a plant. Vegetables do not contain seeds.

Yogurt

A dairy product made by fermenting milk. Bacterial cultures are added to fresh milk. These bacteria then transform lactose, or milk sugar, to lactic acid, thickening the product.

Appendix B
Menus

Dinner for the Boss
Quick Crab Cakes
Avocado Citrus Salad
Steak Stroganoff
Curried Cauliflower
Strawberry Angel Cake

Picnic
Tortilla Chips
Peach Pita Sandwiches
Chili Pepper Potato Salad
Buttermilk Pops

Lunchbox Special
Chicken Pocket Sandwiches
Seafood Pasta Salad
Savory Tomato Soup
Peanut Butter Chocolate Bars

Family Dinner
Bean and Corn Tartlets
Caesar Salad
Chimichangas
Dilled Green Beans
Lemon Meringue Pie

Birthday Dinner
Garlic Red Pepper Dip
Peach Spinach Salad
Apricot Pork Pinwheels
Stuffed Baked Potatoes
Peachy Angel Cake

Summer Cookout
Oven-Baked Fries
Lean, Juicy Burgers
California Turkey Burgers
Summer Potato Salad
Strawberry Pie

Holiday Dinner
Stuffed Parmesan Mushrooms
Surf and Turf Pasta
Peach Spinach Salad
Glazed Baby Carrots
Lemon Cheesecake

Holiday Breakfast
Baked Apple Pancake
Cheese Egg Casserole
Spicy Cold Pears

Lunch on the Porch
Thai Beef Salad
Chilled Cucumber Mint Soup
Cranberry Sherbet

Breakfast on the Run
Apple Date Bread
Blueberry Muffins
Apple Gemelli Salad

Birthday Dinner
Pumpkin Cheese Chowder
Pineapple Pear Mold
Crab-Stuffed Chicken
Wonderful Risotto
Coriander Carrots
Angel Food Cake

Appendix C
Resources

Books

Alexander, Devin and Karen Kaplan, *The Biggest Loser Cookbook.* (New York: Rodale Books, 2006).
This book is based on recipes and diet information from the TV show The Biggest Loser. Good recipes, lots of photographs, and weight loss information.

American Heart Association, *American Heart Association Low-Fat, Low-Cholesterol Cookbook, 3rd Edition.* (New York: Clarkson Potter, 2005).
The American Heart Association created this book for people with high cholesterol who must eat a low-fat diet. The book contains flavorful recipes and lots of tips.

Betty Crocker Editors, *Betty Crocker's Low-Fat, Low-Cholesterol Cooking Today*, 3rd Edition. (New York: John Wiley & Sons, 2000).
Recipes are based on the Food Guide Pyramid, focusing on reducing fat without sacrificing flavor. Nutrition information includes carbs, fiber, protein, and dietary exchanges.

Lowery, Deborah Garrison and Allison Chappell Cain, *Cooking Light Low-Fat, Low-Calorie Quick & Easy Cookbook.* (Birmingham, AL: Oxmoor House, 1998).
The home economists at *Cooking Light* magazine have collected delicious, easy to make recipes and lots of information about a low-fat diet in this excellent cookbook.

Websites

About.com Low Fat Cooking
http://lowfatcooking.about.com
This site focuses on good-tasting, low-fat recipes, with lots of tips about cutting fat and health information.

Low Fat Lifestyle.com

www.lowfatlifestyle.com

This site has lots of low-fat, healthy recipes and information. It stresses an overall healthy lifestyle, including exercise. There are also tips on how to eat out at restaurants and fast food places.

Delicious Decisions

www.deliciousdecisions.org

The American Heart Association runs this Web site, which offers recipes and guides to eating out and achieving a healthy lifestyle.

Food Fit

www.foodfit.com

Sign up for newsletters and join this site to learn about healthy lifestyles and food choices, including information about healthy food choices.

Magazines and Newsletters

Cooking Light

This is an excellent magazine with delicious recipes and sensible advice.

Prevention

This general health magazine stresses prevention, a good diet, and exercise as the road to good health.

Eating Well

This magazine offers lots of delicious recipes concentrating on lifestyle, healthy fats, and good taste.

Index

Note: Page references in **bold** indicate detailed lists of category recipes.

Alcohol, 13, 17, 119
Alfredo Sauce, Light, 281
Almonds, 114
Angel Food Cakes, 254–55, 257
Angry Ziti, 179
Antioxidants, 215
Appetizers, **19–30**
Apple Bread Pudding, 42
Apples
    about: choosing, 294; squash and, 130
    Apple Bread Pudding, 42
    Apple Date Bread, 32
    Apple Gemelli Salad, 189
    Applesauce Pound Cake, 267
    Apple Squash Soup, 130
    Baked Apple Pancake, 41
    Cooked Applesauce, 293
    Pear and Apple Sauce, 282
    Sweet Potato Apple Bake, 230
    Sweet Potato Apple Purée, 233
    Uncooked Applesauce, 293
Apricots
    about: dried, 69
    Apricot Green Salad, 101
    Apricot Pork Pinwheels, 69
    Southwestern Apricot Salsa, 275
Asparagus, Lemon, and Carrots, 234
Autumn Soup, 219
Avocados
    about: preparing, 149
    Avocado-Citrus Salad, 202

Baked desserts, **253–68**
Baked goods, 16
Barley, 132
BBQ Sauce, 287
Beans. See also Pasta and bean salads
    about: black beans, 158; cooking, 84; preparing, 217; tomatoes and, 125
    Bean and Corn Tartlets, 27
    Black Bean and Rice Salad, 157

Black Bean Dip, 20
Black Bean Stew, 215
Black Bean Veggie Dip, 21
Chili Bean Dip, 22
Cuban Black Beans and Rice, 158
Curried Beans and Rice Salad, 159
Four Bean Salad, 205
Hearty Bean Stew, 57
Italian Bean Soup, 125
Lima Bean Casserole, 136
Slow-Cooker Chili Tortilla Bake, 129
Soulful Black-Eyed Peas, 138
Southwest Ham Succotash, 74
Spicy Pink Bean Stew, 217
Bean sprouts, 109
Beef, **45–64**
    about: grilling hamburgers, 62; grinding, and controlling fat, 47; ground beef, 47, 64; stir-frying, 55, 60
    Beef and Snow Peas, 60
    Beef and Veggie Pitas, 145
    Beef Burgundy, 54
    Beef Stew, 53
    Caribbean Beef, 51
    Chimichangas, 63
    Curried Beef Stir-Fry, 61
    Ginger Peach Steak, 58
    Hearth Meat Loaf, 47
    Hearty Bean Stew, 57
    Lean, Juicy Burgers, 62
    Marinated Steak Kebabs, 58
    Orange Beef and Broccoli Stir-Fry, 56
    Pastitsio, 48
    Roast Beef Pitas, 141
    Savory Pot Roast, 50
    Spicy Beef and Cabbage, 52
    Spicy Chinese Beef, 55
    Steak Stroganoff, 49
    Steak Subs, 147
    Surf and Turf Pasta, 59
    Texan Rice, 64
    Thai Beef Salad, 46
Berry Sauce, 251

Black beans. See Beans; Pasta and bean salads
Black-eyed peas, 138
Blueberry "Ice Cream," 249
Blueberry Muffins, 44
Borscht, Creamy, 220
Bread crumbs, making, 115
Bread pudding, 42
Breads, **31–44**
Brining, 17
Broccoli
    Broccoli-Leek Soup, 212
    Broccoli Pasta Toss, 176
    Orange Beef and Broccoli Stir-Fry, 56
Burgers, 62, 97, 104
Busy Day Salad, 205
Buttermilk
    about: in baking, 35
    Buttermilk Dressing, 272
    Buttermilk Fruit Sherbet, 238
    Buttermilk Mashed Potatoes, 236
    Buttermilk Pops, 246
    Herbed Buttermilk Quick Bread, 35
    Mid-East Buttermilk Shake, 293

Cabbage, 208. See also Coleslaws
Caesar Salad, 198
Cajun Chicken Strips, 80
Cakes and baked desserts, **253–68**
California Black Bean Salad, 184
California French Bread Pizza, 151
California Rice, 166
California Salsa, 277
California Vegetable Pizza, 144
Caramelization, 13
Caribbean Beef, 51
Carrots
    about: shredded, 148
    Coriander Carrots, 235
    Glazed Baby Carrots, 235
    Lemon Asparagus and Carrots, 234
Cashews, 162
Cauliflower
    about, 226
    Cauliflower Purée, 226
    Curried Cauliflower, 230

Celery, Stuffed, 27
Cheese
   about: Romano, 151
   Cheese Coins, 38
   Cheese Egg Casserole, 131
   Cheesy Chicken Rolls, 91
   Light Alfredo Sauce, 281
   Low-Fat Cheese Sauce, 280
   Welsh Rarebit, 137
Cheesecakes, 260
Cherries
   Sherry Custard with Spiced
      Cherries, 268
   Spiced Cherry Sauce, 252
Chicken, **18**–92
   about: breasts and thighs, 81;
      coating, 89; grilling, 92;
      pounding, 91
   Broiled Spicy Chicken in Yogurt, 82
   Cajun Chicken Strips, 80
   Cheesy Chicken Rolls, 91
   Chicken and Dumpling Stew, 223
   Chicken Breasts with Curried
      Stuffing, 90
   Chicken in Buttermilk, 89
   Chicken Lime Soup, 224
   Chicken Marsala, 85
   Chicken Pasta Salad, 186
   Chicken Pizza, 149
   Chicken Pocket Sandwiches, 141
   Chicken Salad Plate, 84
   Crab-Stuffed Chicken, 88
   Curried Chicken Mushroom Soup,
      213
   Easy BBQ Chicken, 79
   Fruity Chicken Salad, 78
   Garlicky Grilled Chicken, 92
   Grilled Tarragon Chicken Sandwich,
      143
   Nutty Chicken Fingers, 79
   Poached Chicken, 85
   Quick Chicken Parmesan, 83
   Sesame Teriyaki Chicken, 87
   Skillet Chicken and Rice, 82
   Very Lemon Chicken, 86
   Yogurt Chicken Paprika, 81
Chili Bean Dip, 22
Chili Pepper Potato Salad, 206

Chilled desserts, puddings, and
   sorbets, **237**–52
Chimichangas, 63
Chinese Rice Salad, 156
Chocolate
   Chocolate "Ice Cream," 247
   Peanut Butter Chocolate Bars, 264
   Sweet Cocoa Sauce, 248
Chunky Pasta Sauce, 170
Chutneys, 97, 284, 288
Citrus, 13, 86
Citrus Rice Salad, 154
Citrus Shrimp and Scallops, 113
Coffee
   about: as flavoring, 279
   Coffee Almond Float, 242
Coleslaws, 199, 201, 208
Condiments and extras, 11, **283**–94
Cooking tricks and tips, 15–18
Corn
   about: making popcorn, 285
   Bacon Corn Chowder, 216
   Bean and Corn Tartlets, 27
   Candy Corn, 285
   John Barleycorn Casserole, 132
   Light Corn Chowder, 214
   Spicy Corn Bread, 38
Corn syrup, 240
Crab-Stuffed Chicken, 88
Crab Surprise, 118
Cranberry Chutney, 288
Cranberry Sherbet, 240
Cream of Mushroom Soup, 133
Creamy Mustard Dip, 21
Creamy Tomato Sauce, 171
Crostini, 26
Cuban Black Beans and Rice, 158
Cucumbers
   about: English cucumbers, 186
   Chilled Cucumber Mint Soup, 212
Curry
   about: cooking with, 111; powder,
      164, 213
   Curried Beans and Rice Salad, 159
   Curried Beef Stir-Fry, 61
   Curried Cauliflower, 230
   Curried Chicken Mushroom Soup,
      213
   Curried Cod with Apricots, 119

Curried Pork Chops, 66
Curried Shrimp and Vegetables, 111
Curried Turkey Pockets, 142
Curried Turkey Strawberry Salad, 97

Daikon Salsa, 291
Deli meals, 141
Desserts (baked), **253**–68
Desserts (chilled, sorbets, and
   puddings), **237**–52
Dilled Green Beans, 232
Dips. *See* Appetizers
Doubling recipes, 83
Dressings. *See* Sauces and dressings
Dumplings, 223

Egg white foams, 263
Egg whites, pasteurized, 244
En papillote, 122

Fat
   calories and, 4, 8
   cooking tricks and tips, 15–18
   definition and functions, 2
   high-fat foods, 14–15
   high-flavor substitutes, 9–13, 33
   low-fat foods, 14
   moderate intake of, 4–6
   recent studies, 4–5
   saturated and unsaturated, 3
   too low or too high, 5–6
   types of, 2–3
Fiesta Turkey, 98
Five-spice powder, 199
Flavor
   color and, 7
   cooking tricks and tips, 15–18
   factors impacting, 6–9
   fats carrying, 6
   high-flavor fat substitutes, 9–13
   smell and, 7
   taste and, 8–9
   temperature and, 7–8
   texture and, 9
Freezer Jam, 289
French Bread Pizza, 148
French bread tins, 37
Fruit. *See also specific fruits*

about: baked, 265; canned, 275; fruit cocktail, 197; purées as substitutes, 15, 33
Buttermilk Fruit Sherbet, 238
Fruit Smoothie, 284
Fruity Chicken Salad, 78
Fruity Coleslaw, 201

Garden Pasta, 180
Garlic
   about: roasting, 24
   Garlic Kasha with Pork, 74
   Garlicky Grilled Chicken, 92
   Garlic Red Pepper Dip, 24
   Roasted Garlic, 23
Garlic Red Pepper Dip, 24
Gazpacho Salad, 207
Gelatin, about, 241, 257
Ginger Peach Steak, 58
Glorified Brown Rice, 197
Glossary, 295–301
Graham Cracker Crust, 258
Grapes, 193
Gravy, Country, Low-Fat, 279
Greek Lamb Pizza, 147
Green beans
   about, 231
   Dilled Green Beans, 232
   Green Beans with Garlic, 231
   Potato Green Bean Salad, 196
Green Salsa, 274
Grilled Fish and Spinach Packets, 122
Grilled Tarragon Chicken Sandwich, 143
Grilled Vegetable Sandwich, 140

Hearts of Palm Salad, 200
Heat, 11, 98
Herbed Buttermilk Quick Bread, 35
Herbed Pasta Salad, 190
Herbed Rice Pilaf, 154
Herbs, 10, 271
High-flavor fat substitutes, 9–13
Hoisin Dressing, 273
Horseradish Salad Dressing, 272

Ice cream makers, 249
"Ice creams," 247, 249
Indian Rice, 164
Indian Turkey Pilaf, 99

Italian Bean Soup, 125
Italian Pistachio Pasta, 178
Italian Salad Dressing, Low-Fat, 273
Italian Vegetable Bake, 126

Jambalaya, 110
John Barleycorn Casserole, 132

Lamb Pizza, Greek, 147
Lemons
   about: lemon zest, 86
   Lemon Asparagus and Carrots, 234
   Lemon Cheesecake, 260
   Lemon Meringue Pie, 261
   Lemon Sesame Tuna, 28
   Lemon Tarragon Sole, 120
   Light Lemon Pudding, 246
   Very Lemon Chicken, 86
Lentils
   Lentil Stew, 128
   Mediterranean Lentil Bean Salad, 189
Lima Bean Casserole, 136
Limes
   about, 278
   Chicken Lime Soup, 224
   Lime Turkey Tenderloin, 100
   Margarita Pie, 259
   Sweet Potato Sticks with Lime, 29
   Tangy Lime Pie, 241

Macaroni and Bean Salad, 190
Macaroni and Cheese, 181
Manhattan Deli Salad, 206
Margarita Pie, 259
Marinades and rubs, 17
Marinara Sauce, 171
Marmalade, 276
Meat, as flavor, 16
Mediterranean Lentil Bean Salad, 189
Melons, ripening, 25
Menus, 302
Microwave cooking, 117
Microwave Sole Florentine, 117
Milk, 17–18
Mozzarella Basil Crostini, 26
Muffins, 43–44
Mushrooms
   about: cleaning, 133; shitake, 167
   Baked Mushroom Dip with Spinach, 24

Cream of Mushroom Soup, 133
Curried Chicken Mushroom Soup, 213
Portobello Sandwiches, 134
Stuffed Parmesan Mushrooms, 30
Mussels, 107
Mustard Sauce, Creamy, 280

Nuts, toasting, 288
Nutty Chicken Fingers, 79

Oat Bran French Bread, 37
Onions
   about: taming, 146
   Onion Soup, 211
   Scallion Tabbouleh, 229
Orange Beef and Broccoli Stir-Fry, 56
Orange Pilaf, 168
Orange Sherbet, 239
Orzo Salad, 187

Pad Thai, 109
Paella, 108
Pasta, 72, 169–82
   about: baking, 72; cooking, 174
   Angry Ziti, 179
   Broccoli Pasta Toss, 176
   Chunky Pasta Sauce, 170
   Creamy Tomato Sauce, 171
   Fusilli and Ricotta, 177
   Garden Pasta, 180
   Italian Pistachio Pasta, 178
   Macaroni and Cheese, 181
   Marinara Sauce, 171
   Pasta Shells with Zucchini, 177
   Pasta with Summer Squash, 182
   Salmon with Fettuccine, 121
   Seafood Linguine Fra Diavolo, 173
   Shells with Scallops, 172
   Surf and Turf Pasta, 59
   Tuna Tomato Sauce, 175
   Vermicelli with Tuna and Anchovies, 174
Pasta and bean salads, **183**–94
Pastitsio, 48
Peaches
   about: peeling, 192
   Fresh Peach Pie, 262
   Peach Leather, 290
   Peach Pita Sandwiches, 144

Peach Sorbet, 243
Peach Spinach Salad, 204
Peachy Angel Cake, 257
Summer Peach Pasta Salad, 192
Tangy Peach Salsa, 276
Peanut Butter Chocolate Bars, 264
Pears
about: puréed as fat substitutes, 33
Baked Pears, 265
Pear and Apple Sauce, 282
Pears in Orange Sauce, 250
Pear Tea Bread, 33
Pineapple Pear Mold, 207
Spicy Cold Pears, 245
Peppers
about: bell peppers, 194; hot, 11, 98
Garlic Red Pepper Dip, 24
Tricolor Pepper Pasta Salad, 194
Pesto, 172, 187, 286
Pesto Potatoes, 226
Phyllo shells, 27
Pies, **253**, 258–63
Pineapple
Pineapple Pear Mold, 207
Pineapple Rice, 162
Pineapple Sherbet, 239
Pistachios, 178
Italian Pistachio Pasta, 178
Pistachio Turkey Salad, 103
White Bean Pistachio Salad, 191
Pita breads, 142
Pizza, **139**
crust/dough recipes, 39, 40
recipes, 144, 147–52
sauce, 150
Pork, **65**–76
about: ham hocks, 67
Apricot Pork Pinwheels, 69
Bacon Corn Chowder, 216
Baked Ziti, 72
Curried Pork Chops, 66
Garlic Kasha with Pork, 74
Peach Pita Sandwiches, 144
Pork and Bean Salad, 75
Pork and Garbanzo Bean Curry, 75
Pork and Veggie Casseroles, 76
Pork Chops Dijon, 70
Pork Corn Dogs, 73
Pork Medallions, 68

Raspberry Pork Chops, 70
Southwest Ham Succotash, 74
Split Pea Soup, 67
Summer Potato Salad, 198
Sweet and Sour Pork, 71
Tenderloin in BBQ Sauce, 66
Portobello Sandwiches, 134
Potatoes
about: mashing, 228; roasting, 236;
types of, 135
Buttermilk Mashed Potatoes, 236
Chili Pepper Potato Salad, 206
Chilled Potato Soup, 216
Oven-Baked Fries, 25
Pesto Potatoes, 226
Potato Cheese Casserole, 135
Potato Corn Chowder, 127
Potato Garbanzo Stew, 220
Potato Green Bean Salad, 196
Potato Vegetable Soup, 131
Roasted Potatoes with Rosemary, 236
Stuffed Baked Potatoes, 228
Tomato Potatoes, 227
Pound cakes, 267
Puddings, chilled desserts, and
sorbets, **237**–52, 258
Pumpkin
Low-Fat Pumpkin Pie, 259
Pumpkin Cheese Chowder, 218
Pumpkin Nut Bread, 36
Pumpkin Pudding, 242
Pumpkin Nut Bread, 36
Purées, as fat substitutes, 15, 33

Quinces, 282

Raspberry Pork Chops, 70
Recipes, about, 18
Recipes, doubling, 83
Resources, 303–4
Rhubarb Muffins, 43
Rice, **153**–68
about: basmati rice, 156; brown rice,
155; cooking, 160; wild rice, 165
Black Bean and Rice Salad, 157
California Rice, 166
Chinese Rice Salad, 156
Citrus Rice Salad, 154
Cuban Black Beans and Rice, 158

Curried Beans and Rice Salad, 159
Glorified Brown Rice, 197
Herbed Rice Pilaf, 154
Indian Rice, 164
Indian Turkey Pilaf, 99
Orange Pilaf, 168
Pineapple Rice, 162
Rice with Black Beans and Ginger, 160
Risotto with Vegetables, 163
Risotto with Winter Squash, 161
Seafood Rice, 155
Skillet Chicken and Rice, 82
Texan Rice, 64
Vegetable Fried Rice, 163
Wild Rice Casserole, 167
Wild Rice Pilaf, 165
Wonderful Risotto, 137
Rosie's Pizza Dough, 39
Rosie's Pizza Sauce, 150

Salad dressings, **269**–73
Salads. *See* Chicken; Pasta and bean
Salads; Rice; Side salads; Turkey
Salmon with Fettuccine, 121
Salsas, 25, **269**, 274–78, 292
Sandwiches, **139**–44, 145–47
Sauces and dressings, **269**–82, 287
about: freezing sauces, 252
dessert sauces, 248, 250–52
pasta sauces, 170–71, 175
Scallion Tabbouleh, 229
Scallop and Pepper Stir-Fry, 106
Seafood
about: cleaning shrimp, 112;
doneness of, 173; fresh mussels,
107; stretching, 116; tuna, 175
Baked Scrod, 118
Baked Sole Amandine, 114
Baked Sole with Bread Crumbs, 115
Cioppino, 210
Citrus Shrimp and Scallops, 113
Crab-Stuffed Chicken, 88
Crab Surprise, 118
Curried Cod with Apricots, 119
Curried Shrimp and Vegetables, 111
French Country Mussels, 107
Grilled Fish and Spinach Packets, 122
Herbed Clam Dip, 23
Jambalaya, 110

Lemon Sesame Tuna, 28
Lemon Tarragon Sole, 120
Louisiana Seafood, 106
Microwave Sole Florentine, 117
Pad Thai, 109
Paella, 108
Poached Cod with Spicy Buttermilk
    Sauce, 120
Quick Crab Cakes, 26
Salmon Tortellini Toss, 188
Salmon with Fettuccine, 121
Scallop and Pepper Stir-Fry, 106
Seafood Pasta Salad, 185
Seafood Rice, 155
Shells with Scallops, 172
Shrimp Scampi, 112
Stuffed Fillet of Sole, 116
Surf and Turf Pasta, 59
Tuna Chowder, 221
Tuna Tomato Sauce, 175
Vermicelli with Tuna and
    Anchovies, 174
Seeds, toasting, 87, 176
Sesame Noodles, Cold, 203
Sesame Teriyaki Chicken, 87
Shells with Scallops, 172
Sherbets/sorbets, chilled desserts, and
    puddings, **237**–52
Sherry Custard with Spiced Cherries, 268
Shrimp. *See* Seafood
Side dishes, **225**–35
Side salads, **195**–208
Slow-Cooker Chili Tortilla Bake, 129
Slow cookers, 18, 53
Smokiness, 13
Smoothies, 284
Snow Pea Penne Salad, 188
Sorbets, chilled desserts, and
    puddings, **237**–52
Soups and stews, 53, 57, 67, **209**–24
    about: chowders, 127
    dessert, 238
    vegetarian, 124, 125, 128, 130, 131, 133
Sour Cream, Mock, 286
Spice Cake, 266
Spices, 12. *See also* Heat; *specific spices*
Spicy Beef and Cabbage, 52
Spicy Chinese Beef, 55
Spicy Turkey Enchiladas, 96

Spinach
    Baked Mushroom Dip with Spinach, 24
    Low-Fat Spinach Pesto, 286
    Peach Spinach Salad, 204
    Stuffed Triangles, 28
Split Pea Soup, 67
Squash, 161
    about: apples and, 130; preparing, 219
    Autumn Soup, 219
    Baked Acorn Squash, 232
    Pasta Shells with Zucchini, 177
    Pasta with Summer Squash, 182
Steak. *See* Beef
Stir-frying, 55, 60
Stocks, 17
Stone Fruit Salsa, 276
Strawberries
    Berry Sauce, 251
    Strawberry Angel Cake, 255
    Strawberry Pie, 263
    Strawberry Sorbet, 244
    Strawberry Soup, 238
Surf and Turf Pasta, 59
Sweet and Sour Pork, 71
Sweet and Sour Turkey Burgers, 104
Sweet potatoes
    about: yams vs., 29
    Orange Sweet Potatoes, 233
    Sweet Potato Apple Bake, 230
    Sweet Potato Apple Purée, 233
    Sweet Potato Pudding, 258
    Sweet Potato Sticks with Lime, 29
    Sweet Potato Tart, 256

Taco shells, 103
Tenderloin in BBQ Sauce, 66
Texan Rice, 64
Thai Beef Salad, 46
Toasting seeds and nuts, 87, 176, 288
Tomatoes
    about: beans and, 125; peeling, 180;
        tomato paste, 49
    pasta sauces, 170–71, 175
    sauces. *See* Sauces and dressings
    Savory Tomato Soup, 221
Top Hat Pizza, 152
Tortilla Chips, 20
Tricolor Pepper Pasta Salad, 194
Tropical Salsa Bruschetta, 25

Tuna. *See* Seafood
Turkey, **93**–104
    about: ground turkey, 104
    California Turkey Burgers, 97
    Curried Turkey Pockets, 142
    Curried Turkey Strawberry Salad, 97
    Fiesta Turkey, 98
    Indian Turkey Pilaf, 99
    Lime Turkey Tenderloin, 100
    Mai Fun Turkey Salad, 95
    Pistachio Turkey Salad, 103
    Spicy Turkey Enchiladas, 96
    Sweet and Sour Turkey Burgers, 104
    Turkey Jerusalem, 101
    Turkey Shish Kebabs, 95
    Turkey Tetrazzini, 102
    Turkey with Couscous, 100
    Warm Chinese Turkey Salad, 94

Vanilla Sauce, Sweet, 247
Vegetables. *See also specific vegetables*
    about: steaming, 234
    Beef and Veggie Pitas, 145
    California Vegetable Pizza, 144
    Creamy Vegetable Soup, 222
    Garden Pasta, 180
    Grilled Vegetable Sandwich, 140
    Top Hat Pizza, 152
    Vegetable Fried Rice, 163
Vegetarian entrees, **123**–38, 161, 205, 227
Vinegars, 11–12

Waldorf Pasta Salad, 193
Watermelon Salsa, 291
Welsh Rarebit, 137
Whole Grain Bread, 34
Whole wheat pastry flour, 44
Wild rice. *See* Rice
Wine. *See* Alcohol
Wintertime Chili, 124

Year in Provence Sandwiches, 146
Yogurt
    about: cooking with, 171
    Broiled Spicy Chicken in Yogurt, 82
    Frozen Yogurt with Berry Sauce, 251
    Herbed Yogurt Dressing, 271
    Yogurt Cheese, 22
    Yogurt Chicken Paprika, 81

THE EVERYTHING SERIES!

BUSINESS & PERSONAL FINANCE

Everything® Accounting Book
Everything® Budgeting Book, 2nd Ed.
Everything® Business Planning Book
Everything® Coaching and Mentoring Book, 2nd Ed.
Everything® Fundraising Book
Everything® Get Out of Debt Book
Everything® Grant Writing Book, 2nd Ed.
Everything® Guide to Buying Foreclosures
Everything® Guide to Fundraising, $15.95
Everything® Guide to Mortgages
Everything® Guide to Personal Finance for Single Mothers
Everything® Home-Based Business Book, 2nd Ed.
Everything® Homebuying Book, 3rd Ed., $15.95
Everything® Homeselling Book, 2nd Ed.
Everything® Human Resource Management Book
Everything® Improve Your Credit Book
Everything® Investing Book, 2nd Ed.
Everything® Landlording Book
Everything® Leadership Book, 2nd Ed.
Everything® Managing People Book, 2nd Ed.
Everything® Negotiating Book
Everything® Online Auctions Book
Everything® Online Business Book
Everything® Personal Finance Book
Everything® Personal Finance in Your 20s & 30s Book, 2nd Ed.
Everything® Personal Finance in Your 40s & 50s Book, $15.95
Everything® Project Management Book, 2nd Ed.
Everything® Real Estate Investing Book
Everything® Retirement Planning Book
Everything® Robert's Rules Book, $7.95
Everything® Selling Book
Everything® Start Your Own Business Book, 2nd Ed.
Everything® Wills & Estate Planning Book

COOKING

Everything® Barbecue Cookbook
Everything® Bartender's Book, 2nd Ed., $9.95
Everything® Calorie Counting Cookbook
Everything® Cheese Book
Everything® Chinese Cookbook
Everything® Classic Recipes Book
Everything® Cocktail Parties & Drinks Book
Everything® College Cookbook
Everything® Cooking for Baby and Toddler Book
Everything® Diabetes Cookbook
Everything® Easy Gourmet Cookbook
Everything® Fondue Cookbook
Everything® Food Allergy Cookbook, $15.95
Everything® Fondue Party Book
Everything® Gluten-Free Cookbook
Everything® Glycemic Index Cookbook
Everything® Grilling Cookbook
Everything® Healthy Cooking for Parties Book, $15.95
Everything® Holiday Cookbook
Everything® Indian Cookbook
Everything® Lactose-Free Cookbook
Everything® Low-Cholesterol Cookbook

Everything® Low-Fat High-Flavor Cookbook, 2nd Ed., $15.95
Everything® Low-Salt Cookbook
Everything® Meals for a Month Cookbook
Everything® Meals on a Budget Cookbook
Everything® Mediterranean Cookbook
Everything® Mexican Cookbook
Everything® No Trans Fat Cookbook
Everything® One-Pot Cookbook, 2nd Ed., $15.95
Everything® Organic Cooking for Baby & Toddler Book, $15.95
Everything® Pizza Cookbook
Everything® Quick Meals Cookbook, 2nd Ed., $15.95
Everything® Slow Cooker Cookbook
Everything® Slow Cooking for a Crowd Cookbook
Everything® Soup Cookbook
Everything® Stir-Fry Cookbook
Everything® Sugar-Free Cookbook
Everything® Tapas and Small Plates Cookbook
Everything® Tex-Mex Cookbook
Everything® Thai Cookbook
Everything® Vegetarian Cookbook
Everything® Whole-Grain, High-Fiber Cookbook
Everything® Wild Game Cookbook
Everything® Wine Book, 2nd Ed.

GAMES

Everything® 15-Minute Sudoku Book, $9.95
Everything® 30-Minute Sudoku Book, $9.95
Everything® Bible Crosswords Book, $9.95
Everything® Blackjack Strategy Book
Everything® Brain Strain Book, $9.95
Everything® Bridge Book
Everything® Card Games Book
Everything® Card Tricks Book, $9.95
Everything® Casino Gambling Book, 2nd Ed.
Everything® Chess Basics Book
Everything® Christmas Crosswords Book, $9.95
Everything® Craps Strategy Book
Everything® Crossword and Puzzle Book
Everything® Crosswords and Puzzles for Quote Lovers Book, $9.95
Everything® Crossword Challenge Book
Everything® Crosswords for the Beach Book, $9.95
Everything® Cryptic Crosswords Book, $9.95
Everything® Cryptograms Book, $9.95
Everything® Easy Crosswords Book
Everything® Easy Kakuro Book, $9.95
Everything® Easy Large-Print Crosswords Book
Everything® Games Book, 2nd Ed.
Everything® Giant Book of Crosswords
Everything® Giant Sudoku Book, $9.95
Everything® Giant Word Search Book
Everything® Kakuro Challenge Book, $9.95
Everything® Large-Print Crossword Challenge Book
Everything® Large-Print Crosswords Book
Everything® Large-Print Travel Crosswords Book
Everything® Lateral Thinking Puzzles Book, $9.95
Everything® Literary Crosswords Book, $9.95
Everything® Mazes Book
Everything® Memory Booster Puzzles Book, $9.95

Everything® Movie Crosswords Book, $9.95
Everything® Music Crosswords Book, $9.95
Everything® Online Poker Book
Everything® Pencil Puzzles Book, $9.95
Everything® Poker Strategy Book
Everything® Pool & Billiards Book
Everything® Puzzles for Commuters Book, $9.95
Everything® Puzzles for Dog Lovers Book, $9.95
Everything® Sports Crosswords Book, $9.95
Everything® Test Your IQ Book, $9.95
Everything® Texas Hold 'Em Book, $9.95
Everything® Travel Crosswords Book, $9.95
Everything® Travel Mazes Book, $9.95
Everything® Travel Word Search Book, $9.95
Everything® TV Crosswords Book, $9.95
Everything® Word Games Challenge Book
Everything® Word Scramble Book
Everything® Word Search Book

HEALTH

Everything® Alzheimer's Book
Everything® Diabetes Book
Everything® First Aid Book, $9.95
Everything® Green Living Book
Everything® Health Guide to Addiction and Recovery
Everything® Health Guide to Adult Bipolar Disorder
Everything® Health Guide to Arthritis
Everything® Health Guide to Controlling Anxiety
Everything® Health Guide to Depression
Everything® Health Guide to Diabetes, 2nd Ed.
Everything® Health Guide to Fibromyalgia
Everything® Health Guide to Menopause, 2nd Ed.
Everything® Health Guide to Migraines
Everything® Health Guide to Multiple Sclerosis
Everything® Health Guide to OCD
Everything® Health Guide to PMS
Everything® Health Guide to Postpartum Care
Everything® Health Guide to Thyroid Disease
Everything® Hypnosis Book
Everything® Low Cholesterol Book
Everything® Menopause Book
Everything® Nutrition Book
Everything® Reflexology Book
Everything® Stress Management Book
Everything® Superfoods Book, $15.95

HISTORY

Everything® American Government Book
Everything® American History Book, 2nd Ed.
Everything® American Revolution Book, $15.95
Everything® Civil War Book
Everything® Freemasons Book
Everything® Irish History & Heritage Book
Everything® World War II Book, 2nd Ed.

HOBBIES

Everything® Candlemaking Book
Everything® Cartooning Book
Everything® Coin Collecting Book
Everything® Digital Photography Book, 2nd Ed.

Everything® Drawing Book
Everything® Family Tree Book, 2nd Ed.
Everything® Guide to Online Genealogy, $15.95
Everything® Knitting Book
Everything® Knots Book
Everything® Photography Book
Everything® Quilting Book
Everything® Sewing Book
Everything® Soapmaking Book, 2nd Ed.
Everything® Woodworking Book

HOME IMPROVEMENT

Everything® Feng Shui Book
Everything® Feng Shui Decluttering Book, $9.95
Everything® Fix-It Book
Everything® Green Living Book
Everything® Home Decorating Book
Everything® Home Storage Solutions Book
Everything® Homebuilding Book
Everything® Organize Your Home Book, 2nd Ed.

KIDS' BOOKS

All titles are $7.95

Everything® Fairy Tales Book, $14.95
Everything® Kids' Animal Puzzle & Activity Book
Everything® Kids' Astronomy Book
Everything® Kids' Baseball Book, 5th Ed.
Everything® Kids' Bible Trivia Book
Everything® Kids' Bugs Book
Everything® Kids' Cars and Trucks Puzzle and Activity Book
Everything® Kids' Christmas Puzzle & Activity Book
Everything® Kids' Connect the Dots
    Puzzle and Activity Book
Everything® Kids' Cookbook, 2nd Ed.
Everything® Kids' Crazy Puzzles Book
Everything® Kids' Dinosaurs Book
Everything® Kids' Dragons Puzzle and Activity Book
Everything® Kids' Environment Book $7.95
Everything® Kids' Fairies Puzzle and Activity Book
Everything® Kids' First Spanish Puzzle and Activity Book
Everything® Kids' Football Book
Everything® Kids' Geography Book
Everything® Kids' Gross Cookbook
Everything® Kids' Gross Hidden Pictures Book
Everything® Kids' Gross Jokes Book
Everything® Kids' Gross Mazes Book
Everything® Kids' Gross Puzzle & Activity Book
Everything® Kids' Halloween Puzzle & Activity Book
Everything® Kids' Hanukkah Puzzle and Activity Book
Everything® Kids' Hidden Pictures Book
Everything® Kids' Horses Book
Everything® Kids' Joke Book
Everything® Kids' Knock Knock Book
Everything® Kids' Learning French Book
Everything® Kids' Learning Spanish Book
Everything® Kids' Magical Science Experiments Book
Everything® Kids' Math Puzzles Book
Everything® Kids' Mazes Book
Everything® Kids' Money Book, 2nd Ed.
**Everything® Kids' Mummies, Pharaoh's, and Pyramids
    Puzzle and Activity Book**
Everything® Kids' Nature Book
Everything® Kids' Pirates Puzzle and Activity Book
Everything® Kids' Presidents Book
Everything® Kids' Princess Puzzle and Activity Book
Everything® Kids' Puzzle Book

Everything® Kids' Racecars Puzzle and Activity Book
Everything® Kids' Riddles & Brain Teasers Book
Everything® Kids' Science Experiments Book
Everything® Kids' Sharks Book
Everything® Kids' Soccer Book
Everything® Kids' Spelling Book
Everything® Kids' Spies Puzzle and Activity Book
Everything® Kids' States Book
Everything® Kids' Travel Activity Book
Everything® Kids' Word Search Puzzle and Activity Book

LANGUAGE

Everything® Conversational Japanese Book with CD, $19.95
Everything® French Grammar Book
Everything® French Phrase Book, $9.95
Everything® French Verb Book, $9.95
Everything® German Phrase Book, $9.95
Everything® German Practice Book with CD, $19.95
Everything® Inglés Book
Everything® Intermediate Spanish Book with CD, $19.95
Everything® Italian Phrase Book, $9.95
Everything® Italian Practice Book with CD, $19.95
Everything® Learning Brazilian Portuguese Book with CD, $19.95
Everything® Learning French Book with CD, 2nd Ed., $19.95
Everything® Learning German Book
Everything® Learning Italian Book
Everything® Learning Latin Book
Everything® Learning Russian Book with CD, $19.95
Everything® Learning Spanish Book
Everything® Learning Spanish Book with CD, 2nd Ed., $19.95
Everything® Russian Practice Book with CD, $19.95
Everything® Sign Language Book, $15.95
Everything® Spanish Grammar Book
Everything® Spanish Phrase Book, $9.95
Everything® Spanish Practice Book with CD, $19.95
Everything® Spanish Verb Book, $9.95
Everything® Speaking Mandarin Chinese Book with CD, $19.95

MUSIC

Everything® Bass Guitar Book with CD, $19.95
Everything® Drums Book with CD, $19.95
Everything® Guitar Book with CD, 2nd Ed., $19.95
Everything® Guitar Chords Book with CD, $19.95
Everything® Guitar Scales Book with CD, $19.95
Everything® Harmonica Book with CD, $15.95
Everything® Home Recording Book
Everything® Music Theory Book with CD, $19.95
Everything® Reading Music Book with CD, $19.95
Everything® Rock & Blues Guitar Book with CD, $19.95
Everything® Rock & Blues Piano Book with CD, $19.95
Everything® Rock Drums Book with CD, $19.95
Everything® Singing Book with CD, $19.95
Everything® Songwriting Book

NEW AGE

Everything® Astrology Book, 2nd Ed.
Everything® Birthday Personology Book
Everything® Celtic Wisdom Book, $15.95
Everything® Dreams Book, 2nd Ed.
Everything® Law of Attraction Book, $15.95
Everything® Love Signs Book, $9.95
Everything® Love Spells Book, $9.95
Everything® Palmistry Book
Everything® Psychic Book
Everything® Reiki Book

Everything® Sex Signs Book, $9.95
Everything® Spells & Charms Book, 2nd Ed.
Everything® Tarot Book, 2nd Ed.
Everything® Toltec Wisdom Book
Everything® Wicca & Witchcraft Book, 2nd Ed.

PARENTING

Everything® Baby Names Book, 2nd Ed.
Everything® Baby Shower Book, 2nd Ed.
Everything® Baby Sign Language Book with DVD
Everything® Baby's First Year Book
Everything® Birthing Book
Everything® Breastfeeding Book
Everything® Father-to-Be Book
Everything® Father's First Year Book
Everything® Get Ready for Baby Book, 2nd Ed.
Everything® Get Your Baby to Sleep Book, $9.95
Everything® Getting Pregnant Book
Everything® Guide to Pregnancy Over 35
Everything® Guide to Raising a One-Year-Old
Everything® Guide to Raising a Two-Year-Old
Everything® Guide to Raising Adolescent Boys
Everything® Guide to Raising Adolescent Girls
Everything® Mother's First Year Book
Everything® Parent's Guide to Childhood Illnesses
Everything® Parent's Guide to Children and Divorce
Everything® Parent's Guide to Children with ADD/ADHD
Everything® Parent's Guide to Children with Asperger's
    Syndrome
Everything® Parent's Guide to Children with Anxiety
Everything® Parent's Guide to Children with Asthma
Everything® Parent's Guide to Children with Autism
Everything® Parent's Guide to Children with Bipolar Disorder
Everything® Parent's Guide to Children with Depression
Everything® Parent's Guide to Children with Dyslexia
Everything® Parent's Guide to Children with Juvenile Diabetes
Everything® Parent's Guide to Children with OCD
Everything® Parent's Guide to Positive Discipline
Everything® Parent's Guide to Raising Boys
Everything® Parent's Guide to Raising Girls
Everything® Parent's Guide to Raising Siblings
**Everything® Parent's Guide to Raising Your
    Adopted Child**
Everything® Parent's Guide to Sensory Integration Disorder
Everything® Parent's Guide to Tantrums
Everything® Parent's Guide to the Strong-Willed Child
Everything® Parenting a Teenager Book
Everything® Potty Training Book, $9.95
Everything® Pregnancy Book, 3rd Ed.
Everything® Pregnancy Fitness Book
Everything® Pregnancy Nutrition Book
Everything® Pregnancy Organizer, 2nd Ed., $16.95
Everything® Toddler Activities Book
Everything® Toddler Book
Everything® Tween Book
Everything® Twins, Triplets, and More Book

PETS

Everything® Aquarium Book
Everything® Boxer Book
Everything® Cat Book, 2nd Ed.
Everything® Chihuahua Book
Everything® Cooking for Dogs Book
Everything® Dachshund Book
Everything® Dog Book, 2nd Ed.
Everything® Dog Grooming Book

Everything® Dog Obedience Book
Everything® Dog Owner's Organizer, $16.95
Everything® Dog Training and Tricks Book
Everything® German Shepherd Book
Everything® Golden Retriever Book
Everything® Horse Book, 2nd Ed., $15.95
Everything® Horse Care Book
Everything® Horseback Riding Book
Everything® Labrador Retriever Book
Everything® Poodle Book
Everything® Pug Book
Everything® Puppy Book
Everything® Small Dogs Book
Everything® Tropical Fish Book
Everything® Yorkshire Terrier Book

REFERENCE

Everything® American Presidents Book
Everything® Blogging Book
Everything® Build Your Vocabulary Book, $9.95
Everything® Car Care Book
Everything® Classical Mythology Book
Everything® Da Vinci Book
Everything® Einstein Book
Everything® Enneagram Book
Everything® Etiquette Book, 2nd Ed.
Everything® Family Christmas Book, $15.95
Everything® Guide to C. S. Lewis & Narnia
Everything® Guide to Divorce, 2nd Ed., $15.95
Everything® Guide to Edgar Allan Poe
Everything® Guide to Understanding Philosophy
Everything® Inventions and Patents Book
Everything® Jacqueline Kennedy Onassis Book
Everything® John F. Kennedy Book
Everything® Mafia Book
Everything® Martin Luther King Jr. Book
Everything® Pirates Book
Everything® Private Investigation Book
Everything® Psychology Book
Everything® Public Speaking Book, $9.95
Everything® Shakespeare Book, 2nd Ed.

RELIGION

Everything® Angels Book
Everything® Bible Book
Everything® Bible Study Book with CD, $19.95
Everything® Buddhism Book
Everything® Catholicism Book
Everything® Christianity Book
Everything® Gnostic Gospels Book
Everything® Hinduism Book, $15.95
Everything® History of the Bible Book
Everything® Jesus Book
Everything® Jewish History & Heritage Book
Everything® Judaism Book
Everything® Kabbalah Book
Everything® Koran Book
Everything® Mary Book
Everything® Mary Magdalene Book
Everything® Prayer Book

Everything® Saints Book, 2nd Ed.
Everything® Torah Book
Everything® Understanding Islam Book
Everything® Women of the Bible Book
Everything® World's Religions Book

SCHOOL & CAREERS

Everything® Career Tests Book
Everything® College Major Test Book
Everything® College Survival Book, 2nd Ed.
Everything® Cover Letter Book, 2nd Ed.
Everything® Filmmaking Book
Everything® Get-a-Job Book, 2nd Ed.
Everything® Guide to Being a Paralegal
Everything® Guide to Being a Personal Trainer
Everything® Guide to Being a Real Estate Agent
Everything® Guide to Being a Sales Rep
Everything® Guide to Being an Event Planner
Everything® Guide to Careers in Health Care
Everything® Guide to Careers in Law Enforcement
Everything® Guide to Government Jobs
Everything® Guide to Starting and Running a Catering Business
Everything® Guide to Starting and Running a Restaurant
Everything® Guide to Starting and Running a Retail Store
Everything® Job Interview Book, 2nd Ed.
Everything® New Nurse Book
Everything® New Teacher Book
Everything® Paying for College Book
Everything® Practice Interview Book
Everything® Resume Book, 3rd Ed.
Everything® Study Book

SELF-HELP

Everything® Body Language Book
Everything® Dating Book, 2nd Ed.
Everything® Great Sex Book
Everything® Guide to Caring for Aging Parents, $15.95
Everything® Self-Esteem Book
Everything® Self-Hypnosis Book, $9.95
Everything® Tantric Sex Book

SPORTS & FITNESS

Everything® Easy Fitness Book
Everything® Fishing Book
Everything® Guide to Weight Training, $15.95
Everything® Krav Maga for Fitness Book
Everything® Running Book, 2nd Ed.
Everything® Triathlon Training Book, $15.95

TRAVEL

Everything® Family Guide to Coastal Florida
Everything® Family Guide to Cruise Vacations
Everything® Family Guide to Hawaii
Everything® Family Guide to Las Vegas, 2nd Ed.
Everything® Family Guide to Mexico
Everything® Family Guide to New England, 2nd Ed.

Everything® Family Guide to New York City, 3rd Ed.
Everything® Family Guide to Northern California and Lake Tahoe
Everything® Family Guide to RV Travel & Campgrounds
Everything® Family Guide to the Caribbean
Everything® Family Guide to the Disneyland® Resort, California Adventure®, Universal Studios®, and the Anaheim Area, 2nd Ed.
Everything® Family Guide to the Walt Disney World Resort®, Universal Studios®, and Greater Orlando, 5th Ed.
Everything® Family Guide to Timeshares
Everything® Family Guide to Washington D.C., 2nd Ed.

WEDDINGS

Everything® Bachelorette Party Book, $9.95
Everything® Bridesmaid Book, $9.95
Everything® Destination Wedding Book
Everything® Father of the Bride Book, $9.95
Everything® Green Wedding Book, $15.95
Everything® Groom Book, $9.95
Everything® Jewish Wedding Book, 2nd Ed., $15.95
Everything® Mother of the Bride Book, $9.95
Everything® Outdoor Wedding Book
Everything® Wedding Book, 3rd Ed.
Everything® Wedding Checklist, $9.95
Everything® Wedding Etiquette Book, $9.95
Everything® Wedding Organizer, 2nd Ed., $16.95
Everything® Wedding Shower Book, $9.95
Everything® Wedding Vows Book, 3rd Ed., $9.95
Everything® Wedding Workout Book
Everything® Weddings on a Budget Book, 2nd Ed., $9.95

WRITING

Everything® Creative Writing Book
Everything® Get Published Book, 2nd Ed.
Everything® Grammar and Style Book, 2nd Ed.
Everything® Guide to Magazine Writing
Everything® Guide to Writing a Book Proposal
Everything® Guide to Writing a Novel
Everything® Guide to Writing Children's Books
Everything® Guide to Writing Copy
Everything® Guide to Writing Graphic Novels
Everything® Guide to Writing Research Papers
Everything® Guide to Writing a Romance Novel, $15.95
Everything® Improve Your Writing Book, 2nd Ed.
Everything® Writing Poetry Book